FASHION AND THE CONSUMER

Understanding Fashion series

ISSN 1753-3406

Understanding Fashion is a series of short, accessible, authored books designed to provide students with a map of the fashion field. The books are aimed at beginning undergraduate students and they are designed to cover an entire module. Accessibly written, each book will include boxed case studies, bullet point chapter summaries, guides to further reading, and questions for classroom discussion. Individual titles can be used as a key text or to support a general introductory survey. They will be of interest to students studying fashion from either an applied or cultural perspective.

Titles in the series will include:

Fashion Design
Elizabeth Bye

Fashion and the Consumer
Jennifer Yurchisin and Kim K.P. Johnson

Fashion and Identity
Alison Goodrum

Understanding Fashion and Textiles
Jess Power

Fashion Trends and Forecasting
Eundeok Kim and Ann Marie Fiore

FASHION AND THE CONSUMER

Jennifer Yurchisin and Kim K. P. Johnson

BERG

Oxford • New York

English edition
First published in 2010 by
Berg

Editorial offices:
First Floor, Angel Court, 81 St Clements Street, Oxford OX4 1AW, UK
175 Fifth Avenue, New York, NY 10010, USA

© Kim K.P. Johnson and Jennifer Yurchisin 2010

Berg is the imprint of Oxford International Publishers Ltd.

Library of Congress Cataloging-in-Publication Data

A catalogue record for this book is available from the Library of Congress.

British Library Cataloguing-in-Publication Data

A catalogue record for this book is available from the British Library.

ISBN 978 1 84520 797 7 (Cloth)
       978 1 84520 798 4 (Paper)

Typeset by Apex CoVantage, LLC, Madison, WI.

www.bergpublishers.com

CONTENTS

ILLUSTRATIONS

Chapter 5

Chapter 6

Chapter 7

ACKNOWLEDGEMENTS

The authors wish to thank all of the individuals who contributed their time and talents to the creation of this book. Special thanks are in order for Jean McElvain from the Goldstein Museum of Design at the University of Minnesota. Jean is responsible for the appearance of the wonderful historic items featured in the book. Great appreciation is also extended to the following individuals who helped the authors find and take the photographs in the book: Brian Balster, Kaitlin Johnson, Mark Johnson, Riane Johnson, Sherman Malkerson, Yingjie Ou, Lisa Pruden, Ashley Thompson, Kittichai Watchravesringkan, Beth Yurchisin, and Morticia Yurchisin. The help that Hyo Jung Chang provided with the index must also be recognized by the authors. The authors also wish to thank Hannah Shakespeare, Anna Wright, Julia Hall, and all those individuals at Berg for their support, ideas, and assistance in this project. They are wonderful team members. We would also like to express our appreciation to the anonymous reviewers of this textbook for their constructive comments.

INTRODUCTION

The world of fashion is a very exciting one, indeed. It is a world that we are all a part of because we are all fashion consumers. Every one of us searches for, purchases, wears, and eventually disposes of apparel throughout the course of our lifetimes. Unfortunately, though, the topic of consumption is often given little attention in survey textbooks. Introductory textbooks designed for use by first-year students in fashion studies often cover topics such as the scope and nature of fashion, the environment of fashion, the design of fashion, the materials of fashion, the production and manufacture of fashion, and the retailing of fashion. Rarely do students enrolled in introductory-level courses get the opportunity to examine the role that consumers play in the world of fashion. Thus, we developed *Fashion and the Consumer* to fill this void.

This textbook is designed to serve as an introduction to understanding consumer decision making as it relates to fashion. It is intended to be used in a first-year introductory course. Thus, no prior background in the study of consumption is needed to read and understand the topics contained herein. Much of the material features a rational and what many assume to be a "normal" model of consumer decision making concerning fashion. Additionally, we feature a discussion of nonnormative consumption as we present material on practices such as buying counterfeit merchandise, merchandise borrowing, and shoplifting. Throughout *Fashion and the Consumer* we present the idea that consumers make many decisions that impact the environmental, social, and economic well-being of our planet and its inhabitants. This book can be used to supplement existing textbooks used in an introductory course or it can be used in combination with other texts in Berg's Understanding Fashion Series.

Our position within this text is that fashion impacts more than just apparel because fashion means change. Thus, we have fashion in multiple aspects of our lives including the home furnishings, automobiles, food, and electronic equipment we purchase; the words we speak; the ways we act; and, of course, the apparel we wear. Even though our discussion focuses on the consumption of apparel, the concepts we discuss can easily be applied to other items that are impacted by fashion.

Each chapter features learning objectives at the beginning as well as discussion questions at the end. Key terms are bolded within the text for easy identification. We also have provided suggested additional readings at the end of each chapter if you are interested in delving deeper into chapter content. Boxed case material is featured in each chapter, which allows you to learn about specific content in greater detail or to rate yourself on specific personal qualities concerning your own consumption behavior.

We begin our discussion of fashion consumption in chapter 1 by defining the key terms, such as *fashion* and *consumption,* that will be used throughout the text. We explain the scope of fashion influence and the process of fashion acceptance. In chapter 2 we provide a brief historical overview of how people shopped for products before and after the Industrial Revolution. We present key developments in apparel shopping during the twentieth century and highlight different apparel shopping environments available to consumers. Chapter 3 focuses on a normative decision-making model concerning apparel from the prepurchase stage to the purchase stage. Included are a discussion of consumer needs and how they are met, how consumers search for information before they make purchases, the ways in which consumers evaluate apparel products, and the influence of the retail store environment on purchase decisions. In chapter 4 we review several additional key variables that were introduced in the third chapter for their effect on decision making concerning apparel purchasing. Included is a discussion of selected demographic variables and psychographic variables and how they play a role in consumers' decision making. We also discuss cultural influences and economic influences on decision making concerning apparel. We follow this discussion with postpurchase consumption behaviors in chapter 5. Within this chapter we attempt to answer questions addressing what consumers do with apparel once it is purchased. Do they clean apparel items before they wear them? How do consumers care for apparel items? Do they share items with friends? How do they determine their satisfaction or dissatisfaction with apparel items? How do consumers dispose of unwanted fashion products? Where does all the fashion go? In chapter 6 we take on the topic of nonnormative consumption and consumer misbehavior in the marketplace. We provide a categorization of types of misbehavior and highlight some of the reasoning underlying consumers' decisions to misbehave. Chapter 7 ends the book with a focus on the concept of social responsibility as it relates to fashion consumption. We provide an introduction to the complex issue of being a socially responsible consumer of apparel by examining the environmental impact of the production of the materials of fashion apparel, followed by a discussion of ways in which the apparel footprint on the environment might be reduced. We discuss the benefits of the practice of fair trade in the apparel industry and explain cause-related marketing. We note the dangers associated with the overconsumption of apparel products and discuss the benefits associated with the voluntary simplicity movement.

We offer the following suggestions to the reader who is new to the area of fashion consumption. To gain familiarity with the topics that will be covered, read the chapter objectives and the subheadings of the chapter before you read the entire chapter. Read the boxed case material when it is referred to in the text because this will expand on information provided or further exemplify content. As you read, think of other examples that you have encountered. Reflecting on the material enhances your ability to apply concepts in a variety of situations.

Now join us on our journey through the part of the world of fashion that we participate in every day—consumption.

1

WHAT IS FASHION CONSUMPTION?

After you have read this chapter, you should be able to

- Define the concept of fashion.
- Understand the scope of fashion.
- Explain the process of fashion acceptance.
- Describe the fashion cycle.
- Identify alternatives to the typical fashion cycle.
- Define the concept of consumption.
- Describe the difference between normative and nonnormative consumption.
- Discuss the advantages and disadvantages of different methods of consumer research.

Introduction to the concept of fashion

Fashion is a word that can mean different things. To some it means what models wear on a runway. To others, fashion means the clothing styles that people wear on a daily basis. Because this book is about fashion consumption, a good place to start our discussion is with a definition of the word *fashion*. By defining fashion, we make clear what we are discussing and ensure that we are thinking about the same concept when the term fashion is used throughout this book. When we use the term **fashion**, we mean a way of behaving or doing something that is accepted and used by the majority of a group of people at a given point in time, regardless of the size of the group (Stone, 2008; Tortora & Eubank, 2005). To fully understand this definition, let's examine each of the parts.

First, according to this definition, fashion is a way of behaving. Ways of behaving include a wide variety of activities such as the dances we dance, the words we speak, the clothing we wear, the way we style our hair, and how we spend our leisure time. Fashion influences all of these types of activities and more.

Second, in order for a way of behaving or appearing to become fashion, it must be accepted by many members of a group. The group can be as large as a country or a region of the country, or it can be as small as a group of friends. The point is that the majority of the members of the group must accept and use that way of behaving. For example, if a single member of a group decides to pierce an eyebrow, it is not fashion. However, if most members of the group decide to pierce their eyebrows, eyebrow piercing is a fashion for that group.

Third, our definition of fashion indicates that these ways of behaving will change over time. For a clothing style to be labeled as fashion, it must be accepted by the majority of the group and later rejected. Fashion demands change. On an aggregate level, if there is no change in the ways of behaving within a group of individuals, there is no fashion within that group. This may be the case when individuals participate in groups that require uniforms. They wear the same uniform for many years without changing any aspect of it. Thus, there is no fashion in the apparel of this group.

On an individual level, if you wear the exact same clothing styles and never change them or any aspect of how you wear them, your behavior does not reflect fashion. Think about it—do you still wear the same clothing styles that you wore five years ago? It is likely that you have disposed of at least some of the things you used to wear because they no longer appealed to you or you tired of them. If this is the case, you are participating in fashion.

Scope of fashion

Fashion applies to "an idea, practice, or object" (Rogers, 1983, p. 11). Fashion applies to art, architecture, food, cars, television programs, movies, books, political thoughts, communication styles, and so forth. In many cases, the items that are fashionable in one area (e.g., political thought) will be similar to the items that are fashionable in other areas (e.g., apparel, cars, food). For example, think about the public's recent awareness of global warming and individuals' desire to live in a sustainable environment. Now, think about how the popularity of eco-friendly fashions, hybrid cars, and organic food has risen over the past few years. Do you see the connection?

It is not surprising that there would be a connection between many areas of our lives, because fashions reflect the zeitgeist of a time and place. **Zeitgeist** is a German word that means "spirit of the times." Because people living in a particular place during a particular time are exposed to similar sights and sounds, images, and ideas, parallels can often be found throughout various aspects of a culture. Despite the fact that fashion applies to many areas of our lives, we focus in this book on fashion as it relates to apparel.

Fashion acceptance

Not everyone purchases and wears a new clothing style immediately after she sees it. For example, when a Prada fashion show held in the United States featured cropped pants in 1996 (Cotton Incorporated, 2001), not every woman instantly rushed out and purchased the style. Instead, as usually occurs, a few women began wearing cropped pants after they were introduced. Several more women began wearing cropped pants in 1997 because they saw other women wearing them. By 2007, almost every woman probably either had tried or owned at least one pair of cropped pants. Thus, over time, cropped pants were accepted by the majority of women residing in the United States.

This same process of introduction and imitation is repeated over and over again with different ways of behaving in different parts of the world. Thus, fashion represents social copying. Social copying begins with a new clothing style or way of behaving being introduced into a group by a member. Other members observe the style and decide whether to accept that style or way of behaving. As each individual member makes the decision to accept the style, the style spreads or diffuses throughout the group. If the style is accepted and used by the majority of the members of the group, the style becomes a fashion for the group. Not all styles introduced into the group are accepted by the majority of the group. Thus, not all styles introduced become fashion. A term used to describe a style that never gains mass acceptance is a **flop** (Stone, 2008).

The time that it takes for a style or way of behaving to gain acceptance by the majority of group members varies. Some styles catch on quickly and gain mass acceptance within weeks of being introduced. Other styles are not accepted as quickly. Styles that are inexpensive to try and easy to wear may gain faster acceptance than styles that are expensive or complicated. The speed with which a style gains acceptance is related to the continuity of the style. Continuity in this instance refers to the connections that the new style has with existing styles. Styles that have continuity are accepted more easily than styles that are discontinuous. An example of a **discontinuous style** is the introduction of pants as a style to be worn by women to important social events outside of the home. For example, throughout the 1930s, women wore dresses and skirts to social events outside of the home. Hollywood actresses including Marlene Dietrich and Katherine Hepburn introduced the wearing of pants to social events. Even though these highly visible women were seen wearing pants to important social gatherings, it was not until the 1960s that wearing pants rather than skirts or dresses to important social events was accepted by a majority of women (Buckland, 2005).

The fashion cycle

In order for a style to become a fashion, it must first be introduced into a group of people, next be accepted by a majority of individuals within that group, and ultimately be rejected by the group to make room for the next **innovation** or new style. According to Rogers (1983), an innovation is "an idea, practice, or object perceived as new by an individual" (p. 11). This process of introduction, acceptance, and then rejection is called the **fashion cycle**. The typical fashion cycle can be illustrated graphically using a bell-shaped curve (see Figure 1.1). This bell-shaped curve is often referred to as the **Innovation Adoption Curve**. The curve can be divided into several parts, and within each part the number of individuals that are accepting the innovation is either increasing or decreasing. The vertical axis of the curve represents the number of adopters as represented by their purchase of the item or sales. The horizontal axis represents time.

In the previous discussion of fashion acceptance, we pointed out that Prada introduced an innovation—cropped pants. The part of the adoption curve where the introduction of an innovation is designated is at the far left of the curve. At this point, very few people are purchasing and wearing the apparel item. In other words, very few people have accepted, or, to use Rogers's terminology, adopted the innovation. The term for this stage of the curve is *introduction*.

Individuals who are the first to adopt an innovation (e.g., a new apparel item) are referred to as **fashion innovators**. Fashion innovators are "the brave souls who are always on the lookout for novel developments and will be the first to try a new offering" (Solomon & Rabolt, 2004, p. 96). These men and women are among the first to wear a new apparel item or try a new hairstyle. They may even have contributed to the creation and promotion of the new item (Sproles & Burns, 1994). Fashion innovators may make their own styles or put items together in a unique way that is copied by others. Fashion innovators are looked to by others for their fashion leadership. Although a fashion innovator can come from any walk of life, celebrities have the potential to be fashion innovators because of their high visibility and popularity. Apparel designers may often provide celebrities with their latest designs in an effort to promote these innovations to the general public.

Over time, as more people accept and adopt the innovation, the innovation is described as moving along the curve (i.e., to the right). **Early adopters** and members

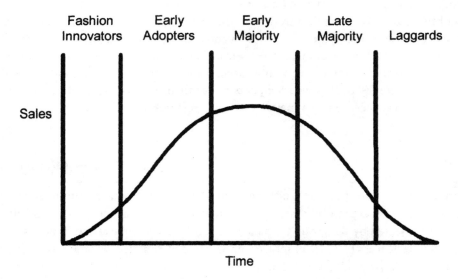

Figure 1.1 The Innovation Adoption Curve has a bell shape. The curve shows the number of people who have accepted an innovation over a period of time.

FASHION AND THE CONSUMER

of the **early majority** are respectively the next groups of consumers to adopt the innovation. In many ways, early adopters and fashion innovators are similar. They are both willing to try new things, but early adopters tend to be more cautious than fashion innovators when adopting items (Value Based Management, 2007). Because of this carefulness, early adopters allow the fashion innovators to "field-test" the item before adopting it themselves (Solomon & Rabolt, 2004, p. 97). Continuing on, consumers who are members of the early majority adopt new items "more quickly than the average" consumer (Value Based Management, 2007). However, members of the early majority are even more cautious than the early adopters, so they wait until they see many other individuals using the item before they adopt it.

As long as the number of new adopters increases, the innovation adoption curve moves upward. However, at some point in time, the adoption of the innovation begins to decrease. This decrease is designated by the downward angle of the curve. Individuals who adopt the innovation at this point are members of the **late majority**. Members of the late majority tend to be "skeptic people" (Value Based Management, 2007). These individuals often wait to adopt an innovation until most other people have adopted it. At this point, it is not unusual for the price of the innovation to be lower than when it was first introduced. This reduction in price may provide members of the late majority with an incentive for purchasing the item (Cornell University, 2006; Solomon & Rabolt, 2004).

Eventually, there are very few new adopters of the innovation. In fact, the item originally called an innovation would not likely be referred to as such at this point in time. The only people who have not already adopted the item and may still be interested in adopting it at this point are referred to as **laggards**. Laggards tend to be "traditional people" who are "critical of new ideas" (Value Based Management, 2007). Waiting to adopt an item may be a choice for bargain-hunting consumers, but other people may be forced to wait until this point due to their economic situation. This latter group of laggards may wish to adopt an innovation earlier in its life cycle, but they may not have the financial wherewithal to purchase the item before it is discounted (Sproles & Burns, 1994). We present further discussion of the ways in which demographic variables, such as income and age, along with psychographic variables, including personality traits, affect purchasing patterns in chapter 4. For now, see which adopter category you are in by taking the questionnaire in Boxed Case 1.1.

BOXED CASE 1.1. ARE YOU A FASHION INNOVATOR?

Beaudoin, Lachance, and Robitaille (2003) created a measure to categorize consumers into groups based on their innovativeness. You can determine your level of fashion innovativeness by responding to the following statements. For each statement, you need to decide how much you think the statement describes your feelings about apparel. There are no right or wrong answers. Indicate how much you agree or disagree with each statement. Circle the number for each statement that corresponds most closely with your own feelings.

To determine your level of fashion innovativeness, first add all of the numbers you circled for a total score. If your total score is 6 to 14, you are a fashion laggard. This means you are among the slowest individuals to accept and adopt an innovation. If your score is 15 to 18, you represent the late majority of fashion adopters. This means you are extremely cautious in your decisions to adopt new apparel styles. Most of the people you know will have accepted the new style before you do. If your total score is 19 to 22, you are a part of the early majority. This means you like to try new styles, but you wait to try them until at least some of the people you know are wearing them. If your score is 23 to 26, you are an early adopter. This means you may be one of the first in your peer group to try the new style. And if your score is 27 to 36, you are a fashion innovator. You are the only one to be wearing the innovation and are the originator of new looks and ways of doing things.

Reference

Beaudoin, P., Lachance, M. J., & Robitaille, J. (2003). Fashion innovativeness, fashion diffusion, and brand sensitivity among adolescents. *Journal of Fashion Marketing and Management, 7*(1), 23–30.

	Strongly Disagree				Strongly Agree	
1. In general, I am among the first in my circle of friends to buy a new apparel item when it appears.	1	2	3	4	5	6
2. If I heard that a new apparel item was available in the store, I would be interested enough to buy it.	1	2	3	4	5	6
3. Compared to my friends, I own a lot of apparel items.	1	2	3	4	5	6
4. In general, I am the first in my circle of friends to know about the latest apparel items.	1	2	3	4	5	6
5. I will buy a new apparel item, even if I haven't seen anyone else wearing it yet.	1	2	3	4	5	6
6. I know about new fashion items before other people do.	1	2	3	4	5	6

Different words are used to describe innovations that are popular for a short period of time versus a long period of time. The term **fad** is used to refer to an innovation that is adopted quickly by a large group of people but remains in acceptance for only a brief period of time. Compare the shape of the innovation adoption curve of a fad versus a fashion in Figure 1.2. The figure shows that a fad is typically adopted by only a subsection of a population, such as young individuals (Cornell University, 2006).

Figure 1.2 also provides an illustration of the adoption curve for a basic product. A **basic product** (also referred to as a classic) is an item that remains popular with many people for a long time (Cornell University, 2006). Can you think of an example of an apparel item that has been popular for most of your lifetime? How about denim jeans? According to Sproles and Burns (1994), very few apparel items possess the characteristics needed to become basics. Basic products possess a "simplicity" and "versatility" that allows them to be "adapted to fit in with current fashionable detailing" (Sproles & Burns, 1994, p. 172). Think about those denim jeans again. Do you still feel comfortable wearing the pair of jeans that you wore several years ago? Chances are you probably do not feel as comfortable wearing those jeans now as you did when you first purchased them. Although we often think of history repeating itself in terms of apparel products, the fact of the matter is that subtle (or maybe not-so-subtle) changes in the design of even basic products render them obsolete after a certain amount of time. If you have any doubt about this claim, imagine wearing light blue, stone-washed, taper-legged, high-waisted jeans when everyone else in the room is wearing dark blue, low-rise, boot-cut jeans. Even basic products change over time and are eventually rejected.

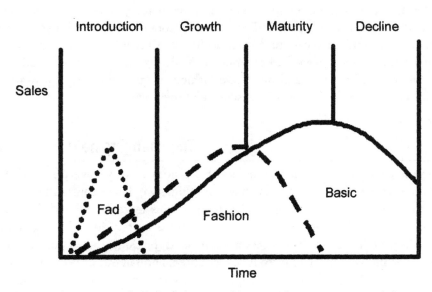

Figure 1.2 Adoption curves for fads, fashions, and basic products vary in size and shape.

Other terms related to fashion include *taste* and *trend*. **Taste** refers to "the prevailing opinion of what is attractive and appropriate for a given occasion or person" (Solomon & Rabolt, 2004, p. 11). In other words, our taste assists us in deciding what we like or dislike. In terms of apparel, our taste influences what we will or will not wear.

Although you may have heard that someone has good taste or bad taste, the truth is that taste, as defined here, has no value associated with it. Tastes differ as a result of the time and the culture in which individuals live. To demonstrate the idea that taste is time specific, look at the women's bathing suits in Figures 1.3 and 1.4. They are both bathing suits, even though the one in Figure 1.3, a Jantzen swimsuit from the 1920s, might not look like something you would like to wear to the beach today. The one in Figure 1.4, a Gucci swimsuit from the 1980s, also might not look like something you would like to wear. However, by looking at these two examples, you can see that what would have been deemed appropriate and attractive bathing attire in the 1920s is very different than what would have been deemed appropriate and attractive attire in the 1980s. The taste reflected in the accepted styles for bathing suits in the 1920s is different from that of the 1980s.

Similarly, the tastes of people from different places and cultural backgrounds vary. For example, the concept of modesty for many Muslim women is very different from the concept of modesty for many non-Muslim women. These differences in tastes are demonstrated in Muslim and non-Muslim women's choice of apparel.

Trend is a term used to describe the movement of an innovation through the adoption curve. A trend is the general direction the innovation is heading. A store owner, when making a buying decision for a product, generally wants to know whether the item is trending upward and gaining in acceptance or trending downward and declining in acceptance. The owner is more interested in buying items to sell that are gaining in acceptance than declining in acceptance. Most innovations initially trend upward or gain in acceptance. Knowing whether an innovation will continue to trend upward and become a fashion or quickly trend downward and turn into a fad or a flop is part of the science of merchandising.

The changing nature of fashion

Fashion is ever-changing. Many scholars throughout history have put forth their ideas concerning why the way we behave and things we do are constantly changing. Note the phrase "throughout history" in the previous sentence. Something to keep in mind is that fashion as a process of change has occurred since the beginning of human history. Although the process has remained the same, the amount of time it takes for an innovation to be introduced, adopted, and fall out of favor has accelerated. In ancient Egypt, for example, apparel items changed very little for hundreds of years. Garments were handmade and used until they were worn out. By our

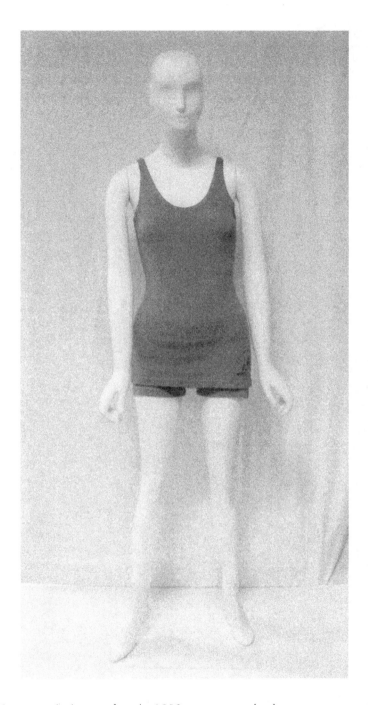

Figure 1.3 Jantzen bathing suit from the 1920s covers more skin than most contemporary bathing suits. From the collections of the Goldstein Museum of Design at the University of Minnesota. Photo by Jean McElvain.

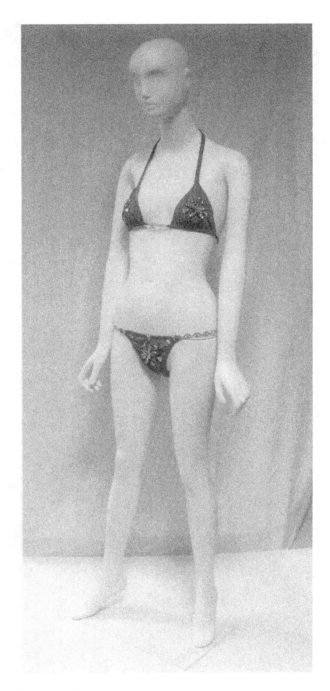

Figure 1.4 Gucci bathing suit from the 1980s allows more skin to show than the Jantzen bathing suit from the 1920s. From the collections of the Goldstein Museum of Design at the University of Minnesota. Photo by Jean McElvain.

definition, we might argue that individuals living at this time did not participate in a fashion system, because styles worn and other ways of behaving did not change over their lifetime.

As time marched on, technological developments enabled improvements in production, transportation, and communication. Following the Industrial Revolution, acceptance and rejection of styles (i.e., fashion) began to occur at a faster pace. Apparel started to become mass produced, as opposed to handmade, and the **fashion system** was born. The fashion system is "a complex industry" that brings "together textile production, clothing design and manufacture, and retail distribution of clothing" (Tortora & Eubank, 2005, p. 6). This system of design, production, and distribution should not be confused with fashion. Fashion would exist in the absence of this system, because ways of behaving have always changed, albeit much slower in the past than in today's global society.

In attempting to explain why fashion changes, Frings (1996) identified three main reasons for fashion change. Fashion changes because fashion "reflects changes in people's life-styles and current events," because "people's needs change," and because "people get bored with what they have" (p. 65). Following are some examples to illustrate how each of these reasons influences fashion change.

After the war in Iraq began in the early 2000s, the use of camouflage fabric in apparel items increased (Thurman, 2003). As the war continued, military influences continued to be seen in women's clothing (Thomas, 2007). In this way, world events appeared to be influencing fashion.

In addition to current events, fashion changes when people's needs change. In the early 1980s, many women, particularly in the United States and Western Europe, started working in corporate environments. These women needed apparel items to wear to the office. In response to this need, the power suit was born (see Figure 1.5).

But even if new needs had not arisen for these women or anyone else in the 1980s, apparel styles would have continued to change. Styles change even when people have no need for new items, because individuals get bored with what they have. Think about your favorite shirt. Would you want to wear that shirt every day? For most of us, the answer is no. People like variety (Postrel, 2004), and this appreciation of the new and different encourages the introduction and adoption of new items into the marketplace.

Although it is true that fashion requires change, the changes that occur within a style are usually evolutionary as opposed to revolutionary. In other words, styles typically change in small increments over short periods of time. In this way, fashion is characterized by **historical continuity**, meaning that "fashion is an evolutionary outgrowth and elaboration of previously existing fashions" (Sproles & Burns, 1994, p. 32). For the most part, the apparel items that appear on the runway in Paris one year are probably similar in many respects to the apparel items that came down the runway the previous year. Colors, fabrics, hemlines, and necklines probably changed slightly. Hemlines did not go from very short to very long, and colors did not change from very dull to extremely bright.

Figure 1.5 The 1980s power suit for women from Chanel features masculine styling, such as square shoulders. From the collections of the Goldstein Museum of Design at the University of Minnesota. Photo by Jean McElvain.

In contrast, revolutionary changes in fashion have typically occurred following dramatic social changes (Sproles & Burns, 1994). For example, fashion revolutions occurred in women's wear following both World War I and World War II. Both the flapper look of the 1920s and Dior's New Look of the 1940s and 1950s were responses to women's new roles in society following each of these wars (i.e., the liberated woman of the 1920s and the respectable suburban housewife of the 1940s and 1950s, respectively).

Fashion and the marketplace

New items can be introduced into the marketplace in a number of ways. For instance, fashion designers like Christian Lacroix can introduce new apparel items. Very few people will actually purchase these particular garments, known as **haute couture** garments. Haute couture apparel items are "the one-of-a-kind, made-to-order collections of famous designers" (Sproles & Burns, 1994, p. 12). Only about 200 people in the world are regular couture customers (Johnson, 2007). You may, however, be wearing an item that looks similar to one of the items from a couture designer's runway show.[1] Fashion editors and buyers interpret the couture designer items for their customers. Then designers and manufacturers produce these reinterpreted looks at a variety of price levels.[2] As a result, in contemporary society, individuals representing "various age ranges, life-styles, tastes, and pocketbooks" can all keep up with the latest fashion changes (Frings, 1996, p. 74). The process of creating lower-priced imitations of haute couture designs is merely controversial in some countries, like the United States, and illegal in other countries, like France, because of copyright infringements (Raustiala & Sprigman, 2006; Wilson, 2007).

Although some new apparel items are introduced by fashion designers and adopted by consumers, consumers themselves may introduce new apparel items or new ways of wearing old styles that are eventually imitated and reintroduced to other consumers by high-end fashion designers. Many of the consumer-introduced changes in styles originate in youth subcultures (Solomon & Rabolt, 2004). Some recognizable examples include denim jeans, hip-hop fashion, and the grunge look of the 1990s (Frings, 1996; Solomon & Rabolt, 2004).

Introduction to the concept of consumption

Now that we have defined how we are going to use the term *fashion*, we focus on defining the term *consumption*. **Consumption** occurs "when individuals select, purchase, use, or dispose of products, services, ideas, or experiences to satisfy needs and desires" (Solomon & Rabolt, 2004, p. 23). It is clear from this definition that consumption includes more than just the act of exchanging money for goods and services. When we consume products, we engage in many behaviors, not just shopping. Think about that favorite shirt of yours. Prior to acquiring that shirt, you may have looked at several different shirts in several different stores before making your decision to purchase. After acquiring or purchasing that shirt, you may have brought it home, cut off the price tags, worn it, and cleaned it or had it cleaned. Since it is your favorite shirt, it probably is still hanging in your closet. But, at some point in time, you will take this shirt out of its regular wearing rotation and dispose of it. You may dispose of it for a number of reasons (perhaps to make room for your next favorite shirt). With disposal comes the end of your consumption of that shirt. We discuss in more detail behaviors related to your apparel product consumption in chapters 3 and 5. Right now, it is important that you understand that consumption is a multistep process, not a singular behavior.

Another important detail about consumption, as defined here, is that it can occur without purchasing. Individuals can consume both tangible things, like apparel, and intangible things, like political thoughts and entertainment experiences. In this sense, the consumption of fashion occurs when you go window shopping at apparel stores, when you read about fashion in a magazine, or when you watch a fashion show on television.

You are probably starting to realize that consumption is a huge part of your life. A former student mentioned on a course evaluation that all of the things that we talked about in the fashion consumer behavior class were things that could be used in daily life. In contemporary, technologically advanced, large, and global-scale societies (Eicher, Evenson, & Lutz, 2008), consumption behaviors are of utmost importance to individuals. Consumption currently plays a key role in many cities around the world, because products and activities have meanings attached to them that transfer from the products and activities to the owners or users (Berger, 2005; McCracken, 1988; Reed, 2002; Solomon & Rabolt, 2004). Or, as Andrea Sachs's friend, Doug, says in the movie *The Devil Wears Prada*, fashion products are "iconography used to express individual identity" (Frankel, 2006). In this way, individuals can use products and activities to create identities for themselves and to communicate those identities to other individuals who are familiar with the products' and activities' meanings (Arnould & Price, 2000; Firat, 1994; Nava, 1992). Think about those jeans mentioned earlier in the chapter. One of the reasons why you might have felt uncomfortable wearing the light blue, stonewashed, taper-legged, high-waisted jeans is because the characteristics associated with those jeans (e.g., old, not fashionable) were inconsistent with ideas you have about yourself. Maybe you would be comfortable wearing the other, dark blue, low-rise, boot-cut jeans because the characteristics associated with those jeans (e.g., young, hip) are characteristics you want other people to know that you possess.

The creation and expression of an identity is one of the needs that consumption fulfills for people in contemporary society. As the definition of consumption indicates, consumption activities and behaviors fulfill both "needs and desires" (Solomon & Rabolt, 2004, p. 23). We will discuss both needs and desires, or wants, in greater depth in chapter 3. For now, just realize that an individual's needs and wants can either be satisfied or not satisfied through the consumption of apparel products.

Normative versus nonnormative consumption

All consumption activities and behaviors can be classified as either normative or nonnormative. **Normative** consumer behaviors follow the established norms of a culture. **Norms** are informal rules "dictating what is right or wrong, acceptable or unacceptable" (Solomon & Rabolt, 2004, pp. 42–43). Consumption norms, then, are consumption-related behaviors that are deemed appropriate in a given culture. When you are in your home country and you engage in normative consumption, everything feels natural to you. For instance, if you live in the United States, you may be one of the millions of individuals who goes shopping on Black

Friday, or the day after Thanksgiving.[3] People who are not familiar with this consumption norm might find it odd for individuals to get up at 4:00 A.M. on this particular Friday just to go shopping, but in the United States, it is quite normal. Normative consumption is not necessarily rational consumption. When women in Australia go shopping to improve their mood (Minahan & Beverland, 2005), they most likely are not purchasing apparel items that reflect prior planning. They are not shopping for items as replacement for other items that have worn out, nor are they typically shopping for items for which they conducted a cost comparison. In this sense, their consumption behavior is not rational. However, given the fact that many women living in Australia, and in the rest of the world, engage in consumption to improve their mood, their behavior is still normative within their culture.

Nonnormative consumer behavior, on the other hand, seems unnatural to people living in a certain culture. **Nonnormative consumption** includes "consumer misconduct in the acquisition, usage or disposition of goods and services" (Callen & Ownbey, 2003, p. 99). Nonnormative consumption may be illegal, unethical, or economically and psychologically unhealthy. Remember that favorite shirt of yours? Well, if you acquired it without purchasing it, then you were engaging in a nonnormative consumer activity known as shoplifting. We discuss examples of illegal, unethical, and unhealthy consumption in chapter 6.

Learning about consumers

Why we wish consumers had tails

Dogs. You've heard about them. You've seen them. Maybe you even have one. We think dogs are great, because to know what a dog is feeling, all you have to do is look at its tail. When dogs are happy, their tails are turned upward and are wagging (see Figure 1.6). When they are unhappy, dogs keep their tails down and do not wag them. And when dogs are nervous or naughty, they put their tails between their legs. It would be great if people had tails. If people had tails, we would know how they felt just by observing their tails. Retailers would know when consumers were satisfied with their shopping experiences, because their tails would be upturned and wagging. Designers would know when consumers were dissatisfied with apparel items because these consumers would keep their tails down and still. And when consumers were uncomfortable when wearing an apparel item or were being naughty by stealing an apparel item, retailers would know immediately, because these consumers would have their tails between their legs. Alas, consumers do not have tails, so it is very difficult to tell how they are feeling by looking at them. Therefore, consumer researchers use other methods to investigate and collect data about fashion consumers and their behavior. These methods can be grouped into two broad categories: quantitative and qualitative techniques.

Figure 1.6 Happy dogs have upright tails. Photo by Jennifer Yurchisin.

Quantitative methods of data collection

When researchers use **quantitative** methods to collect information about consumers, they collect data in numeric form. Two of the main methods researchers use to collect numeric data are surveys and experiments. **Surveys** are used to "determine specific characteristics of a group" (Fraenkel & Wallen, 2003, p. 12). When researchers conduct surveys, they usually use questionnaires. A **questionnaire** is "a document containing questions and other types of items designed to solicit information appropriate for analysis" (Babbie, 2004, p. 244). You may have seen a questionnaire if you have ever completed a customer comment card. When asked to participate in survey research using questionnaires, consumers read through the items listed on the questionnaire and respond to these items. The researcher assigns a numeric value for each item on the questionnaire. The researcher will analyze all of the consumers' responses to all of the items on the questionnaire to find connections between different types of consumers and different types of behaviors.

For instance, Lee and Johnson (2005) were interested in investigating whether personality characteristics were related to unethical consumption among Korean and U.S. undergraduate students. They distributed a questionnaire containing items to assess consumers' personality characteristics as well as their unethical consumption behaviors. They found that differences in Korean and U.S. undergraduates' ethical perspectives did have an impact on their perception of unethical consumption behaviors. The impact of ethical philosophy was more significant for the U.S. participants than for the Korean participants. (See Boxed Case 1.2 for measures of ethical philosophy.)

The advantages of using the survey method include its relative low cost. A survey requires the cost of planning, selecting participants, duplicating the questionnaire,

BOXED CASE 1.2. THE ETHICS POSITION QUESTIONNAIRE

To understand differences between individuals as they make moral judgments, researchers have developed different measures. This is one example of a scale designed to measure individual variations in ethical viewpoints. The Ethics Position Questionnaire (EPQ) was developed by Forsyth (1980). The scale measures the extent to which an individual rejects universal moral rules in favor of relativism. It also measures the role of idealism in contributing to moral judgments. The measure allows the researcher to categorize individuals into one of four different groups: situationists, absolutists, subjectivists, and exceptionists. Situationists reject moral rules and believe that moral decisions are always relative to the situation. Absolutists believe that the best possible outcome can be achieved by following universal moral rules. Subjectivists believe that moral judgments are based in personal values and perspectives. Exceptionists believe that moral absolutes guide judgments but can be violated in situations where breaking the rule benefits the majority.

To evaluate which ethical position reflects your decision making, indicate your degree of agreement with each of the following statements. Each represents a commonly held opinion, and there are no right or wrong answers. You will probably disagree with some items and agree with others. Please read each statement carefully.

The idealism score is obtained by taking the mean of items 1 through 10. The relativism score is obtained by taking the mean of items 11 through 20. The mean score of your responses to the idealism items and the mean score of your responses to the relativism items are taken to be your two EPQ scores. These scores can then be used to identify your ethical ideology. If you have high scores on both scales, you are a situationist. If you have a high score on the idealism scale but a low score on the relativism scale, you are absolutist. If you have a low score on the idealism scale but a high score on the relativism scale, you would be classified as a subjectivist. Finally, if you have a low score on both scales, you would be classified as an exceptionist.

───────────────────── Reference ─────────────────────

Forsyth, D. R. (1980). A taxonomy of ethical ideologies. *Journal of Personality and Social Psychology, 39*(1), 175–184.

	Strongly Disagree							Strongly Agree
1. A person should make certain that his or her actions never intentionally harm another, even to a small degree.	1	2	3	4	5	6	7	8	9
2. Risks to another should never be tolerated, irrespective of how small the risks might be.	1	2	3	4	5	6	7	8	9
3. The existence of potential harm to others is always wrong, irrespective of the benefits to be gained.	1	2	3	4	5	6	7	8	9
4. One should never psychologically or physically harm another person.	1	2	3	4	5	6	7	8	9
5. One should not perform an action that might in any way threaten the dignity and welfare of another individual.	1	2	3	4	5	6	7	8	9
6. If an action could harm an innocent other, then it should not be done.	1	2	3	4	5	6	7	8	9
7. Deciding whether to perform an act by balancing the positive consequences of the act against the negative consequences of the act is immoral.	1	2	3	4	5	6	7	8	9
8. The dignity and welfare of people should be the most important concern in any society.	1	2	3	4	5	6	7	8	9
9. It is never necessary to sacrifice the welfare of others.	1	2	3	4	5	6	7	8	9
10. Moral actions are those that closely match ideals of the most "perfect" action.	1	2	3	4	5	6	7	8	9
11. There are no ethical principles that are so important that they should be a part of any code of ethics.	1	2	3	4	5	6	7	8	9
12. What is ethical varies from one situation and society to another.	1	2	3	4	5	6	7	8	9

	Strongly Disagree								Strongly Agree
13. Moral standards should be seen as individualistic; what one person considers to be moral may be judged to be immoral by another person.	1	2	3	4	5	6	7	8	9
14. Different types of moralities cannot be compared in terms of their "rightness."	1	2	3	4	5	6	7	8	9
15. Questions of what is ethical for everyone can never be resolved, because what is moral or immoral is up to the individual.	1	2	3	4	5	6	7	8	9
16. Moral standards are simply *personal* rules that indicate how a person should behave and are not to be applied in making judgments of others.	1	2	3	4	5	6	7	8	9
17. Ethical considerations in interpersonal relations are so complex that individuals should be allowed to formulate their own individual codes.	1	2	3	4	5	6	7	8	9
18. Rigidly codifying an ethical position that prevents certain types of actions could stand in the way of better human relations and adjustment.	1	2	3	4	5	6	7	8	9
19. No rule concerning lying can be formulated; whether a lie is permissible or not permissible totally depends upon the situation.	1	2	3	4	5	6	7	8	9
20. Whether a lie is judged to be moral or immoral depends upon the circumstances surrounding the action.	1	2	3	4	5	6	7	8	9

distributing and collecting completed questionnaires. The benefit of using of a survey is clear when the people you want to study are spread out across a large geographic area. Additionally, participants can remain anonymous when they complete questionnaires. They might be willing to respond to sensitive questions when they do not have to speak to someone directly. A survey also reduces bias that might result from personal characteristics of the researcher. Sometimes attractive researchers get different responses from participants than less attractive researchers.

Disadvantages of surveys include the requirement of using simple items on the questionnaires. All questions must be understood by the majority of the population. There is also no control over who really completes the questionnaire. Researchers assume that the appropriate person completes the questionnaire, but it is possible that someone other than the intended participant actually completes it. Another major disadvantage of using a survey method is that it is difficult to obtain an adequate **response rate**. A response rate is the percentage of respondents who return completed questionnaires. The response rates for surveys are much lower than for other types of research (Frankfort-Nachmias & Nachmias, 2008).

Researchers use **experiments** when they want to examine potential causes of consumers' behavior (Babbie, 2004; Blackwell, Miniard, & Engel, 2001; Fraenkel & Wallen, 2003). When conducting an experiment, researchers assess the way consumers' behavior changes when particular aspects of the consumption situation change. When the behavior of a majority of the participants in the experiment changes following a change in the consumer situation, researchers can assume that the change in the consumption situation had an impact on the consumers' behavior. Furthermore, the change in the consumption situation should continue to have an impact on other consumers' behavior in the future. For example, suppose you were interested in determining how the use of an attractive model in an advertisement influenced consumers' recall of a brand name. For the experiment, you would develop two advertisements. One advertisement would feature an attractive model with a branded apparel product and one would feature an unattractive model with the same branded apparel product. Participants in the experiment would be randomly assigned to view only one of the advertisements, and they would be asked to write down the brand name of the product they saw featured in the advertisement. With this experiment, you could determine whether the attractiveness of the model in an advertisement had an impact on consumers' ability to remember the brand name of the apparel product featured.

Advantages of using experiments include enabling the researcher to test individual variables for their contribution to causing a change in consumers' behavior. From our example, marketers would know whether to use an attractive model in advertisements if they wanted consumers to be able to remember their brand names. Another advantage is that researchers have control over which variables are tested.

Disadvantages of experiments include that they are not generally carried out in natural settings. If we conducted the experiment about attractiveness in advertisements in a classroom, we might not get the exact same results as if we conducted the experiment in someone's home while he was looking at a magazine containing advertisements. When you are at home, you are probably relaxed, and magazines have lots of advertisements competing for your attention. However, you are probably not as relaxed in the classroom, especially when you know someone is watching you and you only have to focus on one particular advertisement for the experiment. Another disadvantage is that the results of an experiment may apply to only one situation with only one group of participants. If the situation changes or the characteristics of the participants change, the results may change (Frankfort-Nachmias & Nachmias, 2008).

Qualitative methods of data collection

When researchers use **qualitative** methods to collect data, they collect verbal or written information about consumers. Sometimes the words that are being examined originate from the consumers themselves. Researchers can interview consumers, either one on one or in a group, to learn about their behavior. During a qualitative **interview**, the researcher asks the consumers about "a set of topics to be discussed in depth" rather than using a set of standardized questions, as is done with survey research (Babbie, 2004, p. 300). To investigate the ways in which consumers understood fashion and their own use of apparel, Thompson and Haytko (1997) interviewed twenty college students. The students were told that the purpose of the research was to gain an understanding of their feelings, experiences, and perceptions of fashion. The researchers found that students use their clothing styles to communicate messages about themselves every day. Sometimes the meanings the students are trying to send are similar to the ones that marketers assign to the products in advertisements. Other times, the students use their clothing to construct new meanings that are different from the marketer-assigned meanings.

The advantages of using qualitative methods to conduct research include a deeper understanding of the phenomenon under investigation. Consumers can tell you directly what they believe instead of completing a questionnaire with forced responses. Another advantage of qualitative methods is the fact that new, unexpected insights can be gained. The researcher can probe for additional details and explanations for responses.

The disadvantages of using qualitative methods include the problem of potential deception and the impact that the research might have on the lives of the individuals being studied. The deception can occur from either the researcher or the participants. Some researchers interested in studying unethical consumption may hide their true purpose, and some participants may not be completely forthright in their responses. Additionally, researchers could adversely affect the feelings of participants if they were asked to discuss sensitive topics. Another disadvantage of qualitative research is the fact that information is collected from a relatively small number of individuals. Conducting interviews with a small number of participants may yield findings that are not applicable to other consumers (Frankfort-Nachmias & Nachmias, 2008).

While some qualitative data can come directly from consumers, the words that researchers examine in qualitative research studies may also originate from the researcher. Researchers can make observations of consumers and their behavior to learn about them. Conducting **field observations** involves recording descriptions of the actions that are occurring in a specific setting as they are occurring (Babbie, 2004). Researchers who conduct field observations watch people in arenas of consumption and describe what they see happening. Paco Underhill is a world-renowned researcher who examines consumer behavior as it is happening in stores. (You can learn more about Underhill's observation research by reading Boxed Case 1.3).

BOXED CASE 1.3. PACO UNDERHILL: SHOPPING SCIENTIST

Envirosell, Inc. was founded in New York in 1978 by Paco Underhill. Underhill and his colleagues have an interesting way in which to collect information about consumers. Rather than surveying or interviewing consumers, the researchers of Envirosell politely spy on consumers while they are shopping. Sometimes the behavior is recorded on hidden video cameras. At other times, the Envirosell researchers hide among the fixtures in retail stores to directly observe consumer behavior. In either case, the actions and movements of consumers are studied and categorized in an attempt to better understand and explain consumer behavior. The information gleaned from the investigations is shared with retailers and manufacturers, such as H&M, The Gap, Victoria's Secret, and Adidas, so that they may make products or provide services that are desired by consumers. Or, as Underhill explains, the research results teach "retailers and consumer product manufacturers better manners" (CBC News, 2000).

Over the past thirty years, Envirosell has observed many, many consumers. Each year, the researchers observe approximately 50,000 to 70,000 consumers (Smith, 2001). By observing these consumers, Underhill and his colleagues have made the following observations:

- There is a transition zone in every store between the outside and the inside where items can easily be missed by customers.
- Most people when they enter a store will turn to the right. This means that items placed on the left side should be items that customers will search for.
- Customers do not like to bend down to get items.
- Customers do not like too many mirrors. Too much glass can be disorientating.
- Customers do not like long lines.
- Customers do not like obscure price tags.
- Customers do not like intimidating service.

References

CBC News. (2000, November 7). *Paco Underhill: Shopping scientist*. Retrieved May 26, 2009, from http://www.cbc.ca/consumers/market/files/home/shopping/index.html

Smith, S. S. (2001, December). Attention, shoppers! Paco Underhill knows what they look at, what they buy and why, so get ready to put a huge dent in the concept of customers' free will. *Entrepreneur.* Retrieved May 26, 2009, from http://findarticles.com/p/articles/mi_m0DTI/is_12_29/ai_83678101/

Underhill, P. (1999). *Why we buy.* New York: Simon & Schuster.

Summary

Fashion refers to ways of behaving that are accepted by the majority of individuals in a given time and place. In addition to apparel, fashion applies to many different consumer products. In order for an item to be labeled a fashion, it is introduced, accepted, and then ultimately rejected. This process is called the fashion cycle. Individuals who adopt new styles or innovations early in the fashion cycle are called fashion innovators. Not all styles become fashion. Some are flops and others are fads.

Fashion consumption refers to the selection, purchase, use, and disposal of products. Consumption does not always mean purchasing. Individuals can consume products, but they can also consume experiences and thoughts. Normative consumption reflects consumer behaviors that follow the established norms of a culture. Nonnormative consumption reflects consumer behaviors that are outside the normal consumption patterns of a culture.

Researchers use a variety of methods to learn about consumers. Some of these methods involve gathering data through the use of questionnaires. Other methods involve gathering data by talking directly with consumers or by observing their behavior in the marketplace. Each of these approaches has advantages and disadvantages.

Key Terms

- basic product
- classic
- consumption
- discontinuous style
- early adopters
- early majority
- experiment
- fad
- fashion
- fashion cycle
- fashion innovators
- fashion system
- field observation
- flop
- haute couture
- historical continuity
- innovation
- innovation adoption curve
- interview
- laggards
- late majority
- nonnormative consumption
- normative
- norms
- qualitative methods
- quantitative methods

- questionnaire
- response rate
- survey methods

- taste
- trend
- zeitgeist

Questions for review and discussion

1. Some groups of individuals do not participate in fashion. Think about one of those groups of people. Describe that group. Why might they not participate in fashion? In what ways might it be beneficial for them not to participate in fashion? In what ways might it be better if they did participate in fashion?
2. Discuss factors that might accelerate or decelerate the rate of adoption of a new style.
3. Compare and contrast a style labeled as a classic to a style labeled as a fad. Provide an example of a classic. Provide an example of a fad.
4. Draw the typical innovation adoption curve. Label the x and y axes. Label the points on the curve that represent the point in time when fashion innovators, early adopters, early majority, late majority, and laggards would adopt a new fashion innovation.
5. After an innovation is introduced by a high-end designer, that innovation may be copied by other designers and manufacturers as it moves through the adoption process. Do you think it is ethical for designers and manufacturers to copy styles? Identify pros and cons associated with allowing copies of styles to be sold.
6. Explain the difference between normative and nonnormative consumption. Provide an example of a normative fashion consumption behavior. Provide an example of a nonnormative fashion consumption behavior.
7. Describe the differences between quantitative and qualitative research. Identify the advantages and disadvantages associated with each of the methods of conducting research.

Notes

1. To see examples of runway shows, see http://www.cosmopolitan.com/style/fashion-show/.

2. To see examples of similar-looking apparel items at different price points, go to http://www.instyle.com/instyle/celebrities/lookforless/0,,20044918,00.html.

3. Black Friday gets its name from the fact that it is the day many retailers move from running their businesses without making a profit (in the red) to making a profit (in the black).

Suggested Readings

If you are interested in the topics in chapter 1, you may also like reading these other books:

Breward, C. (1995). *The culture of fashion: A new history of fashionable dress*. New York: Manchester University Press.
Rogers, E.M. (1983). *Diffusion of innovations* (3rd ed.). New York: Free Press.
Underhill, P. (1999). *Why we buy*. New York: Simon & Schuster.

References

Arnould, E. J., & Price, L. L. (2000). Authenticating acts and authoritative performances. In S. Rathneshwar, D. G. Mick, & C. Huffman (Eds.), *The why of consumption*. New York: Routledge.

Babbie, E. (2004). *The practice of social research* (10th ed.). Belmont, CA: Wadsworth/Thomson Learning.

Berger, A. A. (2005). *Shop 'til you drop: Consumer behavior and American culture*. Lanham, MD: Rowman & Littlefield Publishers.

Blackwell, R. D., Miniard, P. W., & Engel, J. F. (2001). *Consumer behavior* (9th ed.). Fort Worth, TX: Harcourt College Publishers.

Buckland, S. S. (2005). Promoting American designers, 1940–44: Building our own house. In L. Welters & P. A. Cunningham (Eds.), *Twentieth-century American fashion* (pp. 99–121). Oxford, England: Berg.

Callen, K. S., & Ownbey, S. F. (2003). Associations between demographics and perceptions of unethical consumer behaviour. *International Journal of Consumer Studies, 27*(2), 99–110.

Cornell University. (2006). *Life cycle. The cutting edge apparel business guide*. Retrieved August 27, 2007, from http://instruct1.cit.cornell.edu/courses/cuttingedge/lifeCycle/03.htm

Cotton Incorporated. (2001, August 23). A shorter look with legs: Capris and cropped pants head into fall season. *Womenswear Articles*. Retrieved May 28, 2007, from http://www.cottoninc.com/lsmarticles/?articleID=146

Eicher, J. B., Evenson, S. L., & Lutz, H. A. (2008). *The visible self: Global perspectives of dress, culture, and society* (3rd ed.). New York: Fairchild Books.

Firat, A. F. (1994). Gender and consumption: Transcending the feminine? In J. A. Costa (Ed.), *Gender issues and consumer behavior* (pp. 205–228). Thousand Oaks, CA: Sage.

Fraenkel, J. R., & Wallen, N. E. (2003). *How to design and evaluate research in education* (5th ed.). Boston: McGraw-Hill.

Frankel, D. (2006). *The devil wears Prada* [Motion picture]. Fox 2000 Pictures.

Frankfort-Nachmias, C., & Nachmias, D. (2008). *Research methods in the social sciences* (7th ed.). New York: Worth Publishers.

Frings, G. S. (1996). *Fashion: From concept to consumer* (5th ed.). Upper Saddle River, NJ: Prentice Hall.

Johnson, D. (2007). What is haute couture? Uncovering the business of high fashion. *Infoplease*. Retrieved September 12, 2007, from http://www.infoplease.com/spot/fashionside1.html

Lee, M., & Johnson, K.K.P. (2005). Effects of ethical philosophy on perceptions of unethical clothing shopping behaviors: Comparison between U.S. and Korean consumers. *ITAA Proceedings* (Vol. 62, pp. 380–381). Boulder, CO: International Textile and Apparel Association.

McCracken, G. (1988). *Culture and consumption: New approaches to the symbolic character of consumer goods and activities*. Bloomington: Indiana University Press.

Minahan, S., & Beverland, M. (2005). *Why women shop: Secrets revealed*. Milton, Queensland, Australia: Wrightbooks.

Nava, M. (1992). *Changing cultures: Feminism, youth and consumerism*. London: Sage.

Postrel, V. (2004, June 17). Variety, the spice of life, has measurable value. But it's not easy to determine. *New York Times*. Retrieved September 16, 2007, from http://www.vpostrel.com/articles-speeches/nyt/globalvariety.html

Raustiala, K., & Sprigman, C. (2006). The piracy paradox: Innovation and intellectual property in fashion design. *Virginia Law Review, 92*(8), 1688–1777.

Reed, A., II. (2002). Social identity as a useful perspective for self-concept-based consumer research. *Psychology and Marketing, 19*, 235–266.

Rogers, E.M. (1983). *Diffusion of innovations* (3rd ed.). New York: Free Press.

Solomon, M.R., & Rabolt, N.J. (2004). *Consumer behavior in fashion.* Upper Saddle River, NJ: Prentice Hall.

Sproles, G.B., & Burns, L.D. (1994). *Changing appearances: Understanding dress in contemporary society.* New York: Fairchild Books.

Stone, E. (2008). *The dynamics of fashion* (3rd ed.). New York: Fairchild Books.

Thomas, P.W. (2007, July 28). Key fashion trends for fall 2007 and winter 2008. *Fashion-Era.* Retrieved August 27, 2007, from http://www.fashion-era.com/trends_2008/2008_autumn_looks_key_winter_fashion_2007.htm

Thompson, C.J., & Haytko, D.L. (1997). Speaking of fashion: Consumers' uses of fashion discourses and the appropriation of countervailing cultural meanings. *Journal of Consumer Research, 24*(1), 15–42.

Thurman, R. (2003, November). Camouflage—It's an everywhere fashion statement. *Shooting Industry.* Retrieved July 19, 2010, from http://findarticles.com/p/articles/mi_m3197/is_11_48/ai_1113888350/

Tortora, P.G., & Eubank, K. (2005). *Survey of historic costume: A history of Western dress* (4th ed.). New York: Fairchild Books.

Value Based Management. (2007, May 1). *Innovation adoption curve of Rogers.* Retrieved August 27, 2007, from http://www.valuebasedmanagement.net/methods_rogers_innovation_adoption_curve.html

Wilson, E. (2007, September 4). Before models can turn around, knockoffs fly. *New York Times.* Retrieved September 5, 2007, from http://www.nytimes.com/2007/09/04/us/04fashion.html?_r=1&pagewanted=print

2

HISTORICAL OVERVIEW
OF APPAREL CONSUMPTION

After you have read this chapter, you should be able to

- Describe the ways in which our ancient ancestors shopped for apparel products.
- Understand how and why shopping for apparel changed after the Industrial Revolution.
- Discuss developments in apparel shopping during the twentieth century.
- Explain the popularity of the different types of apparel retail establishments among contemporary consumer groups.
- Compare and contrast apparel shopping across cultures.

The evolution of shopping arenas

Apparel retailing is an exciting topic because the way we buy apparel products is constantly changing right along with what we buy. Just as the apparel products we wear are time- and culture-specific, the way we buy those products and the supplies needed to make those products are also time- and culture-specific. It may be hard to imagine a time and a place when and where there was no such thing as shopping, let alone shopping simply for the pleasure of shopping as many of us do today. But, in reality, our contemporary notions of what it means to shop for apparel are very different from those of individuals who lived before us. In fact, college-aged individuals in the 1980s and 1990s shopped differently than college students do today at the beginning of the twenty-first century. If apparel shopping has changed that much in the past twenty-five years, imagine how much things have changed since ancient times.

Shopping in ancient times (3500 to 300 B.C.)

Evidence of the existence of markets stretches back to ancient Egypt (Hine, 2002). The very first markets were open-air venues in the center of a town. Markets like this still exist in the twenty-first century. Some of these markets appear temporarily for special events, like weekend arts and crafts fairs. But other markets, like the market in Marrakech, Morocco, are permanent shopping venues where local citizens purchase apparel items on a regular basis (see Figure 2.1).

In the earliest Egyptian marketplace, the practice of exchanging money for finished goods and services did not exist. During these early times in human history, apparel was made by hand in the home. Textile supplies for making apparel were available in the marketplace. At this time, there was no such thing as manmade fibers. **Manmade fibers** are "fibers made from cellulose in plants or from chemicals derived from petroleum, gas, and coal" (Frings, 1996, p. 378). The concept of a completely synthetic fiber is quite recent; the first completely manmade fiber, nylon, was created by the DuPont Company in 1939 (Frings, 1996). The only fibers available to people for the greater part of human history have been **natural fibers** like "cotton, wool, ramie, silk, and flax, which come from plant and animal sources and have been used for thousands of years" (Jarnow & Dickerson, 1997, p. 107).

If we were living in Egypt, we would need to make the fabric for our apparel items out of fibers derived from plants or animals. For example, linen fibers from flax plants could be spun by hand into yarns. These yarns could then be woven, again by hand, into linen fabric. And this linen fabric could be made into a stylish tunic. **Tunics** "were simple one-piece and often T-shaped garments with openings for the head and the arms" (Tortora & Eubank, 2005, p. 13). The tunic was a garment that

Figure 2.1 A permanent outdoor shopping venue in Marrakech, Morocco. Photo by Jennifer Yurchisin.

was worn by both men and women in ancient times (Tortora & Eubank, 2005). Figure 2.2 shows a contemporary interpretation of the Egyptian tunic.

The only apparel-related items that appeared in the marketplace were supplies that estate owners had left over after the servants made all the apparel items needed for the estate owner, his family members, and the servants (Hine, 2002; Tortora & Eubank, 2005). There were no finished goods for sale to consumers. So if you were an estate owner who experienced a large crop of flax and your family's servants were particularly efficient at spinning yarns and weaving fabric, your family might end up with more textile supplies (e.g., fabric) than needed for apparel. You might decide to go to the marketplace and exchange these surplus textiles for other household supplies such as food using a barter system. **Bartering** is a "system in which companies or people trade merchandise and services without using money" (Babylon Ltd., 2009, p. 1). The entire process of growing fiber to be woven into fabric and then made into apparel was very difficult and time-consuming. This may explain why most people living in Egypt did not have extensive wardrobes like many of us do now (Welters, 2008). Even the process of shopping at the marketplace sounds more like work than fun.

Figure 2.2 A contemporary version of the Egyptian tunic. Photo by Jennifer Yurchisin.

Of course, not everyone who lived in these very early times in Egypt had to live so modestly. If you were a member of one of the ruling class families, like Cleopatra, you certainly had more than one ensemble to wear. And even though you had to have the fabric for your apparel items made out of natural fibers, the fibers that were used in your apparel would not have to be grown in your own yard. You could have your fabric made out of exotic fibers that were acquired during trips to other countries and other parts of the empire. Your apparel items could be made out of the finest materials, such as silk, cotton, or even gold (Tortora & Eubank, 2005; Welters, 2008). So the members of the ruling classes certainly consumed fashion in a much different way than the rest of the population in ancient times. Compared to the nonruling members of the population (that is, the majority of the population living in Egypt), the wardrobes of the ruling classes differed in size (they had more apparel items) and quality (they had better apparel items). Remember these differences as you read chapter 4. You will find that social class still affects apparel purchasing habits in the twenty-first century.

Shopping prior to the industrial revolution (300 B.C. to 1700)

Apparel shopping styles did not change dramatically immediately after the fall of the Egyptian Empire. Some changes occurred over an extended period of time. As humans became efficient and effective farmers, fewer individuals needed to focus their attention on growing food and harvesting other natural materials (like cotton, flax, and wool). When each farmer's yield began to greatly exceed the amount of supplies needed to feed and clothe the immediate family, fewer individuals had to work as farmers. This development cleared the way for a greater level of job specialization and an increased amount of trade among people (Denslow, 2006). In other words, individuals who were successful at growing and harvesting raw materials (e.g., sheep farmers who cultivate sheep that produce wool fibers) specialized in performing those tasks. They brought to the marketplace those raw materials (e.g., wool fibers, vegetables, meat). The individuals who specialized in producing textiles (e.g., weaving and dyeing) obtained the raw materials, processed them (e.g., wove them into cloth or dyed the cloth a particular color), and brought their finished cloth to the marketplace.

At the end of a busy day at the marketplace, the farmers left the marketplace with the finished cloth they needed for their family. And the textile producers left the marketplace with the raw materials they needed to make cloth as well as the food they needed to feed their families. To obtain the supplies they needed at the marketplace, the farmers and the textile producers could barter, or, as the use of silver and copper coins as currency became commonplace, they could use money to purchase supplies (Klaffke, 2003). And, as money was introduced into the marketplace, the retail trade as we know it was born (Hine, 2002).

In addition to supplies needed to make apparel in the marketplace, finished apparel items began to appear for purchase. Evidence exists to suggest that there was somewhat of a ready-to-wear business during the Roman Empire (Tortora & Eubank, 2005). That is to say, rather than making all of their apparel items by hand at home, people could also purchase some apparel items from tailors and artisans who sold finished apparel items. Furthermore, used apparel items could also be purchased in the marketplace at this time (Tortora & Eubank, 2005; Welters, 2008). As mentioned earlier, some individuals (i.e., those from the ruling classes) had more apparel items than they needed. As a result, these individuals did not wear out their apparel items as did many of the individuals in lower-ranking social positions. As members of the ruling classes acquired a surplus of apparel items, they could sell their old apparel items to traders who then sold these finished apparel items in the marketplace.

By the end of the Renaissance in Europe, a greater number and variety of apparel supplies and items appeared in marketplaces. This variety was a result of continued world exploration and development. As transportation improved, trade in textiles and finished apparel items flourished (Tortora & Eubank, 2005). Marketplaces during this time might have looked something like contemporary Renaissance festivals. If you have been to one of these festivals, you probably remember that shopping is a big part of the event (see Figure 2.3). You might remember, also, that you can buy a wide range of apparel and apparel-related items, from wool sweaters to leather handbags and silver jewelry.

Figure 2.3 Apparel shopping in the Middle Ages would have taken place in outdoor courtyards, like the one pictured here. Photo by Jennifer Yurchisin. With thanks to Sherman Malkerson.

OVERVIEW OF APPAREL CONSUMPTION

During the Renaissance in Europe, no machines were used to create the items being sold in the marketplace. But the Industrial Revolution was about to begin, and things were going to change in a major way.

The industrial revolution and the introduction of the department store (1700 to 1900)

As our ancestors began to invent machines to increase their productivity and reduce costs during the eighteenth and nineteenth centuries, the seed for the practice of apparel shopping as we know it in contemporary society was planted. The **Industrial Revolution** occurred when society moved "from a stable agricultural and commercial society to a modern industrial society relying on complex machinery rather than tools" ("Industrial Revolution," 2008, p. 1).

Some have argued that the textile industry played an important role in the Industrial Revolution. British textile merchants selling domestic wool fabric were having trouble competing with individuals selling lower-cost imports of cotton fabric from India (Tortora & Eubank, 2005; Yafa, 2005). The solution to the British textile producers' problem was the invention and implementation of technology that permitted textile items to be produced faster and less expensively. It was not long before individuals in countries other than England, such as France and the United States, also realized the benefits of mass production. Rather than producing a small number of textile items slowly by hand, a greater number of textile items could be produced much faster after equipment and machines began to be used during the manufacturing process. Several important developments needed for mass production in the textile industry occurred in the 1700s and 1800s. These include the flying shuttle in 1733, the spinning jenny in 1764, the water frame in 1769, and the power loom in 1814 (Frings, 1996). And what was the world to do with all of the fabric that was being produced? Why, make apparel items with it, of course. After the sewing machine, complete with foot treadle, was developed in 1859, the stage was set for mass production of ready-to-wear apparel (Frings, 1996).

If you saw the movie *Field of Dreams*, you probably remember the line, "If you build it, they will come" (Robinson, 1989). Even though the movie is about a baseball field, the quote works for the field of apparel and textiles. When textile mills and apparel manufacturing plants were located in cities, individuals needed to migrate from farms in the countryside to the cities to work in those mills and plants. To be employed in this industry, these individuals needed apparel items to wear when they were at work. However, these employees no longer had time to make their own apparel in the same way that they did when they lived in the country. Now that there were factories producing finished apparel items, these workers did not have to make their own apparel by hand. But where would these employees, as well as the other individuals who were living in the cities, go to purchase these ready-to-wear apparel items? A few options existed. Tailors and artisans still operated small stores in the cities. Also, general or dry goods stores started opening in the early 1800s. **General stores** evolved out of trading posts and were generally located in rural areas. They sold a wide variety of items, including saddles, guns, seed, fabric, food supplies, dress fabric, bonnets, and sewing supplies. They also provided some services, including marketing crops taken in trade, operating post offices, and providing some elementary banking services. Prices were negotiated between sellers and buyers. There were no returns made on purchases. If you purchased something, it was yours. Individuals could purchase some ready-to-wear apparel items at this type of store. In the mid-1800s, a third option appeared on the retail landscape that would change the way we shop forever. Enter the department store.

Just as a general store met a wide range of customers' needs by stocking a wide variety of merchandise, a **department store** also was designed for a range of customers. Most of the earliest department stores were outgrowths of general stores (Frings, 1996; Klaffke, 2003). A department store generally offers customers a variety of merchandise lines at several different price points. Department stores have evolved over the years, but many continue to offer men's, women's, and children's apparel, cosmetics, jewelry, home furnishings, furniture, small home appliances, and electronics. Some department stores offer other lines of products such as hardware, large home appliances, food, and sporting goods.

The first department store opened in Paris in 1852. The Bon Marché, as it was (and is still) called, carried a variety of merchandise, including apparel items and home goods, all under one roof (Klaffke, 2003). Like department stores in any city, all of the prices on the merchandise available for purchase at the Bon Marché were fixed. Furthermore, consumers were allowed to enter and leave the Bon Marché without making a purchase. While the practices instituted at the Bon Marché do not sound revolutionary to us, they were very unusual for the time. At other stores in the 1850s, consumers had to make a purchase if they entered a store and negotiated with salespeople over prices (Klaffke, 2003). Merchants in other cities soon followed the Bon Marché's lead, and department stores opened in many other countries in the late 1800s. You may have been to some of these department stores, because some of them are still in business today, including Harrods in London, Macy's in New York, and Eaton's in Toronto (Frings, 1996; Klaffke, 2003).

The new department stores catered to the needs of many women and men, including the members of the newly formed and growing middle class. The middle class developed as a result of the Industrial Revolution. The wives of successful tradesmen and captains of industry had both time to spend shopping at the "theatres of retailing" and money to spend on ready-to-wear apparel, which the enterprising retailers were more than willing to accept (Jarnow & Dickerson, 1997, p. 395).

While members of the so-called leisure class purchased their ready-to-wear apparel items at department stores, individuals in the lowest-ranking social positions, who could not afford to purchase apparel items in department stores, continued to have to make their own apparel items by hand. Additionally, members of the highest levels of society continued to have their apparel made for them by hand in couture houses.

Charles Worth opened the first haute couture establishment in Paris in 1858. Many other couture houses soon followed, including Paquin, Doucet, and Lanvin. As a means of protecting the ideas and designs of couturiers, Charles Worth's sons established the Chambre Syndicale de la Couture Parisienne in the 1880s (Tortora & Eubank, 2005). The **Chambre Syndicale de la Couture Parisienne** was a trade association that "was formed to determine qualifications for a couture house and to deal with their common problems and interests" (Jarnow & Dickerson, 1997, p. 348). The Chambre Syndicale de la Couture Parisienne is still in existence today. As the nineteenth century drew to a close, the work of its members helped to make Paris the fashion capital of the world.

Shopping in the twentieth century (1900 to 1980)

During the first half of the twentieth century, the first two World Wars had a devastating effect on Europe's major cities and the people living in those cities. Buildings were damaged and destroyed. Shopping for new apparel products took a back seat to the pressing concerns of basic survival. Sacrifices of materials typically used for apparel needed to be made to support the war effort in both Europe and the United States. For example, the newly created nylon fiber was diverted from apparel production to defense production (Tortora & Eubank, 2005). Silk was reserved for the production of parachutes. Women had to get creative with material for apparel fabric as many items were rationed. In the countryside, women recycled feed bags for apparel products similarly to the way that we are currently reusing materials in apparel and related products. By the time these dark days were over, people were ready to get back to their normal routines, to raise their families, to have some fun, and to shop again. And a new shopping arena was developed to fulfill these hungry consumers' appetites.

The enclosed shopping mall, an American original

After World War II ended, men came home to the United States. After serving their country for several years, these men were ready to settle down in new homes in the suburbs of cities. The former soldiers and their young wives started families. In fact, these couples had so many children that the children are described as the baby boom generation. Baby boomers are the children who were born during the years immediately following World War II. We will talk more about the baby boomers in chapter 4, when we discuss the apparel consumption behavior of different age cohorts. Right now, we discuss what it was like for the parents of the baby boomers to shop.

For the most part, during this time period, the responsibility for taking care of the home and the people in it fell to the wives and mothers (Tortora & Eubank, 2005). However, it was not very convenient for these women to tote their children all the way to the cities from the suburbs to go shopping. So, instead of forcing the homemakers to travel downtown to shop in department stores, the department stores moved out to the suburbs.

The idea for the suburban shopping center was not completely new. There were about one dozen shopping centers in the United States in 1945 (Klaffke, 2003). However, these suburban shopping centers were more like contemporary strip malls than the multistory, enclosed malls that we typically think of when we use the term *shopping mall* (Klaffke, 2003). The first modern, multistory, enclosed mall in the United States opened in Edina, Minnesota, in 1956. Southdale Center, as it is still known today, opened with two department stores serving as anchors and specialty stores filling in the spaces between. Southdale Center was built as a "refuge for shoppers during the harsh Minnesota winters" (Klaffke, 2003, p. 50). Although the suburban shopping mall was initially opened primarily for suburban homemakers, it was not long before the mall became a place for everyone, including the teenaged baby boomers, to spend their leisure time in the winter and in the summer (Tortora & Eubank, 2005). In this way, the shopping mall ushered in the modern consumer culture. Over the last half of the twentieth century, the shopping mall concept continued to evolve in the United States. Today, the new malls that open tend to be "lifestyle centers," which we will discuss later in this chapter. Additionally, the idea of the shopping mall was exported to other countries around the globe. In fact, today, the world's largest shopping mall is in Dubai in the United Arab Emirates. (See Boxed Case 2.1 for a list of the largest malls in the world.)

Shopping at the end of the twentieth century (1980 to 2000)

As shopping malls evolved, other changes were occurring in the United States and around the world that influenced apparel shopping styles. One of the biggest changes that occurred was the mass entrance of women into the business world in the 1970s and 1980s. During this time, women began "trying to make it up the corporate ladder rather than the social one" (Frings, 1996, p. 24). Rather than working only until

BOXED CASE 2.1. SOME OF THE LARGEST ENCLOSED MALLS AROUND THE WORLD

The following table contains information about the world's largest shopping malls, including their location, square footage, and some of their unique features. As you can see, these contemporary shopping malls are truly destination locations that feature shopping establishments, entertainment venues, and restaurants. Some of these shopping malls may be larger (and maybe more exciting) than your college campus.

Name and location	Square footage	Features	Web site
The Dubai Mall, Dubai, United Arab Emirates	over 9 million square feet	over 1,000 retail shops, the world's largest gold souk market, KidZania, an ice rink, an aquarium, a cinema, and SEGA Republic theme park	http://www.thedubaimall.com/en/
Dream Mall, Taiwan	over 4.3 million square feet	restaurants, movie theater, gym, and a Hello Kitty Ferris wheel in the entertainment facility	http://www.dream-mall.com.tw/
Mall of America, Bloomington, Minnesota, United States	4.2 million square feet	more than 500 specialty stores, 50 restaurants, a cinema, an aquarium, and Nickelodeon Universe amusement park	http://www.mallofamerica.com
West Edmonton Mall, Alberta, Canada	3.8 million square feet	more than 800 stores and services, two unique hotels, over 100 restaurants, a water park, skating rink, casino, and amusement park rides	http://www.westedmall.com

they got married and began having children, women now wanted to keep working throughout their adult lives. This cultural change in the United States and Western Europe forced the apparel industry to change in several ways. First, more women of a variety of ages needed clothing to wear to work, as discussed in chapter 1. Second, women with full-time careers both outside and inside the home found that they had less time for shopping for both themselves and their family members. It was at this time when women began suffering time poverty. **Time poverty** is "a feeling of having less time available than is required to meet the demands of everyday living" (Solomon, 2004, p. 601). Women found that it was difficult to balance the demands of a career and manage busy household. Many women barely had enough time to get all of their home duties done with their work schedules, let alone shop for apparel at the local shopping mall.

To help these overworked women stay up to date with fashion, the apparel retail industry responded by expanding in-home shopping options. First on the scene were catalogs. The mail order catalog business was not a new invention. Both

Montgomery Ward and Sears, Roebuck and Co. had been in operation since the late 1800s. However, the main consumers for these early mail order catalog companies were consumers who lived so far outside of the city that shopping downtown was not a possibility. In the late 1900s, shopping for apparel items via a catalog became popular again, but for other reasons. In the 1980s and 1990s, many women enjoyed purchasing apparel products for themselves and their family members through catalogs because they could shop on their own schedule. These women were not restricted in their shopping by the hours of operation of mall stores. Instead, they could shop for apparel at any time, day or night, in the comfort of their own homes. The success of catalog shopping cleared the path for the introduction of other forms of in-home shopping, including television shopping and later Internet shopping.

Home television shopping

The first home shopping television channel in the United States was the Home Shopping Network (HSN). HSN began broadcasting nationwide in 1985. One year later, rival network Quality Value Convenience (QVC) began offering products (Klaffke, 2003). Today, both HSN and QVC can be seen worldwide in several European and Asian countries. In fact, by 2008, QVC could be seen in approximately 170 million homes around the world (QVC, Inc., 2008). And sales for both home shopping television channels are healthy, with sales on HSN totaling almost $1.9 billion in the third quarter of 2008 (HSN, Inc., 2008) and sales for QVC's 2007 fiscal year totaling more than $7 billion (QVC, Inc., 2008).

At first, the individuals who purchased through home shopping television channels tended to be those who already had experience purchasing apparel through catalogs (Eastlick & Liu, 1997). Through research, a profile of the typical home television shopper in the United States was developed. Most home television shoppers are older women with moderate income levels of less than $50,000 annually. These women tend to live in urban areas and tend to be either unemployed or retired. A majority of these women tend to wear large sizes in apparel. It seems to be the case that these women enjoy shopping via the television because they have trouble finding the sizes they need in apparel stores in their local communities (Stanforth & Lennon, 1996). For these women, it is easier and perhaps more comfortable to shop at home rather than go to the mall to shop for apparel. At the mall, these women risk disappointment and embarrassment when they are unable to locate the sizes they need in the styles they desire. By shopping on television, these women can purchase, without face-to-face contact with a salesperson, the sizes they need from the increased inventory available directly from the home television shopping channel's warehouse.

Unfortunately, the enjoyment these women feel while watching and purchasing products from home shopping television channels is often addictive (Grant, Guthrie, & Ball-Rokeach, 1991; Harden, 1996). Many of the purchases are impulsive and unplanned (Donthu & Gilliland, 1996; Lee, Lennon, & Rudd, 2000). Thus, purchasing apparel products from home shopping television channels can be detrimental to one's bank account. We'll talk more about impulsive consumer behavior and compulsive consumer behavior in chapter 3 and 4. For now, suffice it to say that some negative consequences may result from too much home television shopping.

Internet shopping

Internet shopping is another form of in-home shopping that developed in the last half of the twentieth century and provides the ability to make purchases any day of the week and time of the day. At first, clothing was not purchased very frequently using the Internet. There are several reasons for the lack of electronic apparel commerce. When the Internet was introduced, it tended to be the domain of men (Lohse, Bellman, & Johnson, 2000). Women purchase more apparel, both for themselves and for other members of their families, than men (Underhill, 1999). Ergo, apparel items were not purchased as frequently as other products, such as compact discs, books, and computer software (Pastore, 2000). Another issue related to the lack of electronic apparel commerce was the fact that apparel represents high-risk, high-experience products. There is a great deal of uncertainty associated with purchasing apparel that consumers are unable to touch, feel, and try on before the purchase (Kim, Sullivan, & Forney, 2007). Moreover, consumers were worried about exchanging or returning unwanted apparel, particularly from unknown or Internet-only apparel retailers (Jones & Vijayasarathy, 1998). These purchasing risks further reduced the likelihood of consumers purchasing apparel online.

As time progressed and more women started using the Internet at school or at work, apparel sales on the Internet began to rise. Similarly to home shopping television channels, women consumers who had previous experience purchasing apparel through print catalogs were among the first to adopt the Internet as a channel for purchasing apparel (PriceWaterhouseCoopers, 2000). As both women and men gained experience and confidence using the Internet to make purchases of all kinds, consumers began purchasing high-risk products, including apparel (Bhatnager, Misra, & Rao, 2000). By 2005, consumers, both men and women, in the United States were spending more money ($1.4 billion more, to be exact) purchasing apparel than electronics using the Internet (e-tailing group, 2005). And, in 2007, the apparel, accessories, and footwear category surpassed all other product categories in terms of Internet sales (National Retail Federation, 2007). So, for the first time in the history of the Internet, apparel had reached the top in terms of Internet sales.

These days, consumers all over the world use their computers to purchase apparel from a variety of Internet retailers. Consumers purchase apparel from pure play, Internet-only retailers like bluefly.com and net-a-porter.com as well as from the Web sites of well-known catalog retailers such as Coldwater Creek. Consumers also purchase apparel from the Internet sites of traditional bricks-and-mortar retailers like H&M and Gap. Consumers can even purchase apparel that they see on home shopping television channels using the Internet Web sites for these channels (e.g., HSN.com, QVC.com).

Suffice it to say that apparel retailing in the United States and around the globe has truly become a multichannel affair. **Multichannel retailing** involves "the use of catalogues, stores, and the internet in a coordinated marketing plan" (Rath, Bay, Petrizzi, & Gill, 2008, p. 441). With the exception of pure play, Internet-only retailers, the majority of apparel retailers in the twenty-first century offer their consumers a variety of ways in which to look at and purchase their merchandise.

Meeting a variety of consumer wants and needs in the twenty-first century

Apparel consumers today have more choices than ever before. Not only are there choices about the formats or channels in which to shop, consumers also have many, many choices concerning which stores to patronize. As you may have guessed, the United States has the greatest number of retail stores. For every man, woman, and child living in the United States, there is an estimated twenty square feet of retail space. This number is well above other developed countries, including Sweden (about three square feet per person), the United Kingdom and France (approximately two and a half square feet per person in each country), and Italy (one square foot per person) (Jenkins, 2009). While the numbers are higher in the United States than any country in the world, the situation is similar all over the globe. There is a lot of competition for individuals' hard-earned money these days (Levy & Weitz, 2006; Pine & Gilmore, 1999).

With all of this competition, the power has shifted from the retailers to the consumers. It is a simple equation that you may remember from your economics class. When supply exceeds demand, it is a buyer's market. The buyers get to sit back and relax while the suppliers are forced to compete heavily with each other to win buyers. Enterprising retailers keep coming up with new ways to improve consumers' shopping experience. (You can read about some of these retail inventions in Boxed Case 2.2.) Retailers who sell apparel products, just like every other kind of retailer, have to appeal to the wants and needs of consumers. The various types of wants and needs expressed by consumers are often shaped by the different shopping outcomes that consumers hope to achieve.

BOXED CASE 2.2. CONSUMPTION MADE EASY

Over the years, several key inventions have made shopping and buying easy for consumers. The cash register was first developed by James Ritty in 1878 (Klaffke, 2003). This Ohio tavern owner was concerned that his employees were stealing from his business by taking customers' cash and putting it into their pockets. Two individuals studying at Drexel

Institute of Technology (now Drexel University) developed what would eventually become the universal product code (UPC) or bar code system of tracking inventory. Learning of the need for grocery stores to better track inventory and speed up checkout times, Norman Joseph Woodland and Bernard Silver developed a decoding system that was inspired by Morse code. Used in retailing and industrial manufacturing as well as in libraries and by the medical community, bar code technologically is now a $16 billion a year business (Engineering New Frontiers, n.d.). The father of the credit card was Frank McNamara, who, having left his wallet at home, was unable to pay for a business dinner one evening. This incident stimulated his idea to develop a method so that "consumers could tap into a line of credit with a restaurant instead of having to worry about carrying cash" (Klaffke, 2003, p. 22). McNamara launched the first credit card as we know it today in 1951, getting 27 New York City restaurant owners to accept it. The name of the card was McNamara's Diners Club, and there were 200 members (Klaffke, 2003).

References

Engineering new frontiers. (n.d.). Retrieved May 28, 2009, from http://www.drexel.edu/academics/coe/cae/publications/coe.brochure.pdf

Klaffke, P. (2003). Spree: A cultural history of shopping. Vancouver, BC, Canada: Arsenal Pulp Press.

Utilitarian and hedonic consumer behavior

People shop for lots of different reasons. Some people shop because they like to shop. Some people shop because they have to shop. And sometimes people who like to shop find that they are shopping because they have to shop. Confused? Think about your shopping behavior. If you had spare time on the weekend, would you like to spend the time visiting apparel stores, trying on different outfits (many of which you have no intention of actually buying), talking to the salespeople, enjoying the music playing in the stores, and watching other consumers? Or are you a person who only shops for apparel when it is absolutely necessary, planning in advance exactly what and where you are going to buy so you can enter and exit an apparel store with what you need as quickly as possible? Which scenario best describes your approach to shopping?

The first scenario describes hedonic shopping. **Hedonic consumer behavior** is consumption that is directed at satisfying needs for fantasy, excitement, and fun. Products acquire hedonic meanings when they are associated with "specific feelings or when they facilitate or perpetuate feelings" (Arnould, Price, & Zinkhan, 2004, p 131). Shopping that provides entertainment value and emotional worth reflects hedonic consumption (Arnould, Price, & Zinkhan, 2004). When we shop for hedonic reasons, we shop for shopping's sake (Kim, Sullivan, & Forney, 2007). We feel satisfied when the entire experience associated with shopping is pleasurable. Hedonic shopping is often seen as a fun recreational activity by those who engage in it (Babin, Darden, & Griffin, 1994; Holbrook & Hirschman, 1982). When we are shopping hedonically, it does not matter whether we leave the store with any merchandise. Our ultimate objective while shopping hedonically is not necessarily to purchase anything in particular. If we find something to buy while we are shopping, that is great. If not, that is great, too. It is the shopping experience from start to finish that is the important part when we are shopping hedonically. Hence, if we had a good time while we were shopping, then we will most likely be pleased with the experience.

On the other hand, if we were engaging in utilitarian shopping, we would be very disappointed if we left the store with no merchandise. **Utilitarian consumer behavior** is consumption designed to meet functional needs (Arnould, Price, & Zinkhan, 2004). There are basic items that everyone cannot go without like food and light bulbs. The experience of shopping for these items is routine, and the goal is to get the item. Utilitarian shopping most resembles the second scenario presented above. When we shop in a utilitarian fashion, we tend to view the act of shopping as work, a chore, or a job (Babin, Darden, & Griffin, 1994; Solomon & Rabolt, 2004). We behave practically and rationally when we engage in utilitarian shopping (Holbrook & Hirschman, 1982). We do not have time to worry about our emotional reactions while we are shopping in a utilitarian fashion because we are focusing on accomplishing our goal of obtaining a particular item that we need (Babin, Darden, & Griffin, 1994; Kim, Sullivan, & Forney, 2007). In other words, if we set out to buy a new pair of khaki pants at Carrefour or Wal-Mart, then we will only be satisfied at the end of the utilitarian shopping trip if we leave Carrefour or Wal-Mart with a pair of khaki pants.

Hedonic consumer behavior focuses more on an enjoyment of the entire shopping process, while utilitarian consumer behavior focuses almost exclusively on the attainment of the desired products. The way people shop and the outcomes they desire has been a focus of research for many years. Initially, researchers attempted to identify people who innately tended to be hedonic shoppers or utilitarian shoppers. (You can complete one of the questionnaires used to categorize consumers as hedonic or utilitarian in Boxed Case 2.3.) While it is true that we as individuals are inclined to shop hedonistically or in a utilitarian fashion, researchers have learned that variations in consumption contexts can influence whether we act in a hedonic or utilitarian manner. For example, some products tend to bring the hedonist out of even the most utilitarian shopper. Because women are typically trained by their mothers to enjoy shopping (which is a good thing when we consider the fact that women buy most of the products used by themselves and their family members), women tend to behave more hedonistically in the marketplace than men (Minahan & Beverland, 2005). However, more men than women behave hedonistically in computer stores (Underhill, 1999). Thus, rather than simply identifying who is a hedonic shopper and who is a utilitarian shopper, retailers need to provide consumers with a "balanced consumption experience" (Kim, Sullivan, & Forney, 2007, p. 71). Remember, after all, consumers are demanding and they want retailers to provide them with what they want when they want it. Period. This means that sometimes consumers want extravagant, time-consuming, emotion-invoking experiences when they go shopping for apparel, and sometimes consumers just want to be able to quickly purchase reasonably priced apparel when they go shopping. This also means that a variety of retail establishments, including experiential retailers and value retailers, can coexist in today's marketplace.

BOXED CASE 2.3. ARE YOU A HEDONIC OR UTILITARIAN SHOPPER?

Babin, Darden, and Griffin (1994) created a measure to categorize consumers as hedonic shoppers or utilitarian shoppers. You can determine if you tend to be hedonic or utilitarian by responding to the following statements concerning the last time you went shopping for apparel products. You need to decide how much the statement describes your feelings about apparel. There are no right or wrong answers. Indicate how much you agree or disagree with each statement. Circle the number for each statement that corresponds most closely with your own feelings.

		Strongly Disagree				Strongly Agree
1.	This shopping trip was truly a joy.	1	2	3	4	5
2.	I continued to shop, not because I had to, but because I wanted to.	1	2	3	4	5
3.	This shopping trip truly felt like an escape.	1	2	3	4	5
4.	Compared to other things I could have done, the time spent shopping was truly enjoyable.	1	2	3	4	5
5.	I enjoyed being immersed in exciting new products.	1	2	3	4	5
6.	I enjoyed this shopping trip for its own sake, not just for the items I may have purchased.	1	2	3	4	5
7.	I had a good time because I was able to act on the "spur of the moment."	1	2	3	4	5
8.	During the trip, I felt the excitement of the hunt.	1	2	3	4	5
9.	While shopping, I was able to forget my problems.	1	2	3	4	5
10.	While shopping, I felt a sense of adventure.	1	2	3	4	5

	Strongly Disagree				Strongly Agree
11. This shopping trip was not a very nice time out.	1	2	3	4	5
12. I accomplished just what I wanted to on this shopping trip.	1	2	3	4	5
13. I couldn't buy what I really needed.	1	2	3	4	5
14. While shopping, I found just the item(s) I was looking for.	1	2	3	4	5
15. I was disappointed because I had to go to another store(s) to complete my shopping.	1	2	3	4	5

To determine whether you tend to be more hedonic or utilitarian while shopping for apparel products, first reverse your score for items 11, 13, and 15. In other words, if you circled 1, change your score to 5; if you circled 2, change your score to 4; if you circled 4, change your score to 2; and if you circled 5, change your score to 1. Next, add all of the numbers you circled for items 1 to 11. Then divide this number by 11. This number is your score for section 1. Next, add all of the numbers you circled for items 12 to 15. Then divide this number by 4. This number is your score for section 2. If your score for section 1 is greater than your score for section 2, you tend to be a hedonic shopper. If your score for section 2 is greater than your score for section 1, you tend to be a utilitarian shopper. If your scores for section 1 and section 2 are about the same, then you are a balanced shopper because you do not show a preference for hedonic or utilitarian shopping.

─────────────────────── Reference ───────────────────────

Babin, B. J., Darden, W. R., & Griffin, M. (1994). Work and/or fun: Measuring hedonic and utilitarian shopping value. *Journal of Consumer Research, 20*(4), 644–656.

Experiential retailers

An **experiential retailer** is one "that satisfies the consumers' emotional or expressive desires as well as their rational or functional needs" (Kim, Sullivan, & Forney, 2007, p. 3). Experiential retailers offer customers not only high-quality apparel products available for purchase, but also an enjoyable shopping atmosphere that appeals to consumers' physical, mental, and emotional senses (Pine & Gilmore, 1999). In other words, consumers' hedonic needs are fulfilled by experiential retailers who "dazzle their senses, touch their hearts, and stimulate their minds" (Schmitt, 1999, p. 22). When you shop at an experiential retailer, you don't feel like you are going in to a store to purchase apparel products. Instead, you feel like you are going in to a

───────────────────── 43 ─────────────────────

cabana on a beach in California (see Figure 2.4). Furthermore, at experiential retailers, you can engage in activities besides just trying on and purchasing apparel products. For instance, at Niketown in Chicago, you can shoot some hoops while you ponder which shoes to purchase, and at Nicole Farhi, you can eat lunch while you contemplate which color shirt looks best on you.

Serious consideration goes into a store's design when the retailer is an experiential retailer. However, individual stores are not the only arenas of consumption that can provide shoppers with an experience. To separate themselves from the competition, entire shopping malls are being designed to create unique experiences for consumers. The Fashion Show Mall in Las Vegas is an example of an enclosed mall with an interesting design (see Figure 2.5). Not only is the outside of the mall designed to resemble the tents that appear in Bryant Park in New York during Fashion Week, but each day at noon the center of the mall becomes a runway on which a live fashion show takes place. Another mall in the United States that transports consumers away from the mall to another place and time is the Venetian in Las Vegas, which is designed to look like the canals in Venice, Italy. Wafi City Mall in Dubai gives shoppers a taste of ancient Egypt, and Yokohama Bayside Marina in Yokohama, Japan, virtually transports consumers to a quaint fishing village in the northeastern United States (Beyard, Braun, McLaughlin, Phillips, & Rubin, 2001).

A special kind of shopping mall that is designed to provide consumers with a positive, engaging experience is known as a lifestyle center. A **lifestyle center** is "a

Figure 2.4 Hollister, which sells apparel for young adults, looks like a beach cabana. Photo by Jennifer Yurchisin.

FASHION AND THE CONSUMER

Figure 2.5 The exterior of the Fashion Show Mall in Las Vegas, Nevada. Photo by Jennifer Yurchisin.

shopping center that caters to the retail needs and lifestyle pursuits of consumers in its trading area" (Tubridy & Uiberall, 2004, p. 1). Like regional shopping malls, lifestyle centers are typically located in the suburbs, but lifestyle centers are usually located closer to the homes of more affluent consumers than regional malls (Kim, Sullivan, & Forney, 2007; Tubridy & Uiberall, 2004). As a result, the tenants in lifestyle centers typically cater to the affluent consumer (Martin & Turley, 2004). Although lifestyle centers tend to be smaller than regional shopping centers, the tenant mix usually includes upscale stores along with restaurants and movie theatres. Thus, lifestyle centers contain tenants that can satisfy a variety of consumer needs while providing an enjoyable experience for visitors (Kim, Sullivan, & Forney, 2007).

The design of the lifestyle center often contributes to the experience of consumers who visit. Unlike the modern, boxy, windowless design of many enclosed regional shopping centers, lifestyle centers typically mimic an idealized version of the old-fashioned Main Street in small rural communities (Owens, 2002). The retailers in lifestyle centers often have stores that are fully accessible to consumers from the outside of the center rather than from a common area inside the center. This shopping center design featuring outward-facing stores allows natural light to enter stores through their front windows and provides a unique, aesthetically pleasing look to each lifestyle center. The outward-facing stores also help to create a "community or town center experience" for visitors (Kim, Sullivan, & Forney, 2007,

p. 295). And, apparently, consumers in the United States do enjoy the experience created by lifestyle centers, because they visit lifestyle centers an average of 3.8 times each month—that's almost once a week (Martin & Turley, 2004). (See Figure 2.6 for a picture of a lifestyle center.)

Value retailers

If you cringe when you hear the words *value retailer*, then you may be stuck in the last century. Value "used to convey images of bargain hunting, purchases of second merchandise, and even poor or cheap quality" (Kim, Sullivan, & Forney, 2007, p. 311). It used to be, dare we say, embarrassing to shop at a value retailer for apparel items. However, things have certainly changed with respect to value retailing. All of the free spending consumers were doing during the past twenty years led to a bleak financial situation. In the United States, consumer debt rose while personal savings dropped ("Consumer Debt Avalanche," 2009). While spending decreased by 1 percent and savings increased to 3.6 percent in December 2008 (Healy, 2009), the average U.S. household also had $8,329 worth of credit card debt at the end of 2008 ("2009 Personal Credit Card Debt Trend," 2009). Consumers are spending in other parts of the world as well; average household debt in the United Kingdom is approximately £9,280 (Credit Action, 2009). As a result of today's negative economic situation, value retailing is "associated with intelligence and has become a

Figure 2.6 The Shoppes of Arbor Lakes, a lifestyle center in Maple Grove, Minnesota, is designed to look like an old-fashioned main street in a small town. Photo by Jennifer Yurchisin.

46

status symbol" (Kim, Sullivan, & Forney, 2007, p. 312). Consumers are now proud to say that they got a good deal on a desired apparel item. No longer are consumers embarrassed to "trade down" and purchase apparel items at value retailers (Silverstein & Butman, 2006). In fact, if we look at the list of the world's top retailers in 2007, the top two retailers in terms of sales, Wal-Mart and Carrefour, are value retailers (Deloitte & Stores Media, 2009). And, in terms of fashion goods retailers, we do not have to look too far down the list to see a value retail corporation listed. While Macy's was the world's top fashion retailer in 2007, TJX Corporation, which operates TJ Maxx and Marshall's, was the third largest fashion goods retailer in 2007 (Deloitte & Stores Media, 2009).[1] Lists like these provide evidence that all consumers, even some of whom shop at lifestyle centers, enjoy getting a good deal when they purchase apparel products, at least some of the time. You can see why being a successful apparel retailer can be difficult!

Shopping across cultures

The apparel industry is a global industry. If you need proof of this claim, take a look at the labels in your favorite apparel items. Most likely these items were not made in the country where you are currently living. Your apparel probably has taken at least one trip around the world on its way to you. Your apparel items may have been designed in one country, manufactured in another country, and sold to you in still another country (Rivoli, 2005).

The trade of apparel items or the components to make the apparel items between people of different national origins is not a new phenomenon. As early as 100 A.D., traders were using the Silk Road (Denslow, 2006), a trade route that went through Europe, the Middle East, and Asia. Europeans used the trade route to exchange their metals, woods, and glass for spices, silks, and ceramics that were carried along the route by Asian and Middle Eastern individuals (Denslow, 2006).

While the concept of trading within the apparel industry is not new, the scale of that trading has changed over the past 1,900 or so years. Today, with improvements in communications and transportation, people all over the globe manufacture apparel products for consumers located around the world. We refer to this interdependency of people from every country in the world as globalization. **Globalization** is "the process whereby the world's people are becoming increasingly interconnected in all facets of their lives" (Kunz & Garner, 2007, p. 6). These days, virtually every country participates in the global production and consumption cycle that takes place within the apparel industry. A consumer in any part of the world can use a credit card to purchase anything he or she desires from any part of the world using the Internet.

You may be thinking now that, because of this global interdependence within the apparel industry, people all over the world must be buying and wearing the same kinds of apparel items at the same time. Well, to some extent, that does happen. In our travels, we have seen people in many different countries wearing jeans and

T-shirts (global fashion staples) and participating in the same fashion movements (wearing capri pants) simultaneously. We have also seen the same apparel retailers, like Zara and H&M, in many different countries. So there does exist, on the one hand, a "transnational, homogenized global consumer segment" (Kim, Sullivan, & Forney, 2007, p. 388) within the apparel industry.

On the other hand, there are still many differences in apparel consumption behavior in different parts of the world. As you may have guessed, people in some parts of the world spend much more on apparel items each year than others. For instance, people living in countries in Western Europe, North America, and the Asia Pacific region spent more on apparel and footwear than people living in other regions (see Table 2.1). At times, different particular apparel items become popular in certain areas. For example, when traveling in New Zealand and Australia in 2006, professional women there were wearing tailored shorts with suit jackets. This combination of items has yet to gain mass acceptance in many areas of the United States. In Spain, it is not uncommon to see retail stores that sell apparel and accessories for women flamenco dancers (see Figure 2.7). What, when, where, how, and why people purchase apparel products sometimes differs around the globe. We've collected some fun stories about shopping for apparel in countries around the globe. Read Boxed Cases 2.4, 2.5, and 2.6 to see if it sounds like something that people you know would like to do.

Table 2.1 Consumer Spending on Apparel and Footwear in 2007 around the Globe

Region	Spending in U.S. Dollars
World	1,641,776
Asia Pacific	303,989
Australasia	22,084
Eastern Europe	112,727
Latin America	105,007
Middle East and Africa	80,648
North America	462,770
United States	224,651
Western Europe	545,741

From *Consumer Expenditure on Clothing and Footwear,* by Euromonitor International, 2008. Retrieved July 18, 2008, from http://libproxy.uncg.edu:6038/portal/server.pt?control=SetCommunity&Comm unityID=207&PageID=720&cached=false&space=CommunityPage; *Current Business Reports, Annual Revision of Monthly Retail and Food Services: Sales and Inventories—January 1992 through March 2008,* by U.S. Census Bureau, 2009. Retrieved June 15, 2009, from http://www.census.gov/ compendia/statab/cats/wholesale_retail_trade/retail_trade_sales.html

Figure 2.7 A retail store dedicated to flamenco dance apparel and accessories in Spain. Photo by Jennifer Yurchisin.

49

─────────────────────────────── References ───────────────────────────────

Klaffke, P. (2003). *Spree: A cultural history of shopping*. Vancouver, BC, Canada: Arsenal
     Pulp Press.
McLinden, S. (2008, February). Retail is the reason for the season. *Shopping Centers
     Today*, 32–35.

BOXED CASE 2.5. THE RISE OF THE MIDDLE CLASS IN "CHINDIA"

Have you ever seen a Chuppie? No, it's not a prehistoric fish. It is a new demographic segment in China that mirrors the yuppie (young urban professional) of the 1980s in the United States (Fang, 2006). The Chinese urban professionals are members of a new middle class of consumers. As a result of globalization in several sectors of the world's economy, including apparel production, individuals in developing countries like China and India are quickly finding that their old ways of life are changing. Young Chinese and Indians who are employed in these expanding sectors of the economy are not living the same way that their parents lived. These "Chuppies" and "Induppies" are saving less and spending more of their discretionary income. And they are not simply interested in buying practical, well-priced products with that discretionary income. Instead, these young Asian consumers are brand conscious and are in the market for high-end, luxury goods, including designer handbags and accessories (Fang, 2006). In fact, Chuppies and Induppies are willing to make sacrifices in other areas of their lives in order to purchase certain kinds of products. Much to the distress of members of the older generations in these countries, young Chinese and Indian consumers are opening credit card accounts and even delaying marriage and having children to buy Nike shoes and Louis Vuitton handbags (Friedman, 2004).

─────────────────────────────── References ───────────────────────────────

Fang, B. (2006, May 1). Spending spree. *U.S. News & World Report, 140*(16), 42–48, 50.
Friedman, T. (2004). *The other side of outsourcing* [DVD]. New York: Discovery Communications.

BOXED CASE 2.6. FASHION GOES TO THE DOGS IN THE UNITED STATES

If you thought New York Fashion Week was just for humans, guess again. Since 2006, dogs have been strutting their stuff on the runway during the Pet Fashion Week NY trade show (MD Productions, Inc., 2008). The doggie couture shown at Pet Fashion Week NY is just one part of the growing pet products industry. In 2008, pet parents spent an estimated $10 billion on pet products, including dog apparel, and an additional $3 billion on pet services, including grooming and day care (Bennett, 2009). This spending is not expected to slow down, even with the recent economic downturn. In fact, in a poll of pet owners, 85 percent said that they had no intention of reducing their spending on their pets during the recession (Recession, 2009). What is fueling this purchasing frenzy? Industry insiders have suggested that pets have become child substitutes for older Americans whose children have grown up and left the home and for young, professional Americans who have delayed child rearing to focus on their careers (American Veterinary Medical Association, 2006; Brady & Palmeri, 2007). As a result of the demand for products to pamper the pooch, several well-known designers and high-end fashion brands have begun offering apparel, accessories, and cosmetics for dogs. These days, furry fashionistas can don Gucci caps, Ralph Lauren sweaters, Coach collars, and Burberry boots (or designer knock-offs, like the barrette you can see in the following figure). And no self-respecting doggie would leave the house without a spritz of Juicy Critture dog cologne or Mungo and Maud's Petite Amande eau de toilette for dogs.

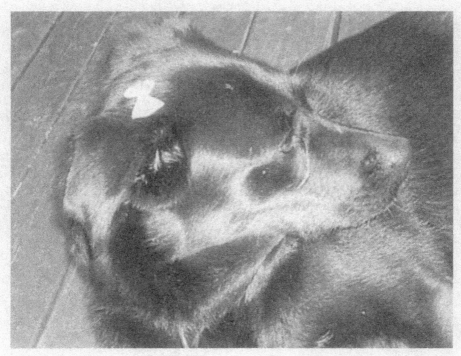

Morticia wearing a faux Louis Vuitton barrette. Photo by Jennifer Yurchisin.

References

American Veterinary Medical Association. (2006, August 1). Spending on pets projected to hit all time high. *JAVMA News*. Retrieved February 7, 2009, from http://www.avma.org/onlnews/javma/aug06/060801c_pf.asp

Bennett, L. (2009, January 15). Pet industry trends for 2009. *Small Business Trends*. Retrieved February 7, 2009, from http:// http://smallbiztrends.com/2009/01/pet-industry-trends-2009.html

Brady, D., & Palmeri, C. (2007, August 6). The pet economy: Americans spend an astonishing $41 billion a year on their furry friends. *Business Week*. Retrieved February 7, 2009, from http://www.businessweek.com/print/magazine/content/07_32/b4045001.htm?chan=gl

MD Productions, Inc. (2008). *About us*. Retrieved February 7, 2009, from http://www.petfashionweek.com/aboutus/aboutus.html

Recession having an impact on consumer spending, survey finds. (2009, January 1). *Veterinary News*. Retrieved February 7, 2009, from http://veterinarynews.dvm360.com/dvm/Veterinary+news/Recession-having-an-impact-on-consumer-spendingfo/ArticleStandard/Article/detail/574390?contextCategoryId=44923

Summary

When and where we shop has changed dramatically over time. Early retailers sold a variety of goods in general stores, and prices were negotiated between buyers and sellers. This early retail store evolved into the department store format that we are familiar with today. The first department store originated in France and offered its customers fixed prices. Department stores quickly grew in number and offered consumers wide assortments of merchandise at various price points. Department stores were generally located in large cities. As consumers moved into the suburbs of these cities, retailers followed. Retailers located in enclosed shopping malls offered customers geographic convenience and a variety of choices.

Today's suburban shopping malls compete with lifestyle centers for customers. Shoppers can satisfy both their utilitarian and hedonic shopping needs by visiting these traditional venues, or they can shop utilizing technological developments including television and the Internet that make products available to consumers around the world seven days a week and twenty-four hours a day.

Key Terms

- bartering
- Chambre Syndicale de la Couture Parisienne
- Charles Worth
- department store
- experiential retailer

- general store
- globalization
- hedonic consumer behavior
- Industrial Revolution
- lifestyle center
- manmade fibers

- multichannel retailing
- natural fibers
- time poverty
- tunic
- utilitarian consumer behavior

Questions for review and discussion

1. Compare apparel shopping in ancient Egypt to apparel shopping today. In what ways are the two processes different? In what ways are the two processes similar?
2. Explain why apparel shopping behavior changed dramatically after the Industrial Revolution. Identify at least three specific changes in society that had an impact on apparel shopping.
3. Describe the relationship between changes in women's social roles and changes in apparel shopping behavior. Provide an example to illustrate your point.
4. Compare and contrast hedonic shoppers with utilitarian shoppers. Which types of apparel retail stores today would appeal most to hedonic shoppers? Which types of apparel retail stores today would appeal most to utilitarian shoppers? Why?
5. Think about your favorite apparel retail store. Why is this store your favorite store? Now think about your least favorite apparel store. Why do you not like this store? In what ways is the experience provided to you by your favorite store different from the experience provided to you by your least favorite store?
6. What is a lifestyle center? Why do you think lifestyle centers are popular with today's apparel consumers?
7. Imagine that it is the year 2025. Describe what apparel shopping might be like. What aspects of the way we shop today will change? What aspects of the way we shop today will not change? Why?

Note

1. Both TJ Maxx and Marshalls are categorized as off-price retailers. Off-price retailers are stores that offer high fashion styles at discounted prices early in the fashion cycle.

Suggested Readings

If you are interested in the topics in chapter 2, you may also like reading the following books:

Farrell, J.J. (2003). *One nation under goods: Malls and the seductions of American shopping*. Washington, DC: Smithsonian Books.

Hine, T. (2002). *I want that! How we all became shoppers*. New York: HarperCollins.

Klaffke, P. (2003). *Spree: A cultural history of shopping*. Vancouver, BC, Canada: Arsenal Pulp Press.

Leach, W. (1993). *Land of desire: Merchants, power, and the rise of a new American culture*. New York: Vintage Books.

Miller, D. (1998). *A theory of shopping.* Ithaca, NY: Cornell University Press.

Pine, B.J., II, & Gilmore, J.H. (1999). *The experience economy: Work is theatre and every business a stage.* Boston: Harvard Business School Press.

Schmitt, B., & Simonson, A. (1997). *Marketing aesthetics: The strategic management of brands, identity, and image.* New York: Free Press.

References

2009 Personal credit card debt trend and the consequences. (2009, June 14). *Online earning guide.* Retrieved June 15, 2009, from http://onlinearnings.com/2009/06/14/2009-personal-credit-card-debt-trend-and-the-consequences/

Arnould, E., Price, L., & Zinkhan, G. (2004). *Consumers.* (2nd ed.). Boston: McGraw-Hill.

Babin, B.J., Darden, W.R., & Griffin, M. (1994). Work and/or fun: Measuring hedonic and utilitarian shopping value. *Journal of Consumer Research, 20*(4), 644–656.

Babylon, Ltd. (2009). *Definition of barter system.* Retrieved June 11, 2009, from http://dictionary.babylon.com/

Beyard, M.D., Braun, R.E., McLaughlin, H., Phillips, P.L., & Rubin, M.S. (2001). *Developing retail entertainment destinations* (2nd ed.). Washington, DC: Urban Land Institute.

Bhatnagar, A., Misra, S., & Rao, H.R. (2000). On risk, convenience, and Internet shopping behavior. *Communications of the Association for Computing Machinery, 43*(11), 98–105.

Consumer debt avalanche ready to roll in 2009. Is there any help? (2009, January 8). *Small commercial mortgage online.* Retrieved June 15, 2009, from http://www.smallcommercialmortgageonline.com/blog/2009/01/03/consumer-debt-avalanche-ready-to-roll-in-2009-is-there-any-help/ Consumer Debt Avalanche Ready To Roll in 2009. Is There Any Help?

Credit Action. (2009, May). *Debt statistics.* Retrieved May 28, 2009, from http://www.creditaction.org.uk/debt-statistics.html

Deloitte & Stores Media. (2009). *Feeling the squeeze: Global powers of retailing 2009.* Retrieved March 22, 2009, from: http://www.nxtbook.com/nxtbooks/nrfe/stores_globalpowers0109/

Denslow, L. (2006). *World wise: What to know before you go.* New York: Fairchild Books.

Donthu, N., & Gilliland, D. (1996). Observations: The infomercial shopper. *Journal of Advertising Research, 36*(2), 69–76.

Eastlick, M.A., & Liu, M. (1997). The influence of store attitudes and other nonstore shopping patterns on patronage of television shopping programs. *Journal of Direct Marketing, 11*(3), 14–24.

e-tailing group. (2005). *E-facts.* Retrieved February 10, 2009, from http://www.e-tailing.com/newsandviews/facts.html

Frings, G.S. (1996). *Fashion: From concept to consumer* (5th ed.). Upper Saddle River, NJ: Prentice Hall.

Grant, A., Guthrie, K., & Ball-Rokeach, S. (1991). Television shopping: A media system dependency perspective. *Communication Research, 18,* 773–798.

Harden, A. (1996). TV shopping: A summary of women's attitudes gained through focus group discussions. *Journal of Family and Consumer Sciences, 88,* 58–62.

Healy, J. (2009, February 2). Consumers are saving more and spending less. *New York Times.* Retrieved June 15, 2009, from http://www.nytimes.com/2009/02/03/business/economy/03econ.html

Hine, T. (2002). *I want that! How we all became shoppers.* New York: HarperCollins.

Holbrook, M.B., & Hirschman, E. (1982). The experiential aspects of consumption: Consumer fantasies, feelings, and fun. *Journal of Consumer Research, 9,* 132–140.

54

HSN, Inc. (2008). *HSN, Inc. reports third quarter results.* Retrieved February 7, 2009, from http://www.hsni.com/common/download/download.cfm?companyid=HSNI&fleid=247586&filekey=fbd96fd7-eebb-44d2-953f-b77defed323c&file

Jarnow, J., & Dickerson, K. G. (1997). *Inside the fashion business* (6th ed.). Upper Saddle River, NJ: Prentice Hall.

Jenkins, L. (2009, January 12). Recession forces thinking outside the big box. *SignOnSanDiego.com.* Retrieved February 10, 2009, from http://www3.signonsandiego.com/stories/2009/jan/12/1m12jenkins21153-recession-forces-thinking-outside/

Jones, J. M., & Vijayasarathy, L. R. (1998). Internet consumer catalog shopping: Findings from an exploratory study and directions for future research. *Internet Research: Electronic Networking Applications and Policy, 8*(4), 322–330.

Kim, Y.-K., Sullivan, P., & Forney, J. C. (2007). *Experiential retailing: Concepts and strategies that sell.* New York: Fairchild Books.

Klaffke, P. (2003). *Spree: A cultural history of shopping.* Vancouver, BC, Canada: Arsenal Pulp Press.

Kunz, G. I., & Garner, M. B. (2007). *Going global: The textile and apparel industry.* New York: Fairchild Books.

Lee, S.-H., Lennon, S. J., & Rudd, N. A. (2000). Compulsive consumption tendencies among television shoppers. *Family and Consumer Sciences Research Journal, 28*(4), 463–488.

Levy, M., & Weitz, B. A. (2006). *Retailing management* (6th ed.). Boston: McGraw-Hill/Irwin.

Lohse, G. L., Bellman, S., & Johnson, E. J. (2000). Consumer buying behavior on the Internet: Findings from panel data. *Journal of Interactive Marketing, 14*(1), 15–29.

Martin, C. A., & Turley, L. W. (2004). Malls and consumption motivation: An exploratory examination of older generation Y consumers. *International Journal of Retail and Distribution Management, 32*(10), 464–475.

Minahan, S., & Beverland, M. (2005). *Why women shop: Secrets revealed.* Milton, Queensland, Australia: Wrightbooks.

National Retail Federation. (2007, May 14). *Online clothing sales surpass computers, according to Shop.Org/Forrester Research study.* Retrieved February 7, 2009, from http://www.nrf.org/modules.php?name=News&op=viewlive&sp_id=292

Owens, A. M. (2002, October 21). The mall is being turned inside out. *National Post,* A6.

Pastore, M. (2000, May 10). Two-thirds of Americans online. *CyberAtlas.* Retrieved February 15, 2002, from http://www.cyberatlas.internet.com/big_picture/demographics/article/0,1323,5901_358791,00.html

Pine, B. J., II, & Gilmore, J. H. (1999). *The experience economy: Work is theatre and every business a stage.* Boston: Harvard Business School Press.

PricewaterhouseCoopers. (2000). *Shopping for apparel online gains popularity.* Retrieved February 11, 2002, from http://www.pwcglobal.com/extweb/ncpressrelease.../4797ED89EC3FB6DF8525691B004F971

QVC, Inc. (2008). *About QVC.* Retrieved February 7, 2009, from http://www.qvc.com/qic/qvcapp.aspx/app.html/params.file.%7Ccp%7Cmainhqabout,html/left.html.file.%7Cnav%7Cnavhqabout,html/walk.html.%7Cnav%7Cnavhqwel,html

Rath, P. M., Bay, S., Petrizzi, R., & Gill, P. (2008). *The why of the buy: Consumer behavior and fashion marketing.* New York: Fairchild Books.

Rivoli, P. (2005). *The travels of a T-shirt in a global economy.* Hoboken, NJ: John Wiley.

Robinson, P. A. (1989). *Field of dreams* [Motion picture]. Universal Pictures.

Schmitt, B. H. (1999). *Experiential marketing: How to get customers to sense, feel, think, act, and relate to your company and brands.* New York: Free Press.

Silverstein, M. J., & Butman, J. (2006). *Treasure hunt: Inside the mind of the new global consumer.* New York: Portfolio.

Solomon, M. R. (2004). *Consumer behavior: Buying, having, and being* (6th ed.). Upper Saddle River, NJ: Prentice Hall.

Solomon, M. R., & Rabolt, N. J. (2004). *Consumer behavior in fashion*. Upper Saddle River, NJ: Prentice Hall.

Stanforth, N. F., & Lennon, S. J. (1996, June). *Clothing consumption via television: The woman's perspective*. Paper presented at the Third Conference on Gender, Marketing, and Consumer Behavior, Salt Lake City, UT.

Tortora, P. G., & Eubank, K. (2005). *Survey of historic costume: A history of Western dress* (4th ed.). New York: Fairchild Books.

Tubridy, M., & Uiberall, J. (2004). Lifestyle center tenant space allocation. *ICSC Research Quarterly, 11*(2), 1–6.

Underhill, P. (1999). *Why we buy*. New York: Simon & Schuster.

Welters, L. (2008). The fashion of sustainability. In J. Hethorn & C. Ulasewicz (Eds.), *Sustainable fashion: Why now? A conversation about issues, practices, and possibilities* (pp. 7–29). New York: Fairchild Books.

Yafa, S. H. (2005). *Big cotton: How a humble fiber created fortunes, wrecked civilizations, and put America on the map*. New York: Viking Penguin.

3

NORMATIVE FASHION CONSUMER DECISION MAKING: PREPURCHASE TO PURCHASE STEPS

After you have read this chapter, you should be able to

• Identify the stages in the fashion consumer decision process model.
• Describe the different types of needs consumers have.
• Compare and contrast consumer needs and consumer wants.
• Explain the concept of planned obsolescence as it relates to apparel.
• Define the different types of searches that consumers engage in.
• Describe the ways in which consumers evaluate purchase alternatives.
• Discuss the different ways in which consumers make their purchase decisions.
• Recognize the influence that the retail store environment has on consumer behavior.
• Define the concept of impulse buying.

The fashion consumer decision process model

Think about the last time you purchased jeans. How did you know that you needed to buy jeans at that time? How did you find out about what kind of jeans you could buy and where you could buy them? How did you decide which jeans to buy and where to buy them? With so many choices of jeans (Figure 3.1 shows the many styles that are available for just one brand, Levi's, at just one store, JCPenney), it can be a daunting task to decide. Now think about the last time you purchased socks. How did you know that you needed to buy socks? How much time did it take you to find out about what kind of socks were available for purchase? How long did it take you to make your purchase decision? Did it take more time for you to select jeans or socks? Are you sensing that there may be some differences in the amount of time and energy expended by different kinds of consumers when they are shopping for different kinds of fashion merchandise? Good!

Normally, when men and women purchase apparel items (or any other type of item for that matter), they engage in a series of cognitive and behavioral activities.

Figure 3.1 Buying jeans can be confusing when there are so many choices available. Photo by Jennifer Yurchisin.

This series of activities is collectively referred to as the **consumer decision process model** (Blackwell, Miniard, & Engel, 2001). The seven stages in the consumer decision process model are shown in Figure 3.2. The main reason why consumers have to think before they act is based on economics. Most people have a limited amount of money to spend on apparel items. As a result, we cannot possibly purchase everything that is available for purchase. (If we did purchase everything that was available, where would we store it?)

When we behave in an economically rational manner, we need to make choices about what we purchase so that we do not spend more money than we have access to. When individuals purchase more apparel items than they can afford or acquire apparel items from stores without paying for them, these individuals are engaging in nonnormative forms of consumer behavior. We will discuss nonnormative consumer behaviors in chapter 6. For now, we are going to concentrate on the rational, normative model of consumer decision making that most of us engage in most of the time.

Of course, as you have most likely deduced from the opening paragraph of this chapter, the consumer decision process model is not as rigid as it may appear from the diagram in Figure 3.2. While the consumer decision process model presents "a roadmap of consumers' minds" as they make choices about which products to purchase (Blackwell, Miniard, & Engel, 2001, p. 71), each individual's consumption

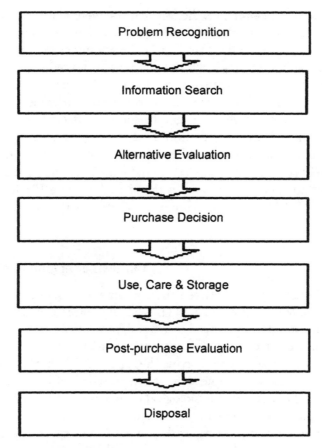

Figure 3.2 The consumer decision process model shows the steps that occur during the consumption process.

experience is unique to him or her. The amount of time and energy you put into each step of the process depends on several factors, including your personal characteristics and the product's characteristics. In this chapter, we focus on the prepurchase steps, or the first four steps, in the consumer decision process model.

Step 1: Problem recognition for consumption of apparel products

Remember those jeans? How did you know it was time to buy new jeans? Did your old jeans have a hole in them when distressed denim was not popular? Did you gain or lose weight so your old jeans no longer fit? Did you have a date and decide a new pair of jeans would impress the object of your affection? Were you just really bored one day so you decided to purchase a new pair of jeans? Regardless of the reason why you felt that you needed to purchase new jeans, the one thing that all of the reasons listed have in common is the fact that you were motivated to purchase new jeans because you realized that you had a problem that you wanted to solve.

Problem recognition is the first step in the consumer decision process model. **Problem recognition** "occurs when the consumer's desired state of affairs departs sufficiently from the actual state of affairs to place the consumer in a state of unrest so that he or she begins thinking of ways to resolve the difference" (Dunne & Lusch, 2005, p. 90). Basically, individuals begin the consumer decision process model when they feel that their lives could be improved in some way. This improvement will occur as consumers move from their actual, present state to their ideal state through the purchase of some good or service. An individual's actual state is his or her as-is state, and an individual's ideal state is the should-be state (Rath, Bay, Petrizzi, & Gill, 2008, p. 276). What might cause dissatisfaction with your actual state? There are several reasons.

Our own changing needs and wants

A **need** is "the discrepancy between the consumer's present state and some ideal state" (Solomon & Rabolt, 2004, p. 111). When it comes to apparel items, few of us reading this book right now actually have real, physiological needs for new apparel items. **Physiological needs** "are the most fundamental type of consumer needs" and "our very survival depends on satisfying these needs" (Blackwell, Miniard, & Engel, 2001, p. 233). These are the needs that we are born with as Homo sapiens. An apparel-related example of a physiological need is protection from the elements in the environment. If we live in a cold climate and need to venture outside, we need to have apparel items to protect our skin so we do not get frostbite. Perhaps those socks we were buying at the beginning of the chapter represent an example of a physiological need for many of us in our advanced societies. We, the authors, know that we would not enjoy tromping through several feet of snow during a Minnesota winter without shoes and a thick pair of socks on to protect our feet.

These types of physiological needs are not the only type of needs that humans have. And when it comes to apparel items, it is usually not the physiological needs that have the most impact on our apparel consumption behavior. Instead, it is our psychogenic needs that typically cause a discrepancy between our actual and ideal states. **Psychogenic needs** are psychosocial needs that are shaped by both our own personalities as well as the culture of which we are a part (Solomon, 2004). Rather than being born with psychogenic needs, we attain these needs as we live our lives within the constraints of time and space. Take, for example, one psychogenic need— the need for affiliation (Solomon, 2004). Some people have a high need for affiliation, while others have a low need for affiliation. Ask yourself how you would feel if you showed up to a party wearing the exact same outfit as one of your friends. Would you feel embarrassed? Maybe you have a low need for affiliation and would rather be perceived by your peers as an individual. On the other hand, if the situation would make you laugh and feel good because it would indicate how close you and your friend were to each other, then maybe you have a high need for affiliation. Do you see the difference?

As you move through life, your psychogenic needs may change. Remember those jeans you were buying at the beginning of the chapter? Well, right now in your life as a college student, you probably feel a strong need for affiliation with your friends and classmates. It is perfectly natural for you to feel this way at this age (Sirgy, Grewal, & Mangleburg, 2000). You probably feel a need to buy the style of jeans or brand of jeans that are the most popular among your peers. You certainly would not want to show up wearing "mom jeans" with a high waist and straight legs if the most popular style of jeans with your friends is low-rise, boot-cut jeans. But as you get a little older, your need for affiliation may decrease. Perhaps you will not feel the need to announce to others who your friends and family members are. Maybe you will make it a point to seek out apparel items that your coworkers are not wearing so that you can demonstrate your individuality to onlookers. In this case, your new, lower need for affiliation will create a new need for you in terms of apparel items.

Now that we have considered needs, what about our wants? How are they different from our needs? Actually, the truth is that our needs are related to our wants. A **want** has been defined as "the particular form of consumption used to satisfy a need" (Solomon, 2004, p. 117). We can think of wants as choices. How many choices does someone have? Let's try to think of a few concerning the purchase of jeans. You can go to a discount store and buy inexpensive, plain jeans. You can go to a department store and buy a midpriced brand of jeans. Or, if you had the financial means, you could go to the True Religion store to buy a pair of those jeans. In this case, your choice of which jeans to purchase may be determined by more than one of your needs. You have a physiological need to cover your body, but your final jean selection may be driven by one of your psychogenic needs. If you have a high need for affiliation, you might buy the kind of jeans that all of your friends are wearing. Or, if you have a high need for status, yet another psychogenic need (Solomon, 2004), maybe you would buy the True Religion jeans to demonstrate your social standing.

The options available to us at any given time are always limited in some way. Perhaps in our culture women and men must wear certain apparel items while they are in public (e.g., a head covering like the ones shown in Figure 3.3). Maybe we have only one store that sells apparel items for women of our height and weight in our town (a problem for many so-called plus-sized women in the United States). Or, as is the case for many, our choices are limited by what we can afford to purchase. As a college student, you may feel that your choices for satisfying your needs are limited. You may not have very much money to spend, or the store where you would like to go to shop to purchase apparel items may not be located near you. When you graduate, get a job, and move to a new location, your life situation will change. You may find that you have many ways to satisfy your needs at your disposal. When you get to your new location, how will you find out what new apparel items are available for you to purchase and where to purchase them? That is the job of marketers.

Figure 3.3 It is customary for Berber men who live in northern Africa to cover their heads when they go out of their homes. Photo by Jessica Havlicek.

Problems created for us by the fashion industry

Your own needs and wants are not the only things that change to cause a discrepancy between your actual state and your ideal state. The fashion industry relies on the planned obsolescence of apparel items for its survival. The **planned obsolescence** of a product occurs when the owners of that product feel a desire "to buy something newer, better and sooner than might otherwise have been necessary" (Wolff, 2007, p. 1). Apparel designers, marketers, and retailers need all of us to believe that the apparel items we wore last year are no longer adequate if they are going entice us to go out and buy apparel items next year. Remember those fashion shows we talked about in chapter 1? Fashion shows are a good example of one of the many ways in which the fashion industry creates problems for us. Every fall and spring, we see the new styles that we "need" to purchase coming down the runway during the fashion week shows. The most marketable styles are promoted to us via the media (e.g., magazines like *Vogue*, in newspapers like the *New York Times*, and on television channels like Fashion Television) and in the stores where we shop. We see all of these new items and we feel that we have a problem on our hands. In our actual state, we are individuals who do not have the new styles. Ideally, we want to be individuals who have the new styles. Thus, there is a discrepancy between our actual states and our ideal states. To solve our problem and to avoid any social stigma we may experience if we are forced to wear last year's apparel items, we go out and buy this year's apparel items. The level of discomfort you feel when you are forced to wear last year's apparel styles varies, of course, by the amount of importance you place on following fashion. Most young adults probably place at least some importance on following fashion.

Related products and purchases

We are all guilty of it. You pass a sweater on a clearance rack that is marked 75 percent off the regular price. You think to yourself, "It's perfect. It's in my size. It's a great price. I am fairly sure that I have some pants that will match with the colors in that sweater." So you head for the cash register, pay for your sweater, and head home. Upon arrival at your closet with your new sweater, you realize that the pants that you thought would match the sweater are definitely not going to match. Who knew there were so many different shades of black and white available? "Well," you think, "it is still okay. The sweater was a great deal, so I can go out and buy some pants to match this sweater." And so it begins, the endless cycle of purchasing that begins simply because you purchased a sweater that was in your size and 75 percent off the regular price. In your ideal state, you would have an outfit put together, complete with the sweater, a pair of coordinating pants, and some matching shoes. However, you feel a need to keep shopping because the only apparel item you possess in your actual state is the discounted sweater.

This need to buy related products is not a new phenomenon. French philosopher Denis Diderot wrote about this need to purchase more items after purchasing one item in 1772. In Diderot's case, he needed to purchase new furniture after he purchased a new dressing gown because his old furniture no longer seemed appropriate

BOXED CASE 3.1. EXCERPTS FROM DIDEROT'S "REGRETS ON PARTING WITH MY OLD DRESSING GOWN" FROM 1772

"Why on earth did I ever part with it? It was used to me and I was used to it. It draped itself so snugly, yet loosely, around all the curves and angles of my body—it made me look picturesque as well as handsome. This new one, stiff and rigid as it is, makes me look like a mannequin. . . .

Wrapped in my old dressing gown I didn't need to worry about the servant's clumsiness or my own awkwardness. Neither did I have to watch out for flying sparks from the fire or for water leaking in through the roof. I was absolute master of my old dressing gown, but I have become a slave to my new one. The dragon that kept guard over the Golden Fleece was no more uneasy than I am—I go about under a cloud of anxiety. . . .

My friends, see to it that you hold fast to your old friends. And, oh, my friends, beware of the contamination of sudden wealth. Let my example be a lesson to you. The poor man may take his ease without thinking of appearances, but the rich man is always under a strain. . . .

My old dressing gown was in perfect accord with the rest of the poor bric-a-brac that filled my room. A chair made out of woven straw, a rough wooden table, a cheap Bergamo tapestry, a pine board that served for a bookshelf, a few grimy engravings without frames, tacked by the corners to the tapestry, and three or four plaster casts that hung between the engravings—all these harmonized with my old dressing gown to make a perfect picture of honest poverty.

Now the harmony is destroyed. Now there is no more consistency, no more unity, and no more beauty. . . .

My study would have presented just such an incongruous appearance if the imperious scarlet robe had not forced everything else to conform with its own elegant tone.

I have seen my Bergamo tapestry compelled to give up its place on the wall where it has hung for so many years to make room for a damask wall covering. . . .

My old straw chair has been relegated to the vestibule; its place has been usurped by an armchair covered with Morocco leather. . . .

The wooden table held its ground, protected as it was by a great heap of pamphlets and loose papers piled up helter-skelter. . . . But . . . Fate at last worked its will with my table: the papers and pamphlets are now neatly stacked in the drawers of an expensive new desk. . . .

The remaining space between the top of my new desk and Vernet's seascape, which hangs directly above it, was displeasing to the eye on account of its blankness, so this void was filled by a pendulum clock—and what a clock! A clock chosen by the wealthy Mme. Goeffrin, made of bronze inlaid with gold!

Then there was an empty corner beside the window. There was just room for a secretary, and one was put there. . . .

Of my former modest surroundings I have kept only one reminder: an old braided carpet. This pitiable object, I know very well, hardly goes with my other splendid furnishings. . . . Every morning when I come into my study, sumptuously robed in scarlet, I shall look down at the floor and I shall see my old braided rug. It will remind me of what I used to be, and Pride will have to come to a standstill at the threshold of my heart. . . .

In time I shall have paid off my creditors, and my sense of guilt will be less lively. Then I shall be able to take undiluted pleasure in all my new possessions. But you need not fear that I shall fall victim to the frenzy that makes men want to go on endlessly heaping up beautiful things. I still have the same friends I used to have, and I have made no new ones."

--------- Reference ---------

Diderot, D. (1772). Regrets on parting with my old dressing gown. In J. Barzun & R. H. Bowen (Translators), *Rameau's nephew and other works* (pp. 309–317). Indianapolis, IN: Hackett Publishing.

FASHION AND THE CONSUMER

after he bought the new outfit. In honor of Diderot's observation, we often refer to the need to purchase related items as the **Diderot effect**. (You can read excerpts from Diderot in Boxed Case 3.1.)

Step 2: Information search for consumption of apparel products

Continuing with our jeans example, let's say that you need new jeans to move from your actual state, as someone with old jeans, to your ideal state, as someone with new jeans. Next, you must figure out how to go about obtaining new jeans by starting your **information search**. You need to "begin searching for information and solutions to satisfy" your need for new jeans by making a purchase decision (Belch & Belch, 2004, p. 75). You need to learn about the characteristics of the jeans that are available for you to purchase, and you need to find out where you can purchase them. There are two kinds of searches in which apparel consumers engage: internal search and external search. **Internal search** "consists of an attempt to scan information stored in memory to recall past experiences and/or knowledge regarding various purchase alternatives" (Belch & Belch, 2004, p. 112). Unless you have amnesia or a problem with your long-term memory, you can probably remember several different times that you purchased jeans in the past. Your experiences of purchasing jeans are stored in your memory, and you can call upon these memories each time you need to buy new jeans. These memories may include information concerning what brands of jeans you purchased in the past (e.g., Levi's, 7 For All Mankind, Rock & Republic, Diesel), where you purchased these jeans (e.g., a specialty store, a department store, a discount store, a Web site), how these jeans looked and performed (e.g., quality, comfort), and how you felt when you wore them (e.g., attractive, unattractive, happy, sad). Typically, if you are an experienced jeans buyer who has been satisfied with your previous jeans purchases, the information stored in your mind may be all that you need to direct you to the appropriate location to purchase the appropriate pair of jeans (Blackwell, Miniard, & Engel, 2001). On the other hand, if you don't have much experience buying jeans or it has been a long time since you had to purchase a pair of jeans, you probably need to do more than just search in your own memory for the information you need to guide your current purchase (Blackwell, Miniard, & Engel, 2001).

If your internal search proves to be inadequate, you will engage in external search behavior when you are investigating the types of jeans that are available for purchase. **External search** involves "collecting information from peers, family, and the marketplace" (Belch & Belch, 2004, p. 75). Every time you talk to your friends or your parents about apparel items, you are engaging in a form of external search behavior. Every time you look at *Elle* magazine or watch a program on E! Television's Style Network to find information about apparel items, you are engaging in a form of external search behavior. These types of external search behavior occur more frequently for those who are interested in fashion. In fact, there is a specific term, *ongoing search*, that is used to describe the type of searching that occurs outside of a specific purchase event. **Ongoing search** is a type of search in which "information acquisition takes place on a relatively regular basis regardless of sporadic purchase needs" (Blackwell, Miniard, & Engel, 2001, p. 107). Individuals who browse at the mall, engage in window shopping, read fashion magazines, and watch television programs about fashion are all performing ongoing searches. It is likely that much of this information collected during ongoing external searches will be stored in consumers' minds and will be available through internal search for the consumers' use when they need to make a specific purchase.

There are four types of external sources of information that consumers use while becoming familiar with the different apparel items available on the market. **Personal sources** include "friends, relatives, or coworkers" (Belch & Belch, 2004, p. 112). **Marketer-controlled sources** include "information from advertising, salespeople, or point-of-purchase displays and the Internet" (Belch & Belch, 2004, p. 112). **Public sources** include "articles in magazines or newspapers or reports on TV" (Belch & Belch, 2004, p. 112). Public sources of information are generally considered to be neutral sources of information about products because the designer, manufacturer, or retailer does not have as much control over the article or the report as they would have over an advertisement (Solomon & Rabolt, 2004). Lastly, **objective sources** include "unbiased third parties" (Solomon & Rabolt, 2004, p. 358). A classic example of an objective external source is *Consumer Reports* magazine. This magazine compares various brands of products from the same category on various criteria and provides ratings so readers can make informed purchase decisions. The magazine accepts no advertising so that its ratings can be seen as completely neutral. Although *Consumer Reports* does not typically focus on apparel items, articles about apparel and apparel-related products have appeared in both *Consumer Reports* as well as a spinoff magazine designed for women called *Shop Smart*. See Boxed Case 3.2 for an excerpt from a *Consumer Reports* feature concerning wrinkle-free shirts.

BOXED CASE 3.2. AN EXCERPT FROM *CONSUMER REPORTS*

Toss the iron

Wrinkle-free shirts that work

Our textile expert, Pat Slaven, checks out the Lands' End Pinpoint, a CR Best Buy.

To make consumers happy, cotton has to suffer. "Soaking the fabric in formaldehyde and pressing it flat makes it wrinkle-resistant," said Eva Osborne, project manager of women's apparel at JCPenney. "The molecules line up like little soldiers and remember where they're supposed to be." But there's a downside, Osborne says: The molecular change makes the fabric more brittle, so its life expectancy may be cut by 25 percent.

People willing to trade durability for wash-and-wearability shouldn't choose just any no-iron shirt. Our tests of nine men's 100 percent cotton, no-iron (or wrinkle-free) shirts found that some stay smooth far better than others.

How we tested. We corralled 13 male employees who were spied wearing long-sleeve dress shirts on scorching days in July and gave each man two to four of the test shirts. Each man wore a test shirt for a day, then filled out a questionnaire. They followed that procedure two or three times per shirt. We also had trained testers look for wrinkles and seam puckers after 10 wash cycles. Scores are based on their assessment. Note: All but the Jos. A. Bank shirt say they should be removed immediately from the dryer, which we did in our tests. That, of course, can be a hassle.

What we found. Shirts from Lands' End, L.L.Bean, Stafford, Brooks Brothers, and Jos. A. Bank stayed wrinkle-free throughout the day, kept sharp creases, "breathed" well, and were often called soft or supple. The first three, all $40, are CR Best Buys. All come in white, at least one shade of blue, and at least one other pastel color. Jos. A. Bank, L.L.Bean, and Stafford have somewhat thicker fabric than the others. Jos. A. Bank, $75, offers the most colors: nine. None of the shirts showed excessive wear after 10 washes. Some panelists said they wouldn't buy the Kenneth Cole or Merona shirts whatever the cost.

CR's take. Consider one of the CR Best Buys. Whichever shirt you choose, look for "no iron," "wrinkle resistant," or a similar claim on the label; some tested shirts have wrinkly siblings.

References

Toss the iron. (2007, March). *Consumer Reports.* Retrieved June 2, 2009, from http://www. consumerreports.org/cro/home-garden/beauty-personal-care/apparel/wri.../0307_ shirts_ov_1.htm?resultPageIndex=1&resultIndex=2&searchTerm=apparel brands
Excerpt copyright 2007 by Consumers Union of U.S., Inc. Yonkers, NY 10703-1057, a nonprofit organization. Excerpted with permission from the March 2007 issue of CONSUMER REPORTS® for educational purposes only. No commercial use or reproduction permitted. www.ConsumerReports.org

So how much and which type of external search behavior do different kinds of people engage in? Individuals tend to engage in extensive search behavior when the purchase is important and when the product is expensive (Blackwell, Miniard, & Engel, 2001). Think about those jeans again. Except for the True Religion jeans, most jeans that people typically buy are around thirty dollars. Compare that price with the price of a wedding dress. Many wedding dresses cost thousands of dollars, with the average cost being $1,300 ("Getting Dream Wedding Dresses," 2008).

Which purchase situation do you think most women will remember? For most young women, the process of buying a wedding gown takes months as they seek the advice of their friends and family members and devour information in magazines like *Modern Bride* and on Web sites like The Knot. Do you think these same women worry as much about which pair of jeans they are going to purchase?

With respect to the types of external search sources that are used, differences have been found between fashion leaders and fashion followers. Fashion leaders tend to use market-controlled sources to collect information about apparel products, while fashion followers tend to rely on the information they can collect from personal sources, like friends (Solomon & Rabolt, 2004).

Step 3: Alternative evaluation for consumption of apparel products

So now that you have all of this information about the types of jeans that are available, it is time to narrow down your choices and engage in the third step in the consumer decision process model. During **alternative evaluation**, "consumers compare what they know about different products and brands with what they consider most important and begin to narrow the field of alternatives before they finally resolve to buy one of them" (Blackwell, Miniard, & Engel, 2001, p. 76). Perhaps during your internal and external searches, you found out that there were many, many brands of jeans that had characteristics that seemed appealing to you. You remembered that the last time you purchased jeans, you really liked the ones that you saw at the Gap. You saw advertisements for 7 For All Mankind jeans and Diesel jeans that indicated that those jeans were an appropriate choice for you. And your best friend told you that she really likes her Rock & Republic jeans, and she thinks that you will like those also. Additionally, you read an article in *Shop Smart* that rated the quality of the denim used in Levi's and Apple Bottom jeans as the highest. How will you ever make your choice?

In our minds, we have a set of evaluative criteria stored that we use when we need to make sense of all of the information that we have collected during our information search. **Evaluative criteria** are "the standards and specifications used to compare different products and brands" (Blackwell, Miniard, & Engel, 2001, p. 76). At the end of the day, you know best which jeans will be the correct choice for you. Although we all have slightly different lists of product characteristics that we look for when we purchase apparel items, most of us look for similar criteria when we are evaluating our alternatives. Some of these product attributes include appropriateness (i.e., to our personalities or to the wear occasion), usefulness in terms of the price paid (i.e., whether we will get our money's worth out of the garment), aesthetics, quality, product image (i.e., what other people will think of me when I wear this), country of origin (i.e., imported or domestically produced), and fiber or fabric composition (Solomon & Rabolt, 2004). As you can see, some of these criteria are **functional** in nature—that is, they are tangible features of the apparel item that will be "directly experienced by consumers" (Belch & Belch, 2004, p. 117). On the other hand, some of these criteria are **psychological** in nature. They are "intangible, subjective, and personal, such as how a product makes you feel or how you think others will view you for purchasing or using it" (Belch & Belch, 2004, p. 117).

Returning to our jeans purchasing example, you have considered your alternatives and have decided that three brands of jeans meet your evaluative criteria. You think the price of the Gap jeans is reasonable, you believe that 7 For All Mankind jeans would provide you with the best image, and you think that Levi's have the best quality. Armed with this information, you now need to make your final purchase decision.

Step 4: Purchase decision for consumption of apparel products

Formal decision rules

Finally, the time has come to make your jeans purchase selection. To determine which brand of jeans to buy, you frequently use decision rules. **Decision rules** are the "strategies consumers use to decide among purchase alternatives" (Belch & Belch, 2004, p. 119). There are two types of decision rules consumers can use: noncompensatory or compensatory. When we use **noncompensatory decision rules**, we make our decision based on each product's rating on the criterion we feel is most important. A noncompensatory decision criterion is one where "a product's weakness on one attribute cannot be offset by its strong performance on another attribute" (Blackwell, Miniard, & Engel, 2001, p. 117). To illustrate decision criteria, we have created Table 3.1, which reflects a consumer's criteria for selecting and purchasing jeans. This consumer has rated image as the most important attribute in jeans (image is rated at 10 out of 10, price is rated at 7 out of 10, and quality is rated at 5 out of 10). Therefore, regardless of the fact that 7 For All Mankind rates the lowest of the three brands in terms of the price criterion (7 For All Mankind are the most expensive jeans of the three brands) and in terms of the quality criterion, this consumer would purchase the 7 For All Mankind jeans using these criteria.

In contrast, if a consumer were using a compensatory decision rule, using the same criteria shown in Table 3.1, the Gap jeans would be selected for purchase.

Table 3.1 Decision Rules for a Jeans Purchase

Brand	Consumer's Decision Criteria and Ratings		
	Quality (5)	Image (10)	Price (7)
7 For All Mankind	4	9	2
Levi's	8	2	6
Gap	6	6	8

When we use **compensatory decision rules**, "a perceived weakness of one attribute may be offset or compensated for by the perceived strength of another attribute" (Blackwell, Miniard, & Engel, 2001, p. 119). Compensatory decision rules let us look at the big picture, so to speak, and make our decision based on the product's rating on a variety of criteria. So how would this consumer come to the decision to select the Gap jeans? Here is what may happen in this situation. Add the weighted ratings of each product on each attribute. The product with the most points will be the product selected for purchase. In our example, we weight the Gap jeans' ratings on each criterion by the importance of each criterion and then add up these weighted ratings. The Gap jeans score a total of 146 points. Because 146 is the highest number of points obtained by the three brands, the decision would be to purchase the Gap jeans. (Take another look at Table 3.1 to make sure that you understand how we came to these conclusions.)

Heuristics

All of these steps make decision making appear like a lot of work. In some instances, it is. Sometimes, however, we do not want to go through such a long process to decide which product to buy. Sometimes we are lazy. **Cognitive miser** is the term used to describe someone who does not want to exert any extra mental power to make purchase decisions. To some degree, we are all cognitive misers. We all use **heuristics**, or "mental rules of thumb that lead to a speedy decision," (Solomon & Rabolt, 2004, p. 367) at one time or another.

In terms of apparel items, there are several common heuristics that consumers use to make quick purchase decisions. One is a heuristic of price. We tend to believe that the more expensive an item is, the better it is. That is to say, we think there is a positive relationship between price and quality (Solomon & Rabolt, 2004). If you are interested in buying a quality product and are in a hurry to make a decision, you will most likely select an expensive apparel item.

Another common heuristic that consumers use is the heuristic of brand names. We all have favorite brands of apparel items. We get our ideas concerning which brands are for us and which brands are not for us from the brand's image. **Brand image** is the collection of knowledge, feelings, and attitudes an individual has about a specific brand (Arnould, Price, & Zinkhan, 2004). Our default when purchasing apparel is always to go with brands we know, trust, and love. When individuals first started purchasing apparel using the Internet, the most popular sites were those sites that were associated with established brands from the offline world. Consumers felt safer purchasing from brands they already knew and trusted in the new, unfamiliar online shopping environment (Klaffke, 2003).

One last example of a heuristic that consumers use when making purchase decisions is the country-of-origin heuristic. When **country of origin** is labeled on apparel items, it refers to "the country where the goods were wholly obtained or, when more than one country is involved, the country where the last substantial transformation has been carried out" (Kunz & Garner, 2007, p. 112). Although most consumers do not look at the name of the country listed on the tag inside their apparel items (Hester, 1986), country of origin can, in some cases, serve as a signal of product quality in the minds of consumers (Solomon, 2004). For example, some of us associate high fashion items with France, so, if we found out that an apparel item was produced in France, we might think it was inherently better than a similar apparel item that was produced in China. Similarly, we would probably rather buy an Italian leather jacket than a Vietnamese leather jacket or an Irish linen shirt than a Colombian linen shirt. This is not to say that similar apparel items produced in different countries actually represent different levels of quality. But, based on our country-of-origin heuristic, we perceive that apparel items produced in some countries are just better than the ones produced in other countries.

Apparel consumers sometimes use formal decision rules and sometimes are lazy and use heuristics to make purchase decisions. Apparel retailers are aware of the fact that consumers can also be very easily influenced to make purchase decisions that they did not plan to make before entering a store or viewing a Web site. Apparel retailers know that sometimes it is the shopping environment itself that influences consumers in their purchase decisions.

Store-level influences on buying: store image and store environment

What words would you use to describe your favorite apparel retail store? How do you know that those words describe your favorite store? What parts of the store were you thinking about when you thought of those words? Was it difficult for you to think of words to describe your favorite apparel retail store? Most likely, it probably was not too difficult for you to think of a few words to describe your favorite store. After all, it is your favorite store, suggesting that you shop there fairly often, are familiar with the store, and most likely enjoy the store's image. **Store image** refers to the "overall impression of a store as perceived by a consumer" (Keaveney & Hunt, 1992, p. 165). This overall impression is formed as you assess various aspects of the store (Kent, 2003). Some of the aspects that you take into account when forming your impressions of the store include the store's physical characteristics (e.g., size, layout, color scheme), the products sold in the store and their price ranges, the store's personnel, and the type and amount of services offered at the store (Keaveney & Hunt, 1992; Martineau, 1958; Sirgy & Samli, 1985; Sirgy, Samli, Bahn, & Varvoglis, 1989; Zimmer & Golden, 1988).

Store image is an important factor for apparel retailers to consider and to control. Think about it: Which store would you rather go to—one that you liked or one that you did not like? It seems like a silly question, but it is one that continues to challenge retailers worldwide. Consumers who like a store's image will tend to visit the store more often (Darley & Lim, 1999), spend more time in the store (Donovan & Rossiter, 1982), and purchase more than consumers who do not like a store's image (Bloemer & Odekerken-Schroder, 2002; Donovan & Rossiter, 1982). It is clear that retailers need to create a positive store image in the minds of their target consumers. One of the most effective ways that retailers can change consumers' perceptions of their store is to make changes to the store's environment.

Store environment is composed of three categories of environmental cues—ambient, design, and social—that retailers can control in order to influence consumers' perceptions of the store (Baker, Grewal, & Parasuraman, 1994). Environmental cues in the **ambient category** include all "nonvisual, background conditions in the environment, including elements such as temperature, lighting, music and scent" (p. 330). What kind of music does your favorite store play? Is it music that you find enjoyable? If this store is your favorite apparel retail store, you are probably in the target market for both the apparel sold in the store as well as the music played in the store.

The **design category** includes "store environmental elements that are more visual in nature than are ambient factors" and include such elements as store layout (e.g., grid versus open), architectural style, materials used, and color scheme (Baker, Grewal, & Parasuraman, 1994, p. 330). Are you familiar with the women's intimate apparel retailer called Victoria's Secret (see Figure 3.4)? Many of our students in the United States tell us that Victoria's Secret is their favorite apparel retail store. There is a particular color, pink, associated with this store. Many of the architectural elements within the store are painted pink. The shopping bags for Victoria's Secret

Figure 3.4 Victoria's Secret uses the color pink throughout the store and merchandise. Photo by Jennifer Yurchisin.

are pink. The retailer even has a line of apparel called PINK. We think that pink was a good choice for this retailer to use because, in the United States, the color pink is associated with femininity. Thus, the color fits with the store's products and target consumers. And, apparently, those target customers like the color used in the design of the store, because Victoria's Secret is one of the most successful specialty store retailers in the United States.

Lastly, the environmental cues in the **social category** are those related to the "number, type, and behavior of other customers and sales personnel in the environment" (Baker, Grewal, & Parasuraman, 1994, p. 331). Have you ever had a job in an apparel retail store? Did you have to wear a certain type of apparel while you were working there? Why would your employer make you wear something specific? Retailers require certain appearances of their associates because salesperson appearance has an impact on consumer behavior (Baker, Levy, & Grewal, 1992; Baker, Parasuraman, Grewal, & Voss, 2002; Pettinger, 2004). Compared to salespeople dressed in informal styles, consumers believe not only that the salespeople dressed in formal business attire will be more professional, credible, and knowledgeable (Cho, 2001) but also that the salespeople dressed in formal business attire will provide better service (Shao, Baker, & Wagner, 2004). Furthermore, salespeople who project the same image as the store through their appearance tend to be more successful than salespeople who do not (Falk, 2003).

When consumers evaluate the environmental cues in a store positively, they also tend to evaluate the store's image positively (Baker, Grewal, & Parasuraman, 1994). But why does this positive relationship between assessments of environmental cues and store image make sense? Mehrabian and Russell (1974), in their S-O-R model, postulate that it is not the cues per se that affect people's behavior within an environment. Instead, it is their emotional reaction to those cues that mediates the relationship between the environmental stimulus and the behavioral response.

The Mehrabian-Russell model

According to Mehrabian and Russell (1974), all behavioral reactions to an environment can be considered either **approach behavior** (e.g., desire to enter, stay, and explore the environment) or **avoidance behavior** (e.g., desire to leave and not interact with the environment). Operating within a stimulus-organism-response (S-O-R) framework, Mehrabian and Russell (1974) proposed that there were elements in environments (i.e., stimuli) that cued either approach or avoidance behavior toward that environment (i.e., response). However, rather than being a simple, direct relationship between the stimulus and the response, Mehrabian and Russell (1974) theorized that individuals' emotional states were mediating variables within the stimulus-organism-response framework. In other words, it was not the stimulus item itself (e.g., music, color, salesperson appearance) that cued individuals' behavior (e.g., amount of time or money spent in the store), but, rather, it was individuals' emotional reaction to this item that cued their behavior.

Mehrabian and Russell (1974) hypothesized that there were three basic emotional reactions that individuals could have to an environment: pleasure (e.g., feeling good, happy), arousal (e.g., feeling excited, stimulated), and dominance (e.g., feeling in control of the environment). They predicted that people will approach environments they believe they have control over and that they perceive to be pleasurable and arousing.

How well does the Mehrabian-Russell (1974) model work for explaining consumer behavior in retail environments? Pretty well, actually, at least in terms of pleasure and arousal. In research using the model, consumers indicated that they intended to spend money in pleasurable retail store environments and intended to spend time and to interact with salespeople in arousing retail store environments (Babin & Darden, 1995; Donovan & Rossiter, 1982). In terms of the effects of the specific categories of environmental cues, consumers' level of arousal and level of pleasure increased when they were exposed to high ambient conditions (e.g., bright lighting, well-merchandised store, store image-appropriate music) and high social conditions (e.g., helpful, friendly salespeople) (Baker, Levy, & Grewal, 1992). Consequently, this high level of arousal and high level of pleasure led to an increased willingness to purchase from the store (Baker, Levy, & Grewal, 1992).

Dominance, on the other hand, did not have a significant influence on consumers' approach or avoidance behaviors in retail store environments (Babin & Darden, 1995). Hence, it seems that, while the Mehrabian-Russell (1974) model does seem useful for explaining consumer behavior in a retail store environment, the only emotional states that mediate the relationship between the stimulus and the individual's response are pleasure and arousal, not dominance.

Wrapping up our jeans example, you may have decided that you were going to buy a pair of 7 For All Mankind jeans. So you head off to your nearest department store to buy a pair. However, when you get to the department store, you have a terrible experience. The store is dirty and smelly. There is no music playing. The store is badly organized, so it takes you an exceptionally long time to find the section of the store where the jeans are located. When you finally find the section of the store, the salesperson working there is dressed in a dirty T-shirt, a skirt that is too tight, and wearing too much makeup. The salesperson is rude to you when you ask her a question about the jeans. Although the department store has your size, you feel angry and you decide to leave without buying the jeans.

As you are heading to your car, you see a Gap store. Even though you had initially decided against purchasing Gap jeans, you decide to stop in and see whether you like what they have. When you enter the store, you immediately feel welcome. The store is bright and clean. Although the salesperson is folding T-shirts, she looks up from her table and greets you with a warm hello. You notice that she is wearing a cute pair of jeans. You ask her which ones she has on. She tells you the style name and escorts you to the section of the store where they are displayed. She helps you find your size and then opens a dressing room for you. As you are trying on the jeans, you hear your favorite song. And the jeans fit perfectly. You decide that you are definitely going to purchase this pair of jeans. You head out of the dressing room toward the cash register to make your purchase. On your way past a rack of sale items, you spot a pair of pants. The pants are such a great deal, you cannot pass them up. You add them to your jeans and meet the salesperson at the register to pay for your two purchases.

Impulse buying

Although you did not plan to purchase either the Gap jeans or the sale pants, the Gap's store environment encouraged you to purchase. When we are "prompted to buy something while in the store" that we did not plan to buy before we entered the store, we are engaging in **unplanned buying** (Solomon & Rabolt, 2004, p. 447). If you feel "a sudden, often powerful and persistent urge to buy something immediately" without "regard for its consequences," then you are engaging in **impulse buying** (Rook, 1987, p. 191). An impulse purchase is a quick decision and is tied more to emotions than to rational thought. An individual may feel somehow obligated or urged to make the purchase as if she were compelled to purchase. Compared to unplanned buying, impulse buying requires a stronger emotional reaction (e.g., pleasure, arousal, dominance) to the stimulus in the store to drive behavior.

Most of us have participated in the act of impulse buying. Researchers have found that fashion students in particular are especially susceptible to the pull of impulse buying; fashion students engage in more impulse buying than other types of students (Han, Morgan, Kotsiopulos, & Kang-Park, 1991). But it is not just fashion students who are impulsively buying. While probably every person has, at one time or another, purchased an item impulsively, women tend to purchase on impulse more often than men.[1] Additionally, individuals who have completed some college report more impulse buying than individuals with less than a high school education, a high school education, or a college graduate. And, younger consumers tend to purchase more items on impulse than older consumers (Wood, 1998). (To find out how impulsive you are when it comes to buying, complete the questionnaire in Boxed Case 3.3.)

BOXED CASE 3.3. HOW IS IMPULSE BUYING MEASURED?

The Buying Impulsiveness Scale was developed by Rook and Fisher (1995) to measure an individual's impulse buying tendency. Since it was developed, it has been used by numerous researchers in studies of impulse buying. To determine your own tendency to purchase

PREPURCHASE TO PURCHASE STEPS

things on impulse, indicate how much each of the following statements describes your behavior by circling a number next to each of the statements.

	Strongly Disagree				Strongly Agree
1. I often buy things spontaneously.	1	2	3	4	5
2. "Just do it" describes the way I buy things.	1	2	3	4	5
3. I often buy things without thinking.	1	2	3	4	5
4. "I see it, I buy it" describes me.	1	2	3	4	5
5. "Buy now, think about it later" describes me.	1	2	3	4	5
6. Sometimes I feel like buying things on the spur of the moment.	1	2	3	4	5
7. I buy things according to how I feel at the moment.	1	2	3	4	5
8. I do not carefully plan most of my purchases.	1	2	3	4	5
9. Sometimes I am a bit reckless about what I buy.	1	2	3	4	5

To calculate your score, add all of the numbers you circled. You will obtain a number between 9 and 45. The closer your score is to 45, the greater amount of impulsivity you display when buying items. If your score is close to 9, then you tend to not buy items impulsively.

─────────────────────── Reference ───────────────────────

Rook, D., & Fisher, R. (1995). Normative influences on impulsive buying behavior. *Journal of Consumer Research, 22*(1), 305–313.

Just what is everyone purchasing impulsively? That's right—apparel! Numerous researchers have documented that clothing, accessories, and shoes are all items that are frequently purchased on impulse (Bellenger, Robertson, & Hirschman, 1978; Dittmar, Beattie, & Friese, 1995; Mai, Jung, Lantz, & Loeb, 2003). The relatively small size and low cost of apparel and related products contribute to consumers' decision to purchase these types of products on impulse.

An impulse purchase can result from a variety of factors. One factor is the store environment. Consumers can encounter various types of stimuli in the store that can encourage impulse buying. For example, a product itself can serve as a stimulus. Perhaps when shopping you encounter an innovative clothing item or something else you have never seen before. It would be impossible to plan to purchase something you did not know existed. Thus, encountering a novel product can motivate an impulse purchase.

Retailers also employ marketing strategies to entice shoppers to purchase on impulse. For example, retailers arrange certain items to entice shoppers while waiting in line to check out. Where items are placed in the store (e.g., at eye level), what types of visual stimulation a shopper encounters (e.g., displays, signs), and what a shopper hears (e.g., music) while shopping all have the potential to influence.

Two situational factors that retailers utilize are music and scent. Mattila and Wirtz (2001) found that the congruency between scent and music influenced impulse buying. They conducted an experiment employing three levels of music (no music, low arousal, high arousal) and paired each with two different scents. Lavender was classified as the low arousal scent, and grapefruit was used as the high arousal scent. Consumers who experienced the store under congruent conditions—either the high arousal scent and high arousal music or the low arousal scent and low arousal music—indicated that their likelihood of purchasing on impulse was higher than when they experienced the incongruent conditions (i.e., a high arousal scent with low arousal music).

Retailers also may offer in-store promotions to encourage impulse purchases. Sales are great ways to induce impulse buying. In our earlier example, we detailed a shopper who encountered a price reduction of 75 percent on a sweater that prompted an impulse purchase. A steady stream of retail innovations and policies also promote impulse buying. The Internet and home shopping networks provide 24/7 availability of retailing. Consumers are offered instant credit and in-store cash machines, which also facilitate spontaneous purchases (Kacen & Lee, 2003; Rook & Gardner, 1993).

A consumer's mood when shopping influences impulse buying. In general, the happier a consumer is while shopping, the more likely it is that unplanned purchases will be made (Beatty & Ferrell, 1998; Rook & Gardner, 1993). Rook and Gardner (1993) found that 85 percent of the participants in their study indicated a positive mood was more conducive to impulse buying than a negative mood. Why does being happy promote being impulsive? Being in a positive mood can result in engaging in behaviors to maintain the feelings (e.g., buy something nice and you will continue to feel good) as well as cause people to want to reward themselves for previous good behavior (Cunningham, 1979; Rook & Gardner, 1993). The activity of browsing or shopping in a store without an immediate intent to buy can also contribute to positive feelings (Sherry, 1990). Shopping without an agenda can promote positive emotions because there is no pressure to find and purchase a specific item. In addition, for some consumers, the act of shopping alone is fun. Referred to as **recreational shoppers** (Bellenger & Korgaonkar, 1980), these individuals shop longer and obtain more pleasure from the act of shopping than from the products purchased. One's enjoyment of shopping contributes to positive feelings, which, in turn, may cause an individual to browse longer, which subsequently influences one's urge to buy impulsively (Beatty & Ferrell, 1998).

Social needs also may be satisfied during shopping trips. Social needs include the need to interact with friends and family members. The experience of shopping can provide this opportunity. Once again, because satisfaction of the social need is the priority, what is purchased is incidental to the need to interact. Therefore, any products purchased without prior planning on shopping trips intended primarily as social events would represent impulse purchases.

Consumers' involvement with the product category has also been shown to be related to impulse buying. **Involvement** is defined as the perceived relevance of an object to a consumer. Involvement is tied to consumers' needs, interests, and values (Zaichkowsky, 1995). If you are involved in fashion, for example, you probably enjoy reading about it, talking about it with your friends, and studying it in school. If you are involved in fashion, you likely spend more time shopping for fashion items than individuals who are less involved in fashion. Because you spend more time looking at fashion goods, you expose yourself to more opportunities to purchase those goods than an individual who is not involved in fashion. With increased opportunities to purchase fashion goods, it is not surprising that you would buy at least some of these items on impulse. Indeed, it has been documented that product involvement is related to impulse buying. The more involved you are with the product category, the more likely it is you will purchase items on impulse (Kwon & Armstrong, 2002; Park, Kim, & Forney, 2006).

Types of impulsive buying behavior

Stern (1962) outlined four categories of unplanned buying that could occur as a result of product stimuli and promotional stimuli. **Reminder impulse buying** reflected a purchase that was made as a result of something in the store causing consumers to remember that they had run out of the product at home or to recall that they had made a previous decision to purchase that item the next time they went shopping. Perhaps upon seeing a display for socks you remember that you need to get some new ones because the ones you own are beginning to fade or are worn out. Seeing the product in the store activates your memory of your need for the new item. The purchase is impulsive in this instance simply because you did not plan to buy it in advance.[2]

Suggestion impulse buying occurs when a shopper is able to visualize a need for an item after seeing it for the first time. Just by seeing the item for the first time you can recognize how that item would fulfill your need. Continuing with the sock example, upon seeing a new style of socks, you recognize that you could use that style.

While the product serves as the stimulus to buying impulsively in both reminder impulse buying and suggestion impulse buying, it is the promotion that serves as the impetus in **planned impulse buying**. Planned impulse buying occurs in situations where you plan to buy products in response to in-store price specials and other in-store incentives. In planned impulse buying, you are deal hunting. You have no specific item in mind, but you plan to buy based on the type of deal the retailer offers you. You might do this type of impulse buying if you plan to shop at a store that is offering 50 percent off all items for a specific time period. You do not know exactly what you are looking for, but you do plan to purchase. Whatever you purchase you do on impulse because you did not know in advance what you might find. The last category is **pure impulse buying**. This is an instance where you have not planned to purchase anything and you encounter something and buy it.

As you can tell from this discussion, impulse buying is a complex phenomenon that entails more than just making an unplanned purchase. It is a part of everyday life. While the outcomes associated with everyday impulse purchases may not always be positive, buying something on impulse is not necessarily a bad thing to do. There are economic benefits to purchasing on impulse. For example, you can take advantage of in-store promotions that you encounter when shopping. There are also emotional benefits. It is fun to find something new or to locate a great deal on an item. There can be a downside to impulse purchases. Buying things that you do not really need and will never use can be viewed as wasteful.

Summary

The consumer decision process model is based on the notion that consumers behave in an economically rational manner when making consumption decisions. This chapter focused on the first four steps, or the prepurchase steps, of the model. According to this model, consumers first recognize that they have a consumption problem and subsequently make a series of decisions designed to solve that problem. The consumption problem arises as a result of a discrepancy between a consumer's actual state and his or her ideal state. This discrepancy may be a result of unmet needs and wants. Although some physiological needs are met through fashion consumption, many consumers are meeting psychogenic needs with their decisions.

After identifying the consumption problem, consumers engage in information search followed by an evaluation of alternative products. During the information search step, both internal and external searches for information are conducted. During the evaluation step, consumers consider important assessment criteria. The final step in this part of the model is the purchase decision, which is shaped by noncompensatory and compensatory decision rules.

Although the consumer decision process model can be applied in many instances of fashion consumption, consumers also engage in unplanned buying or impulse buying. Impulse buying represents a normative form of consumption that is an exception to the rational consumer decision process model.

Key Terms

- alternative evaluation
- ambient category
- approach behavior
- avoidance behavior
- brand image
- cognitive miser
- compensatory rules
- consumer decision process model
- country of origin
- decision rules
- design category
- Diderot effect
- evaluative criteria
- external search
- functional criteria
- heuristics
- impulse buying
- information search
- internal search
- involvement
- marketer-controlled source

- need
- noncompensatory rules
- objective source
- ongoing search
- personal source
- physiological need
- planned impulse buying
- planned obsolescence
- problem recognition
- psychogenic need
- psychological criteria
- public source
- pure impulse buying
- recreational shoppers
- reminder impulse buying
- social category
- store environment
- store image
- suggestion impulse buying
- unplanned buying
- want

Questions for review and discussion

1. What activities do consumers engage in during each of the prepurchase steps of the consumer decision process model?
2. Why are psychogenic needs more likely to be met by fashion consumption than physiological needs?
3. How does the fashion industry contribute to the development of consumer wants and needs?

4. What is the Diderot effect and how does it impact fashion consumption? What techniques or strategies do fashion retailers use to take advantage of the Diderot effect?
5. Discuss an experience where you conducted an information search. Detail the sources of information used and explain whether they were internal, external, subjective, or objective sources.
6. What is the difference between a compensatory heuristic and a noncompensatory heuristic? Provide examples of each.
7. Under what conditions are consumers more likely to follow the rational decision process model as opposed to engaging in impulse buying?

Notes

1. This gender difference is reversed in the online shopping environment, where men have been found to be more impulsive online shoppers than women (Zhang, Prybutok, & Strutton, 2007).

2. Beatty and Ferrell (1998) do not include this type of purchase as an impulse purchase, because, although you did not necessarily plan to purchase the item during this shopping trip, you did have the intention to purchase the item at some point in time.

Suggested Readings

If you are interested in the topics in chapter 3, you may also like reading these journal articles:

Baker, J., Parasuraman, A., Grewal, D., & Voss, G. B. (2002). The influence of multiple store environment cues on perceived merchandise value and patronage intentions. *Journal of Marketing, 66*(2), 120–141.

Bloch, P. H., Sherrell, D. L., & Ridgway, N. M. (1986). Consumer search: An extended framework. *Journal of Consumer Research, 13*(1), 199–126.

Dittmar, H., Beattie, J., & Friese, S. (1995). Gender identity and material symbols: Objects and decision considerations in impulse purchases. *Journal of Economic Psychology, 16*(3), 495–511.

Donovan, R. J., & Rossiter, J. R. (1982). Store atmosphere: An environmental psychology approach. *Journal of Retailing, 58*(1), 34–57.

Kacen, J., & Lee, J. (2002). The influence of culture on consumer impulsive buying behavior. *Journal of Consumer Psychology, 12*(2), 163–176.

McCracken, G. (2009, February 28). Consumers in a downturn: A new spending habit? *The Atlantic.* Retrieved June 16, 2009, from http://business.theatlantic.com/2009/02/consumers_in_a_downturn_a_new_spending_habit.php

Zimmer, M. R., & Golden, L. L. (1988). Impressions of retail stores: A content analysis of consumer images. *Journal of Retailing, 64*(3), 265–293.

References

Arnould, E., Price, L., & Zinkhan, G. (2004). *Consumers.* (2nd ed.). Boston: McGraw-Hill.

Babin, B. J., & Darden, W. R. (1995). Consumer self-regulation in a retail environment. *Journal of Retailing, 71*(1), 47–70.

Baker, J., Grewal, D., & Parasuraman, A. (1994). The influence of store environment on quality inferences and store image. *Journal of the Academy of Marketing Science, 22*(4), 328–339.

Baker, J., Levy, M., & Grewal, D. (1992). An experimental approach to making retail store environmental decisions. *Journal of Retailing, 68*(4), 445–462.

Baker, J., Parasuraman, A., Grewal, D., & Voss, G. B. (2002). The influence of multiple store environment cues on perceived merchandise value and patronage intentions. *Journal of Marketing, 66*(2), 120–141.

Beatty, S., & Ferrell, M. E. (1998). Impulse buying: Modeling its precursors. *Journal of Retailing, 74*(2), 169–191.

Belch, G. E., & Belch, M. A. (2004). *Advertising and promotion: An integrated marketing communications perspective* (6th ed.). Boston: McGraw-Hill/Irwin.

Bellenger, D., & Korgaonkar, P. (1980). Profiling the recreational shopper. *Journal of Retailing, 58,* 58–81.

Bellenger, D., Robertson, D., & Hirschman, E. (1978). Impulse buying varies by product. *Journal of Advertising Research, 18*(6), 15–18.

Blackwell, R. D., Miniard, P. W., & Engel, J. F. (2001). *Consumer behavior* (9th ed.). Fort Worth, TX: Harcourt College Publishers.

Bloemer, J., & Odekerken-Schroder, G. (2002). Store satisfaction and store loyalty explained by customer- and store-related factors. *Journal of Consumer Satisfaction, Dissatisfaction and Complaining Behavior, 15,* 68–80.

Cho, S. (2001). *Influence of consumer age and clothing type of salesperson on consumer satisfaction on salesperson's performance.* Unpublished master's thesis, Virginia Polytechnic Institute and State University.

Cunningham, M. (1979). Weather, mood and helping behavior: Quasi experiments with the sunshine Samaritan. *Journal of Personality and Social Psychology, 37*(11), 1947–1956.

Darley, W. K., & Lim, J.-S. (1999). Effects of store image and attitude toward secondhand stores on shopping frequency and distance traveled. *International Journal of Retail and Distribution Management, 27*(8), 311–318.

Dittmar, H., Beattie, J., & Friese, S. (1995). Gender identity and material symbols: Objects and decision considerations in impulse purchases. *Journal of Economic Psychology, 16*(3), 495–511.

Donovan, R. J., & Rossiter, J. R. (1982). Store atmosphere: An environmental psychology approach. *Journal of Retailing, 58*(1), 34–57.

Dunne, P. M., & Lusch, R. F. (2005). *Retailing* (5th ed.). Mason, OH: Thomson/SouthWestern.

Falk, E. A. (2003). *1001 ideas to create retail excitement* (2nd ed.). New York: Prentice Hall.

Getting dream wedding dresses at bargain price. (2008, July 1). *CNN.com/living.* Retrieved July 11, 2008, from http://www.cnn.com/2008/LIVING/homestyle/07/01/pared.down.weddings.ap/

Han, Y. K., Morgan, G. A., Kotsiopulos, A., & Kang-Park, J. (1991). Impulse buying behavior of apparel purchasers. *Clothing and Textiles Research Journal, 9*(3), 15–21.

Hester, S. B. (1986). Imported versus domestic apparel: Are attitudes and buying behavior related? In R. H. Marshall (Ed.), *ACPTC proceedings* (p. 149). Monument, CO: ACPTC.

Kacen, J., & Lee, J. (2002). The influence of culture on consumer impulsive buying behavior. *Journal of Consumer Psychology, 12*(2), 163–176.

Keaveney, S. M., & Hunt, K. A. (1992). Conceptualization and operationalization of retail store image: A case of rival middle-level theories. *Journal of the Academy of Marketing Science, 20*(2), 165–175.

Kent, T. (2003). 2D23D: Management and design perspectives on retail branding. *International Journal of Retail and Distribution Management, 31*(3), 131–142.

Klaffke, P. (2003). *Spree: A cultural history of shopping.* Vancouver, BC, Canada: Arsenal Pulp Press.

Kunz, G.I., & Garner, M.B. (2007). *Going global: The textile and apparel industry.* New York: Fairchild Books.

Kwon, H., & Armstrong, K. (2002). Factors influencing impulse buying of sports team licensed merchandise. *Sport Marketing Quarterly, 11*(3), 151–163.

Mai, N., Jung, K., Lantz, G., & Loeb, S. (2003). An explanatory investigation into impulse buying behavior in a transitional economy: A study of urban consumers in Vietnam. *Journal of International Marketing, 11*(2), 13–35.

Martineau, P. (1958). The personality of the retail store. *Harvard Business Review, 36* (January–February), 47–55.

Mattila, A., & Wirtz, J. (2001). Congruency of scent and music as a driver of in-store evaluations and behavior. *Journal of Retailing, 77*(2), 273–289.

Mehrabian, A., & Russell, J.A. (1974). *An approach to environmental psychology.* Cambridge, MA: MIT Press.

Park, E., Kim, E., & Forney, J. (2006). A structural model of fashion-oriented impulse buying behavior. *Journal of Fashion Marketing and Management, 10*(4), 433–446.

Pettinger, L. (2004). Brand culture and branded workers: Service work and aesthetic labour in fashion retail. *Consumption, Markets, and Culture, 7*(2), 165–184.

Rath, P.M., Bay, S., Petrizzi, R., & Gill, P. (2008). *The why of the buy: Consumer behavior and fashion marketing.* New York: Fairchild Books.

Rook, D. (1987). The buying impulse. *Journal of Consumer Research, 14,* 189–199.

Rook, D., & Gardner, M. (1993). In the mood: Impulse buying's affective antecedents. *Research in Consumer Behavior, 6,* 1–28.

Shao, C.Y., Baker, J., & Wagner, J.A. (2004). The effects of appropriateness of service contact personnel dress on customer expectations of service quality and purchase intention: The moderating influence of involvement and gender. *Journal of Business Research, 57,* 1164–1176.

Sherry, J. (1990). A sociocultural analysis of a Midwestern flea market. *Journal of Consumer Research, 17,* 13–30.

Sirgy, M.J., Grewal, D., & Mangleburg, T. (2000). Retail environment, self-congruity, and retail patronage: An integrative model and a research agenda. *Journal of Business Research, 49*(2), 127–138.

Sirgy, M.J., & Samli, A.C. (1985). A path analytic model of store loyalty involving self-concept, store image, geographic loyalty, and socioeconomic status. *Journal of the Academy of Marketing Science, 13*(3), 265–291.

Sirgy, M.J., Samli, A.C., Bahn, K., & Varvoglis, T.G. (1989). Congruence between store image and self-image. In A. C. Samli (Ed.), *Retail marketing strategy: Planning, implementation, and control* (pp. 207–219). New York: Quorum Books.

Solomon, M.R. (2004). *Consumer behavior: Buying, having, and being* (6th ed.). Upper Saddle River, NJ: Prentice Hall.

Solomon, M.R., & Rabolt, N.J. (2004). *Consumer behavior in fashion.* Upper Saddle River, NJ: Prentice Hall.

Stern, H. (1962). The significance of impulse buying today. *Journal of Marketing, 26,* 59–62.

Wolff, B. (2007, January 22). Paper dresses from swinging '60s show off planned obsolescence. *University of Wisconsin-Madison News.* Retrieved July 11, 2008, from http://www.news.wisc.edu/13367

Wood, M. (1998). Socio-economic status, delay of gratification, and impulse buying. *Journal of Economic Psychology, 19,* 295–320.

Zaichkowsky, J. L. (1995). Measuring the involvement construct. *Journal of Consumer Research, 12,* 341–352.

Zhang, X., Prybutok, V., & Strutton, D. (2007). Modeling influences on impulse purchasing behaviors during online marketing transactions. *Journal of Marketing Theory and Practice, 15*(1), 79–89.

Zimmer, M.R., & Golden, L.L. (1988). Impressions of retail stores: A content analysis of consumer images. *Journal of Retailing, 64*(3), 265–293.

4

FACTORS INFLUENCING DECISION MAKING AMONG APPAREL CONSUMERS

After you have read this chapter, you should be able to

- Explain how demographic variables influence apparel consumption behavior.
- Describe the impact that psychographic variables have on apparel consumption.
- Identify ways in which our culture affects our apparel consumption.
- Discuss how different economic factors influence apparel consumption patterns.

As consumers go through the decision-making process concerning apparel and related products, they are not doing it in isolation from other facets of their lives. There are other factors such who you are (your personality, your gender), who you are friends with (group membership), the era in which you live, and where you live (suburban area, urban area, rural area) that affect your choices and behaviors. In this chapter we discuss how some of these factors exert an influence on apparel purchase decisions.

We begin our discussion by reflecting on what might make an individual's decision outcomes both different from and similar to others' decision outcomes. In the television program *Absolutely Fabulous*, the two main characters, Edina Monsoon and Patsy Stone, are dedicated followers of high fashion. Edina's daughter, Saffron, is conservative in her appearance. In one episode, entitled "Fashion," Edina comes down the stairs of her stylish home in a particularly tight and colorful ensemble (French, Saunders, & Spiers, 1992). This outfit is, shall we say, not exactly the most flattering silhouette for Edina's figure. In fact, Saffron remarks that her mother's outfit looks like someone vomited on it. Edina justifies her purchase because the outfit was designed by "Lacroix, sweetie." Although the outfit is not aesthetically pleasing on Edina, the fact that it is an expensive, designer outfit serves to validate her purchase decision to herself and her best friend, Patsy, who shares many personal characteristics. At the same time, Edina's outfit is not pleasing to her daughter, because, although they are from the same family, Saffron and her mother share few personal characteristics and lead very different types of lives.

From this example, we can see that individuals make different decisions about what to purchase in terms of fashion products. But we can also see that similar people tend to make similar decisions about what to purchase. The terms used to describe a group of consumers who behave similarly to each other but differently from consumers who are members of other groups is a segment. A **market segment** is "a group of consumers with similar needs and behavior that differ from those of the entire mass market" (Blackwell, Miniard, & Engel, 2001, p. 39). Consumers of fashion can be divided into market segments. These segments describe people whose consumption of fashion varies on the basis of a variety of characteristics. Some of these characteristics describe who people are (e.g., gender, age), some characteristics reflect associations between people (e.g., group memberships), and other characteristics reflect attributes of the environment (e.g., economy, technology) in which people live.

Fashion consumption: demographics

Think about the last time someone who you did not know very well asked you to describe yourself. This usually happens on the first day of class or during the first few minutes of a job interview. How did you start your description? Did you begin with revealing deep, dark secrets about yourself? Well, if you did, you probably suffered through many strange looks from your classmates and your potential employer. It is unexpected in social situations that you would begin a conversation about yourself with this type of information. Instead, we tend to reveal less personal, more objective information about ourselves in social situations with new people (Rubin, 1972). If you have learned this norm of human interaction in contemporary society, then you probably told your classmates or interviewer that you were enrolled in a particular major (e.g., fashion merchandising) or where you worked. Later, as you continued your conversation, perhaps you started revealing other types of information about yourself that was less objective. But, initially, we tend to start by describing ourselves using an array of **demographic characteristics**.

The word *demographics* refers to "the size, structure, and distribution of a population" (Blackwell, Miniard, & Engel, 2001, p. 188). How does demographic information apply to fashion consumption behavior? Think about the kinds of information that would be collected if we were anthropologists studying a particular country. Maybe we would want to know how many women and men lived in the country and what types of work they did. Maybe we would want to know the ages of the people living there. Maybe we would want to know the ethnicities represented or religions practiced and how those ethnicities and religions affected the behavior of the people living in the country. Maybe we would want to know how wealth was distributed among the people. Why would we want to know these things? Well, even though we all like to think of ourselves as being truly unique, the truth is that we share many things in common with people who are the same gender that we are, who are the same age that we are, who are the same ethnicity that we are, and who have the same income level that we have. Because we, as anthropologists, want to eventually understand the behavior of the people living in the country we are studying, we might begin to try to make sense of the people's behavior by first looking at these fairly easily measured characteristics of individuals (e.g., gender, age, ethnicity, income).

Demographic characteristics can be used to categorize people into groups. The behaviors of different groups can be collected and used to predict future behaviors. For example, consumers can be grouped by age, and certain consumption behaviors can be linked to different age groups. Which group of consumers is more likely to purchase baby clothing for their children? Individuals who are in their 20s or 30s or individuals who are in their 60s or 70s?

Consumer behavior researchers, like anthropologists, are also interested in demographic characteristics because these innocuous bits of information about us are related to our buying behavior. Of course, knowing these broad, overarching demographic characteristics about a group of consumers is less useful for predicting an individual's fashion consumption behavior than knowing specific information about individual consumers. But it cannot be denied that gender, age, ethnicity, religion, and income are associated with purchase decisions. Next, we focus on two demographic characteristics, gender and age, and demonstrate how they are related to differences in apparel consumption.

Gender

Women, we have a question for you. When you want to go shopping for apparel items for yourself, who would you call first to accompany you? Is this person a woman or a man? If you are like most women, you probably would not go shopping for apparel items with a man. In fact only 16 percent of the women participants in a survey indicated that they enjoyed shopping with men (Morse, 2005). If you are a woman, you probably find it easier to shop with other women, because most women like to shop for apparel items and most women tend to shop for apparel items in a similar manner.

And, men, who would you like to go shopping with? If you are like most men, you probably would not like to go shopping for apparel at all. In the same survey mentioned earlier, only 25 percent of the men participants indicated that they liked to shop when they did not have something in particular to purchase (Morse, 2005). Men tend to shop infrequently and stock up on apparel and apparel-related products as they need them (Klein, 1998).

Of course, the idea that women like to shop for apparel items and men do not like to shop for apparel items is a generalization, so you may be an exception to the rule. As the distinctions between men's and women's roles in other areas of society become less well defined (e.g., gender roles in the workplace), men and women are becoming more similar in terms of their shopping patterns (Kim, Sullivan, &

Forney, 2007). In fact, both genders indicate that price is the most important factor they consider when deciding where to shop (Klein, 1998). Despite the growing number of similarities between men and women, other researchers have found that gender-related differences still exist, especially in terms of purchasing particular products like apparel (NPD Group, Inc., 2005). For instance, even though price is the most important factor for both men and women when deciding where to shop, more women than men look at the price tag before they purchase apparel products (Klein, 1998).

Here are some of the other differences in shopping patterns based on gender that have been noted. To put it plainly and simply, women enjoy shopping in general more than men enjoy shopping. Women indicate that shopping is one of their top three favorite leisure time activities. Conversely, shopping is men's least favorite way to spend their spare time (Hine, 2002). More women than men tend to be hedonic shoppers, and more men than women tend to be utilitarian shoppers (Kim, Sullivan, & Forney, 2007). Perhaps women enjoy shopping more than men because women view shopping differently than men. To women, shopping provides more than just an opportunity to purchase an apparel item they need (Minahan & Beverland, 2005). Women use the activity of shopping to escape from their regular, sometimes boring, routines. Women also shop to experience a sense of power and independence while making purchase decisions that they usually do not feel in other areas of their lives. Women, unlike men, feel that shopping allows them an opportunity to express their creativity and to socialize with friends and salespeople. Because women have so much invested in the activity of shopping, it is not surprising to find out that "women demand more of shopping environments than men do" (Underhill, 1999, p. 117). In a way, it is actually good that women enjoy shopping so much, since they are responsible for the majority of the household purchases in both the United States (Hine, 2002; Silverstein & Butman, 2006) and the United Kingdom (Cunningham & Roberts, 2006). Because women view shopping as a means of escaping reality and boosting their spirits, more women than men tend to engage in problematic buying behaviors such as compulsive buying.

Age

When we think of age, we can think of the actual number of years that you have been in existence. As you live, your body changes physically, resulting in changing needs in terms of fashion products. Think about a newborn baby versus a toddler. The physical development of newborns and toddlers dictates different characteristics that their clothing must possess. Infants do little except eat and sleep. They must be carried everywhere because they have little muscle control. Typically, newborns wear the same type of apparel products during the day and at night. The onesie is a fashion staple for infants because they can sleep in it and it is machine washable (see Figure 4.1 for a picture of a stylish onesie). As children age, their wardrobe grows and changes. Within a short time, they are walking and playing. They do much more than eat and sleep. They need clothes that are designed for different activities and occasions, such as play clothes, pajamas, and special occasion clothing. These clothing items still need to be easy to care for because young children are rarely concerned with keeping their clothing clean.

While you might not remember being a baby or a toddler, you probably can remember how your wardrobe has evolved as you have aged from a teenager to a young adult. As you transition from a college student to an adult, you will most likely have to forego wearing T-shirts and sweatpants to your morning meetings and start wearing professional apparel. Eventually, your wardrobe will probably come full circle. As men and women reach retirement age, they typically stop wearing professional apparel on a daily basis and start wearing casual, comfortable clothing once again.

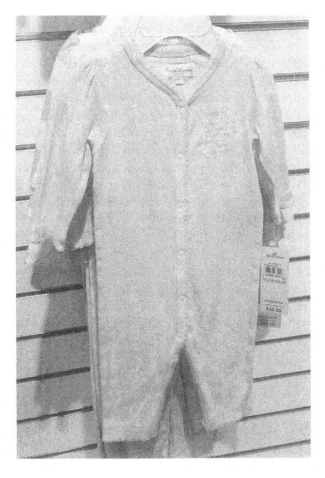

Figure 4.1 Onesies, like the Ralph Lauren one seen here, are a popular apparel choice for babies. Photo by Jennifer Yurchisin.

Changing physical needs is not the only way age influences fashion decision making. Choices about what to wear are also influenced by one's membership in a particular age cohort. An age cohort "consists of people of similar ages who have undergone similar experiences" (Solomon & Rabolt, 2004, p. 178). Members of the same age cohort tend to share similar personal characteristics because they have together experienced "changes that are associated with events of a particular period" (Blackwell, Miniard, & Engel, 2001, p. 326). Individuals who grow up at the same time are exposed to the same political events, technological developments, and cultural happenings when they are approximately the same age. These shared experiences tend to bond the group. As a result, members of the same age cohort tend to share similar beliefs and act in a similar manner.

Think about this: Do you and your friends listen to the same kinds of music? Do you and your grandparents listen to different kinds of music? We do not know a lot of grandparents right now who listen to hip-hop music. Maybe when you are a grandparent you will continue listen to the same style of music that you do now, because, by then, it will remind you of the good times of your youth. But, right now, most grandparents prefer a different sort of music than their grandchildren.

As it is with music preferences, so it is with other consumption behaviors. Membership in an age cohort influences not only what you want to buy but also the way you buy those things. Maybe some of your grandparents lived through the Great Depression or World War II. If that is the case, you may notice when you visit their homes that they tend to stock up on basic necessities such as toilet paper and reuse items such as Ziploc bags. This is a pattern of consumption behavior that individuals in this age cohort learned in their youth when products were regularly unavailable because of forced rationing or their own inability to pay for them. To most of you, this stocking-up behavior may seem very strange. Stores in the current millennium very rarely experience stock-outs of commonly used products, and most of us have credit cards for those moments when we are short on cash and need to purchase something. But major consumer credit cards (e.g., Visa, MasterCard) are a very recent development in the history of consumption. So, although it seems perfectly natural for you to use a credit card at H&M to buy a new outfit, your grandparents' jaws might drop in amazement at this type of purchasing.

As you have probably figured out by now, you and your grandparents are of two different age cohorts. The following sections describe the predominant age cohorts and some of their apparel consumption behaviors.

The gray market

Members of the **Gray Market** were born before 1946. (Perhaps your grandparents are members of this generation). Members of the Gray Market lived through all of the highlights (invention of the television and the Internet) and lowlights (the Great Depression, several major wars) of the twentieth century. Because of advances in medical science and improvements in general health and living habits, members of the Gray

Market typically feel younger than their physical age. This situation is referred to as feeling cognitively young. **Cognitive age** is the "age one perceives one's self to be" (Blackwell, Miniard, & Engel, 2001, p. 198). Trust us when we say that your grandparents are probably keeping up with trends to a much greater extent than our grandparents did. In fact, members of the Gray Market are more fashionable now than ever before (Russell, 1997) and more affluent (Rocha, Hammond, & Hawkins, 2005). The problem for these consumers, though, is that the apparel that is available for purchase often does not fit them properly (Nam et al., 2007). As mentioned previously, physical changes occur as we age. Unfortunately, apparel designers do not always take these changes into consideration when they create apparel for the Gray Market.

Members of the Gray Market seek apparel products that are comfortable and have features such as elastic waistbands, stretch fabrics, Velcro closures that are easier to fasten than buttons, and easily accessible pockets (MacDonald, Keiser, & Mullet, 1998). When consumers find apparel that meets these specifications, it is often not very attractive and does not have up-to-date styling. In other words, the available apparel is frequently not very appealing to these consumers. Thus, although they have money to spend on apparel for themselves, members of the Gray Market often end up spending more money buying apparel for their grandchildren than for themselves (Blackwell, Miniard, & Engel, 2001; Solomon & Rabolt, 2004). This is not to say that no apparel designers or retailers have a good understanding of this consumer group. Coldwater Creek has been very popular among the women members of the Gray Market because the store features apparel with elastic waistbands, a boxy silhouette that can be worn by a variety of body types, and easy care fabrications (Figure 4.2 features a photograph of a Coldwater Creek store). Coldwater Creek is also popular among this age cohort because it is a multichannel retailer that operates stores, a Web site, and a catalog. This consumer group likes catalog shopping because the mall can be confusing and crowded and they often believe that sales associates cannot help them (Nam et al., 2007).

Baby boomers

Baby boomers were born between 1946 and 1964. The baby boomers lived through very turbulent times during their youth. In the United States, members of the baby boomer age cohort "were a part of a philosophical and cultural awakening that created a more open-minded generation" (Kim, Sullivan, & Forney, 2007, p. 38). These consumers lived through Vietnam War protests as well as the civil rights movement. In the United States and throughout much of the Western Hemisphere, the 1960s and 1970s were also a time of experimentation in every sense of the word.

As a result of their broadened horizons from living in a generally accepting society, baby boomer consumers are not afraid to ask for what they want in the marketplace. Baby boomers "are consumers who express their wants, desires, and dreams in their consumption behavior," particularly their behavior with respect to fashion consumption (Kim, Sullivan, & Forney, 2007, p. 38). Baby boomer consumers

Figure 4.2 Coldwater Creek is a popular store for women members of the Gray Market. Photo by Jennifer Yurchisin.

follow fashion and keep up to date with the styles of the times. Baby boomers are willing to pay more for quality when it comes to apparel. In fact, baby boomers spend more on apparel than any other age cohort (Solomon & Rabolt, 2004). Most men and women in the baby boomer cohort need all of these apparel products because, in addition to still being employed full-time in professional occupations, they also have very active social schedules. Hence, they need an extensive wardrobe as they work, travel to exotic locations, go out to eat in restaurants, and go to see performances in the theater (Blackwell, Miniard, & Engel, 2001). Like members of the Gray Market, members of the baby boomer market also feel younger than they actually are. However, unlike the men and women in the Gray Market, men and women baby boomers refuse to age (Kim, Sullivan, & Forney, 2007). To maintain a youthful appearance and attitude, they rely on cosmeceuticals (e.g., over-the-counter face creams to reduce wrinkles), hair coloring, plastic surgery, vitamins, and prescription drugs (Francese, 2003). Baby boomers patronize apparel stores that make them feel young and fashionable.

Generation X

Members of **Generation X** were born between 1965 and 1976. Members of the Generation X cohort have been described as cynical and lazy. However, considering the fact that many of these consumers came of age during an economic recession, it is not surprising that these individuals were a bit unhappy as young adults. Now that Generation X consumers are older adults, some with children of their own, these consumers are being characterized as knowledgeable consumers who "know how to consume, buy, and say no" (Kim, Sullivan, & Forney, 2007, p. 38). Generation X consumers have parlayed their cynicism into marketplace savvy. They are not loyal to brand names but instead seek out the best value (DeBaugh, 2003). They shop for apparel at many different types of stores, including department stores, specialty stores, and discount stores (e.g., Steinmart, TJ Maxx) to find apparel products that possess high quality at a reasonable price (Kim, Sullivan, & Forney, 2007). As a result of their thrifty nature, Generation X consumers typically do not spend as much money on apparel and footwear as the members of their closest age cohorts, the baby boomers and Generation Y (Solomon & Rabolt, 2004). One of their favorite places to shop is bluefly.com because they can purchase high-end, designer apparel products at deeply discounted prices (Kim, Sullivan, & Forney, 2007).

Generation Y

If you are currently a traditional college student, you are a part of **Generation Y**. Generation Y consumers were born between 1977 and 1993. Apparel retailers adore your age cohort because you adore apparel retailers, especially high-end department stores and Internet retailers (van Dyck, 2008). You have been called shopaholics and fashion addicts (Solomon & Rabolt, 2004, p. 182). Do you agree? The statistics show that, among members of Generation Y, "the number one choice for disposing of their wealth is fashion" (Solomon & Rabolt, 2004, p. 183). Generation Y consumers love high-end designer brand names (van Dyck, 2008). Due to their desire for immediate gratification, Generation Y consumers do not want to wait until these expensive apparel products are discounted to purchase them (van Dyck, 2008). These consumers will pay full price for what they want when they want it. This type of spending pattern is not a problem as long as these consumers do not have any other financial obligations.

Unfortunately, the spending patterns displayed by members of Generation Y can quickly become problematic if they live beyond their means and learn to use shopping as way to boost their emotional spirits. **Compulsive buying** is a condition that is marked by repetitive, excessive, uncontrollable purchasing and resulting financial and emotional distress (Hollander & Allen, 2006). Two important criteria must be met to assign the label of compulsive buyer to an individual's behavior. The behavior must be repeated and must be problematic for the individual. The individual may not see that he has a buying problem and may only focus on the relief that buying brings him (O'Guinn & Faber, 1989). The short-term positive rewards, such as mood repair or enhancement (Dittmar, 2000; Faber & Christenson, 1996; Miltenberger et al., 2003), reinforce the behavior, which explains its repetitive nature. As the buying becomes more and more frequent, the individual may begin to recognize that her buying is out of control, which can create additional anxiety, fueling the buying-anxiety cycle (e.g., individual feels anxiety, buys something to alleviate anxiety, feels anxious about uncontrolled buying, then buys more to deal with that anxiety).

Why does the activity of buying alleviate anxiety and make people feel happy? Think about it for a moment. Picture yourself entering your favorite apparel store. How are you treated? Well, if it is your favorite apparel retailer, the sales associate will probably greet you (he may even greet you by name), he may ask you how you are doing today, or how he may help you. When you shop, the center of attention is you. Even when you shop for mundane apparel items, the sales associates are there to assist you (how many of us have personal assistants in our everyday lives?) and to meet your needs. They treat you with respect. They help you find apparel items. They often compliment you with how good you look in those items. When you make a purchase (depending on where you shop), they may carefully place that purchase in tissue paper, fold the tissue around your purchase, and gently place the item in a handled bag for you (to which some retailers tie colorful ribbons). If this description sounds like you are getting a gift, for some apparel retailers that is exactly what the experience is intended to be. The entire apparel purchasing encounter is rewarding, exciting, and you may experience a rush when you are buying. The end result is that you feel good about the experience and forget those problems, if only momentarily, that motivated your going shopping in the first place. Because of the type of experience that shopping and buying apparel can be, it is not too surprising to find that when compulsive buyers are on a buying binge, they frequently make purchases of apparel (Christenson et al., 1994; Schlosser, Black, Repertinger, & Freet, 1994).

Compulsive buying behavior typically begins to occur in early adulthood (Christenson et al., 1994; Schlosser et al., 1994). Because Generation Y consumers are now at the age when they are forming adult consumption patterns, it is imperative for them to avoid developing compulsive buying patterns. Although shopping is an important activity for Generation Y consumers, they must learn to engage in other activities besides shopping to relax and to repair negative mood states in order to avoid developing dangerous consumption habits. (To see if you are currently displaying compulsive buying tendencies, complete the questionnaire in Boxed Case 4.1.)

BOXED CASE 4.1. COMPULSIVE BUYING SCALE

Faber and O'Guinn (1989) developed a scale to assess compulsive buying tendencies. Read the statements below. Circle the number next to each statement to indicate how strongly you agree or disagree with the statement. Remember, there are no right or wrong answers. Just try to be as honest as you can.

Now add the numbers that you circled. You will get a score between 14 and 70. If your score is close to 14, then you do not display many compulsive buying tendencies. If your score is close to 70, then you do display compulsive buying tendencies. If you feel that you need help to control your buying behavior, you should contact one of the professionals in the student services office on your campus.

Reference

Faber, R. J., & O'Guinn, T. C. (1989). Classifying compulsive consumers: Advances in the development of a diagnostic tool. In T. K. Srull (Ed.), *Advances in consumer research* (Vol. 16, pp. 738–744). Provo, UT: Association for Consumer Research.

		Strongly Disagree				Strongly Agree
1.	I have bought things even though I couldn't afford them.	1	2	3	(4)	5
2.	I have felt others would be horrified if they knew of my spending habits.	1	(2)	3	4	5
3.	If I have any money left at the end of the pay period, I just have to spend it.	1	2	3	(4)	5
4.	I make only the minimum payments on my credit cards.	1	2	3	4	5
5.	I have bought something in order to make myself feel better.	1	2	3	(4)	5
6.	I have written a check when I knew I didn't have enough money in the bank to cover it.	1	2	3	4	5
7.	I just want to buy things, and I don't care what I buy.	1	2	3	4	5
8.	I often buy things simply because they are on sale.	1	2	3	4	5
9.	I have felt anxious or nervous on days I didn't go shopping.	1	2	3	4	5
10.	Shopping is fun.	1	2	3	4	5
11.	I have felt depressed after shopping.	1	2	3	4	5
12.	I have bought something and when I got home I wasn't sure why I had bought it.	1	2	3	4	5
13.	I have gone on a buying binge and wasn't able to stop.	1	2	3	4	5
14.	I really believe that having more money would solve most of my problems.	1	2	3	4	5

Look out world—here they come! The oldest members of **Generation Z** are about to hit adulthood. Members of Generation Z were born after 1993. Just as the Gray Market was an interesting age cohort considering all of the developments that its members witnessed during the twentieth century, Generation Z is an interesting age cohort considering the fact that its members have never lived without technology. Because of the access that these consumers have had to information from all over the globe, Generation Z consumers are extremely savvy, sophisticated, and demanding apparel shoppers (Mummert, 2004). In many ways, Generation Z consumers are simply small adult consumers who will not be fooled by retailers' attempts to take advantage of them (Serviss, 2004). Generation Z consumers are conscious of brand names and know the value associated with these apparel items. These consumers seek out apparel products that help them create and express their personality and individuality. In fact, Generation Z consumers represent one of the largest markets for mass-customized apparel products that can be used to communicate aspects of their identity to others (Wellner, 2000).

Fashion consumption: psychographics

Individuals are influenced by the important others with whom they associate. How people choose to spend their time and who they decide to spend it with can be a reflection of shared personality traits and common interests or beliefs. Despite the adage that opposites attract, most people are drawn to others who share their perspectives (Byrne, Griffitt, & Stefaniak, 1967).

Lifestyle is defined as "patterns in which people live and spend time and money, reflecting a person's activities, interests, and opinions (AIOs), as well as demographic variables" (Blackwell, Miniard, & Engel, 2001, p. 219). A lifestyle marketing perspective "recognizes that people sort themselves into groups on the basis of the things they like to do, how they like to spend their leisure time, and how they choose to spend their disposable income" (Solomon & Rabolt, 2004, p. 267). Lifestyle marketers like Ralph Lauren reflect marketing efforts that take a lifestyle approach as they offer consumers not only one category of apparel for themselves but apparel designed for numerous aspects of a consumer's life (e.g., swimwear, golf wear, evening wear) and other family members (e.g., spouses, children) as well as nonapparel items such as home furnishings, colognes, and cosmetics. These marketers offer consumers the opportunity to buy a lifestyle.

Psychographics is "an operational technique to measure lifestyles" (Blackwell, Miniard, & Engel, 2001, p. 220). Demographics identify who buys products, whereas psychographics focus on why they buy. One psychographic technique to measure lifestyle is called VALS™. Originally developed by Arnold Mitchell during the 1970s, VALS was designed around the basic belief that consumers express their personality through their behaviors (Strategic Business Insights, 2001–2008).

Revised as VALS 2 in 1989, the measure was designed to create a link between consumers' personality traits and their purchase behavior. The questionnaire was based on a series of consumer surveys conducted between 1987 and 1992. The data gathered enabled the identification of eight distinct consumer groups. The description of each group identifies key demographics and psychological characteristics that have strong correlations with consumer preferences concerning products, the media, and activities. (See Boxed Case 4.2 for a detailed description of each consumer type.)

BOXED CASE 4.2. VALS 2 CONSUMER SEGMENTS

The VALS 2 questionnaire assigns consumers to one of eight segments based on their primary motivation for purchasing products and the type of resources they have available. The three primary motivations for purchasing include ideals (e.g., acting on knowledge or principles in purchasing), achievement (e.g., demonstrating success by purchasing), or self-expression (e.g., demonstrating personality characteristics by purchasing). The types of resources consumers have access to include their personality traits, such as how much energy they have, their level of self-confidence, intellectualism, and leadership, how much they like novelty, and how innovative, impulsive, and vain they are.

You can take the VALS 2 survey at http://www.sric-bi.com/VALS/presurvey.shtml. By responding to questions designed to assess your type of motivation and level of resources, you will be assigned to one of the following eight segments:

- *Innovators*—Innovators are successful, sophisticated, and have a high level of self-esteem. They are active consumers and most likely fashion opinion leaders. They like variety and independence.
- *Thinkers*—Thinkers are mature, knowledgeable, and responsible. They like to make informed purchasing decisions. They like durable and functional products that represent a good value for the money. They are practical and conservative and respect authority.
- *Achievers*—Achievers are committed to their goals with respect to their careers and families. They prefer products that demonstrate their status to onlookers, so they tend to purchase prestige brands with established reputations. They are conventional and conservative and respect the status quo.
- *Experiencers*—Experiencers love excitement. They tend to be young, enthusiastic, impulsive social butterflies. They place an emphasis on purchasing products that are cool and that make them look good. They like variety and do not mind taking risks.
- *Believers*—Believers like tradition. They value family and honor their religion, and they are active members of the community. They like to buy established brands, particularly products that are manufactured within their own country. They are loyal, conservative, and conventional.
- *Strivers*—Strivers are stylish and love to have fun. For strivers, shopping is a social activity. They tend to purchase products that their peers approve of because they are

FACTORS INFLUENCING DECISION MAKING

Understanding the needs of different consumer groups guides manufacturers in the development of new products and services. The results of VALS 2 assist marketers interested in targeting consumers that are part of these groups. The results help retailers locate new customers for their products, understand consumers' motivations for purchasing different brands, and design convincing selling propositions.

While apparel retailers and designers find VALS 2 useful, there has been limited application of VALS 2 by academic researchers to investigate apparel consumption. Academic researchers interested in this topic have used scales other than VALS 2 to categorize apparel consumers on the basis of their lifestyle (DuPreez & Visser, 2003; Shim & Bickle, 1994). This may have something to do with the high cost of administering the VALS 2. Shim and Bickle, in their study of U.S. women, found three distinct apparel consumer groups: symbolic/instrumentals, practical/conservatives, and apathetics. Symbolic/instrumentals were innovative, independent, and health oriented. They enjoyed shopping at upscale retailers, were fashion conscious, and used credit cards. Practical/conservatives were oriented toward being comfortable, practical, functional, and individual. They did not like shopping, but when they shopped, they did so at department stores. Apathetics did not believe clothing was important. They were less likely to be independent or innovative. They did not enjoy shopping and were not fashion conscious. When they shopped, they liked to shop in discount stores.

DuPreez and Visser (2003), in their study of women consumers in South Africa, also found three distinct groups of apparel consumers: actualizers, strugglers, and aspirationals. Actualizers were found to be individualist, confident apparel shoppers who enjoy shopping. They have high apparel expenditures and shop in and outside of their local community. When they shop, they like to shop in department and specialty chain stores. Strugglers have the lowest apparel expenditures of the three groups. They are individualistic but are neither brand conscious nor innovative. They shop in local stores and prefer to shop in department and discount stores. Aspirationals have high apparel expenditures and are brand conscious. They are active and confident apparel shoppers. They shop in multiple stores but prefer department and chain stores.

Fashion consumption: cultural influences

Social groups operate within a broad context called culture. What is culture? Culture "reflects learned values, mores, and symbols that affect the behavior and consumption" (Kim, Sullivan, & Forney, 2007, p. 7) of a large group of people. Culture is "the collective programming of the mind [that] distinguishes the members of one group or category of people from another" (Hofstede, 2001, p. 9). For example, the United States and the United Kingdom are Western cultures that place an emphasis on individualism. Individualistic cultures stress the values of independence and self-reliance. China and Korea are Eastern cultures that place an emphasis on collectivism. Collectivist cultures stress the value of interdependence and connectedness to others (Hofstede, 2001). Applying this cultural value to an apparel shopping situation, if you were raised in a Western culture, you might be very happy to purchase styles that no one else you know wears or owns. However, if you were raised in an Eastern culture, you might be very happy to purchase styles that most people you know wear or own.

Cultural values "direct attitudes, behaviors, relationships, assessments, and justifications of the self and others" (Kim, Sullivan, & Forney, 2007, p. 120). Because values are related to behavior, an individual's values can be used to predict his or her consumption behavior (Vinson, Scott, & Lamont, 1977). Three categories of interrelated values that affect consumer behavior have been identified: global values, domain-specific values, and evaluative beliefs (Vinson, Scott, & Lamont, 1977). **Global values** are the most abstract of the three categories of values. Their level of abstraction allows them to be generalized to many different sorts of behavior, including consumer behavior. Global values are very important to an individual and, as such, are strongly held by the individual. **Domain-specific values** are acquired from "experiences in specific situations or domains of activity" (Vinson, Scott, & Lamont, 1977). After you participate in an activity, you will develop ideas concerning expectations associated with that activity. For instance, after you become familiar with the purchasing process in an apparel specialty store, you come to expect that salespeople in apparel specialty stores will be friendly and knowledgeable. Thus, a domain-specific value for shopping in an apparel specialty store is friendly, knowledgeable salespeople. **Evaluative beliefs** are specific assessments of particular product classes and brands within those product classes. Hence, these values are the least abstract of the three categories of values. To illustrate the relationships that exist among the three categories of values, consider this example. An individual consumer may, on a global scale, value a world of beauty. This value filtering down into a decision-making context concerning apparel would imply that this person would want to wear apparel products that were visually pleasing. Filtering further down into evaluative beliefs, this global value would suggest this individual would select the brand that reflected the best design.

A society of individuals rarely reflects a single culture. Referred to as **subcultures**, smaller groups of people or consumer segments share values and customs that make them distinctly different from a society as a whole. Consumption subcultures are defined by the multitude of activities and interpersonal relationships that consumers undertake to give their lives meaning. Schouten and McAlexander (1995) define a subculture of consumption as "a distinctive subgroup of society that self-selects on the basis of shared commitment to a particular product class, brand, or consumption activity. Other characteristics of a subculture of consumption include an identifiable, hierarchical social structure; a unique ethos, or set of shared beliefs and values; and unique jargons, rituals, and modes of symbolic expression" (p. 43).

Subcultures can create powerful consumption categories that define how consumers choose to spend their money and time. An example of an international subculture of consumers is the Harley-Davidson Owners Group (HOG). This is a group that individuals are invited to participate in once they have purchased a Harley-Davidson motorcycle. In general, there are HOG chapters associated with each dealership, and members meet monthly to talk about their bikes, plan rides, and socialize. Schouten and McAlexander (1995) did a qualitative study of Harley owners and found that there were visible indicators of commitment to the HOG subculture. These indicators included tattoos, wearing club-specific clothing, wearing sew-on patches and pins, and customization of motorcycles (see Figure 4.3). Participants of the subculture can easily identify each other from want-to-be members or nonmembers. HOG membership easily translates into lifestyle marketing. Harley-Davidson branded products include home furnishings, jewelry, furniture, books, and games.

Fashion consumption: economic influences

While demographics and psychographics certainly influence what type of apparel we purchase, the fact of the matter is that we need money to purchase this apparel.

Figure 4.3 Members of the Harley-Davidson Owners Group often wear branded merchandise. Photo by Kim Johnson.

Yes, you can use a credit card to delay payment for apparel products that you may not be able to afford at the moment of purchase. But, eventually, you will have to pay for everything that you purchase. And, in this sense, you need money to pay for the apparel products that you buy. Your personal income level determines the type and amount of apparel items that you can afford to purchase (not necessarily what you want to purchase) at any given time (Blackwell, Miniard, & Engel, 2001). Most apparel retailers are interested in either your disposable or your discretionary income.

How is disposable or discretionary income arrived at? The basis for arriving at these income levels is total income. **Total income** is "the money or other assets that people receive typically in a year from their work, property, and other investments" (Rath, Bay, Petrizzi, & Gill, 2008, p. 223). If you are currently employed, your total income is what you earn from your job before the government deducts taxes (total income is also referred to as gross wages). If you are still financially dependent on your parents, then your total income would be equal to your disposable income because you do not pay taxes on money you receive from your parents. **Disposable income** is "the amount of money after tax deductions that people have for necessities such as food, shelter, utilities, and transportation" (Rath, Bay, Petrizzi, & Gill, 2008, p. 223). If you are currently employed, then disposable income is the amount of money from your paycheck that you actually take home (disposable income is also referred to as net wages). Your disposable income represents the funds that you use to pay for all of your monthly bills (e.g., rent, groceries, gas, electricity). If you are in need of an apparel item, then you would use your disposable income to pay for that apparel item. For example, if you needed new socks because all of your old socks had holes in them, you would use your disposable income to pay for the socks.

If you are purchasing any apparel item above and beyond what you need (e.g., you are buying something that you want), then you would use your discretionary income to pay for this apparel item. **Discretionary income** is "the amount available about which new decisions can be made when all current obligations have been covered with disposable income and some income remains" (Kunz & Garner, 2007, p. 70). For example, say that you want a new outfit to go out to a club this weekend. The funding for this new outfit would come from your discretionary income. Perhaps it feels like a necessity to you to purchase something new to go to the club. But the truth is that you do not really need this outfit. You probably already have enough apparel in your closet that you would have something to wear to go to the club. You simply want something new.

As you may have guessed, people who have high incomes spend more money on apparel than people with low incomes. As one's total income increases, discretionary income level also increases Thus, one will have more money to spend on apparel items than he or she wants to purchase. However, the percentage of income spent on apparel does not increase at the same level as income increases (Cheng, 2000; Kunz & Garner, 2007). So, for example, if you are lucky enough to receive a 25 percent increase in your salary next year, you might treat yourself to a couple of new outfits. But even with these purchases, you would not end up spending 25 percent more of your discretionary income on apparel than you did in the previous year. So, in absolute terms, you would be spending more money on apparel after you received your pay raise than before, but the percentage of your income that you would be spending on apparel would only increase slightly after your pay raise. Actually, if your income increased at a high enough rate, the percentage of your income that you spent on apparel could decrease from the previous year, even if you spent more money on apparel. The point here is that, even though the amount spent on apparel products increases as income increases, expenditures on apparel do not increase at the same percentage rate.

In addition to personal income level, the economic outlook for an entire nation also has an impact on the amount of money each of us spends on apparel each year. It makes sense that the national economic situation would influence personal spending habits, given the fact that our personal income level will be affected by the state of the economy. If we are worried that we may lose our jobs due to poor economic conditions, then we probably do not want to spend as much on apparel as we would if we felt that our jobs were secure. The term used to describe "how consumers feel about the state of the economy" (Rath, Bay, Petrizzi, & Gill, 2008, p. 223) is **consumer confidence**. You probably hear on the news that the nation's level of consumer confidence is increasing or decreasing each month. Consumer confidence can be measured in several ways. In the United States, the official consumer confidence level is assessed monthly by the Conference Board. Each month, the Conference Board surveys 5,000 random households, asking questions designed to gauge how optimistic consumers are about the state of the nation's economy. The results of the survey are shared with government officials, business leaders, members of the press, and members of the general public (The Conference Board, Inc., 2009). While the official consumer confidence statistics are collected by the Conference Board, other unofficial measures of consumer confidence exist. (You can read about two of these indicators, the Lipstick Indicator and the Necktie Indicator, in Boxed Case 4.3.)

BOXED CASE 4.3. THE LIPSTICK AND NECKTIE INDICATORS

Believe it or not, the economic health of a nation can be determined by counting the number of tubes of lipstick that are sold over a given time period. The term Lipstick Indicator has been attributed to Leonard Lauder, who was the chairman of Estée Lauder during the recession that followed the September 11, 2001, terrorist attacks (Lip Reading, 2009). The idea behind the Lipstick Indicator is this: lipstick sales will increase during an economic downturn because lipstick is an affordable luxury. Rather than spending $300 on a new pair of designer shoes, women "trade down" and purchase a $25 tube of designer lipstick (Silverstein & Butman, 2006). The women, who would feel guilty about spending a great deal of money on a pair of shoes, leave the store happy because they were able to treat themselves to a product they could afford (Schaefer, 2008).

A similar relationship exists between men's necktie sales and economic recessions. The Necktie Indicator suggests that sales of men's neckties will increase during an economic downturn. Men will not be able to purchase new suits because they are too expensive. However, men will be able to purchase new neckties, which are far less expensive than suits, to contemporize their looks at the office (Wisdom, 2007).

Of course, these indicators are not foolproof. Lipstick and necktie sales fluctuate in times of economic prosperity as well as economic deficiency. However, the Lipstick and Necktie Indicators seem logical, given what we know about consumer behavior.

FACTORS INFLUENCING DECISION MAKING

References

Lip reading. (2009, January 22). *The Economist*. Retrieved June 16, 2009, from http://www.economist.com/businessfinance/displayStory.cfm?story_id=12995765&CFID=40641555&CFTOKEN=82729489

Schaefer, K. (2008, May 1). Hard times, but your lips look great. *New York Times*. Retrieved May 17, 2009, from http://www.nytimes.com/2008/05/01/fashion/01SKIN.html?pagewanted=all

Silverstein, M. J., & Butman, J. (2006). *Treasure hunt: Inside the mind of the new global consumer*. New York: Portfolio.

Wisdom, G. (2007, April). Open air indicators. *Ranch and Coast*. Retrieved June 16, 2009, from http://www.ranchandcoast.com/april2007/business-wealth.html

Summary

Decision making concerning apparel and other fashion-related products is a complex phenomenon that is influenced by a variety of factors. Although each decision to purchase is made on an individual basis, people who share characteristics in common often behave in a similar manner. These similarities allow marketers to group consumers into categories based on their shared characteristics and develop market segments. These segments describe people whose fashion consumption is more similar than it is different from each other. One of the ways that consumers are categorized is by demographic characteristics. Two important demographic characteristics are gender and age. Women's apparel shopping patterns differ from men's. There are also several differences in shopping and apparel consumption tied to age.

Apparel consumption is also affected by the activities individuals engage in and the manner in which they spend their leisure time. Individuals' lifestyles reflect the things they like to do in their leisure time and how they spend their disposable income. Marketers have collected lifestyle information that reflects why consumers buy. This psychographic information ties personality characteristics to purchase behavior and allows the identification of distinct consumer groups that marketers can target for their products.

Apparel consumption is also shaped by cultural influences. Broad cultural values determine what is desirable and subsequently shape consumers' attitudes and behaviors. However, a society rarely reflects a single cultural perspective. Numerous subcultures of consumption also exert an influence on what apparel is purchased and worn. Purchasing patterns are tied to an individual's income as well. The type and amount of apparel purchased at any given time is related to the amount of money a person has to spend.

Key Terms

- age cohort
- baby boomers
- cognitive age
- compulsive consumption

- consumer confidence
- culture
- demographic characteristics
- discretionary income
- disposable income
- domain-specific values
- evaluative beliefs
- Generation X
- Generation Y

- Generation Z
- global values
- Gray Market
- lifestyle
- market segment
- psychographic characteristics
- subculture
- total income

Questions for review and discussion

1. Describe how your apparel consumption has evolved as you have matured. Compare and contrast your apparel consumption with that of your parents or your grandparents.
2. Identify additional demographic influences on your decision making concerning apparel consumption. How do these influences enter into your decision making?
3. Think of a consumption subculture that you are a part of. How does your participation in this subculture impact your consumption of apparel and other fashion-related products?
4. There is some evidence that women shop for apparel differently than men. Reread the descriptions of how women versus men shop for apparel. Identify how this description either does or does not fit how you shop for apparel.
5. Reflect on your culture. Identify a global value that people in your culture possess. Describe how this value enters into your decision making concerning apparel.
6. Describe the lifestyle of a college student. Locate an apparel advertisement that you think is specifically designed to appeal to individuals who live this lifestyle. Explain your reasoning.
7. Explain why retailers would be more interested in knowing consumers' discretionary income levels than their disposable income levels?

Suggested Readings

If you are interested in the topics in chapter 4, you may also like reading these other books:

Brooks, D. (2000). *Bobos in paradise.* New York: Touchstone.
Hodkinson, P. (2002). *Goth.* Oxford, England: Berg.
Holland, S. (2004). *Alternative femininities.* Oxford, England: Berg.

References

Blackwell, R. D., Miniard, P. W., & Engel, J. F. (2001). Consumer behavior (9th ed.). Fort Worth, TX: Harcourt College Publishers.
Byrne, D., Griffitt, W., & Stefaniak, D. (1967). Attraction and similarity of personality characteristics. *Journal of Personality and Social Psychology, 5*(1), 82–90.
Cheng, S. (2000). U.S. clothing expenditures: A closer look. *Consumer Interest Annual* (Vol. 46). Retrieved June 16, 2009, from http://www.consumerinterests.org/public/articles/clothing.pdf

Christenson, G.A., Faber, R.J., de Zwaan, M., Raymond, N.C., Specker, S.M., Ekern, M.D., Mackenzie, T.B., Crosby, R.D., Crow, S.J., Eckert, E.D., Mussell, M.P., & Mitchell, J.E. (1994). Compulsive buying: Descriptive characteristics and psychiatric comorbidity. *Journal of Clinical Psychiatry, 55*(1), 5–11.

The Conference Board, Inc. (2009, May 26). The Conference Board Consumer Confidence Index increases sharply. Retrieved June 16, 2009, from http://www.conference-board.org/economics/ConsumerConfidence.cfm

Cunningham, J., & Roberts, P. (2006). *Inside her pretty little head: A new theory of female motivation and what it means for marketing.* London: Marshall Cavendish.

DeBaugh, M. (2003, December 1). Like a gold mine: The new generation of customers. *ABA Bank Marketing.* Retrieved June 16, 2009, from http://www.articlearchives.com/population-demographics/demographic-groups-generation-x/74545-1.html

Dittmar, H. (2000). The role of self-image in excessive buying. In A. Benson (Ed), *I shop, therefore I am* (pp. 105–132). New York: Rowman & Littlefield.

DuPreez, R., & Visser, E.M. (2003). Apparel shopping behavior—Part 2: Conceptual theoretical model, market segments, profiles, and implications. *SA Journal of Industrial Psychology, 29*(3), 15–20.

Faber, R., & Christenson, G. (1996). In the mood to buy: Differences in the mood states experienced by compulsive buyers and other consumers. *Psychology and Marketing, 13,* 803–820.

Francese, P. (2003). Top trends for 2003. *American Demographics, 24*(11), 48–51.

French, D., Saunders, J. (Writers), & Spiers, B. (Director). (1992, November 12). Fashion [Television series episode]. In J. Plowman (Producer), *Absolutely fabulous.* London: British Broadcasting Corporation.

Hine, T. (2002). *I want that! How we all became shoppers.* New York: HarperCollins.

Hofstede, G. (2001). *Culture's consequences: Comparing values, behaviors, institutions, and organizations across nations* (2nd ed.). Thousand Oaks, CA: Sage.

Hollander, E., & Allen, A. (2006). Is compulsive buying a real disorder, and is it really compulsive? *American Journal of Psychiatry, 163,* 1670–1672.

Kim, Y.-K., Sullivan, P., & Forney, J.C. (2007). *Experiential retailing: Concepts and strategies that sell.* New York: Fairchild Books.

Klein, M. (1998). He shops, she shops. *American Demographics, 20*(3), 34–36.

Kunz, G.I., & Garner, M.B. (2007). *Going global: The textile and apparel industry.* New York: Fairchild Books.

MacDonald, N., Keiser, S., & Mullet, K. (1998). United Nations International Year of Older Persons 1999 Clothing Initiative. In *ITAA Proceedings* (Vol. 55, pp. 15–18). Boulder, CO: International Textile and Apparel Association.

Minahan, S., & Beverland, M. (2005). *Why women shop: Secrets revealed.* Milton, Queensland, Australia: Wrightbooks.

Miltenberger, R., Redlin, J., Crosby, R., Stickney, M., Mitchell, J., Wonderlich, S., Faber, R., & Smyth, J. (2003). Direct and retrospective assessment of factors contributing to compulsive buying. *Journal of Behavior Therapy and Experimental Psychiatry, 34,* 1–9.

Morse, David. (2005, March 30). It's a man's world. *RetailWire.* Retrieved June 12, 2009, from http://retailwire.com/Discussions/Sngl_Discussion.cfm/10552

Mummert, J. (2004). The "between" market. *Target Marketing, 27*(1), 49–50.

Nam, J., Hamlin, R., Gam, H.J., Kang, J.H., Kim, J., Kumphai, P., Starr, C., & Richards, L. (2007). The fashion-conscious behaviours of mature female consumers. *International Journal of Consumer Studies, 31*(1), 102–108.

NPD Group, Inc. (2005, February). Shifting roles: How men and women shop today. *NPD Insights, 29.* Retrieved June 16, 2009, from http://www.npdinsights.com/archives/february2005/cover_story.html

O'Guinn, T. C., & Faber, R. J. (1989). Compulsive buying: A phenomenological exploration. *Journal of Consumer Research, 16*(2), 147–157.

Rath, P. M., Bay, S., Petrizzi, R., & Gill, P. (2008). *The why of the buy: Consumer behavior and fashion marketing.* New York: Fairchild Books.

Rocha, M., Hammond, L., & Hawkins, D. (2005). Age, gender, and national factors in fashion consumption. *Journal of Fashion Marketing and Management, 9*(4), 380–390.

Rubin, Z. (1972). *Lovers and other strangers: The development of intimacy in encounters and relationships.* Paper presented at a symposium on theory and research on the development of dyadic relationships, American Psychological Association, Honolulu, Hawaii.

Russell, C. (1997, July). The ungraying of America: Older Americans are the biggest spenders, and their importance to the consumer marketplace is growing. *American Demographics.* Retrieved June 16, 2009, from http:// findarticles.com/p/articles/mi_m4021/is_n7_v19/ai_19570310/

Schlosser, S., Black, D. W., Repertinger, S., & Freet, D. (1994). Compulsive buying: Demography, phenomenology, and comorbidity in 46 subjects. *General Hospital Psychiatry, 16*, 205–212.

Schouten, J., & McAlexander, J. (1995). Subcultures of consumption: An ethnography of new bikers. *Journal of Consumer Research, 22*(1), 43–61.

Serviss, N. (2004). Attracting the teen market. *Global Cosmetic Industry, 172*(3), 24–27.

Shim, S., & Bickle, M. (1994). Benefit segments of the female apparel market: Psychographics, shopping orientations, and demographics. *Clothing and Textiles Research Journal, 12*(2), 1–12.

Silverstein, M. J., & Butman, J. (2006). *Treasure hunt: Inside the mind of the new global consumer.* New York: Portfolio.

Solomon, M. R., & Rabolt, N. J. (2004). *Consumer behavior in fashion.* Upper Saddle River, NJ: Prentice Hall.

Strategic Business Insights. (2001–2008). *The VALS™ Survey.* Retrieved July 19, 2010, from http:// www.strategicbusinessinsights.com/vals/presurvey.shtml

Underhill, P. (1999). *Why we buy.* New York: Simon & Schuster.

van Dyck, D. (2008, Spring). The luxury survey. An in-depth report on how U.S. millennials look at luxury. *Time Style and Design,* pp. 58–59.

Vinson, D. E., Scott, J. E., & Lamont, L. M. (1977). The role of personal values in marketing and consumer behavior. *Journal of Marketing, 41*(2), 44–50.

Wellner, A. S. (2000). Generation Z. *American Demographics, 22*(9), 60–64.

5

NORMATIVE FASHION CONSUMER
DECISION MAKING: POSTPURCHASE STEPS

After you have read this chapter, you should be able to

- Describe what happens to apparel products after they are purchased.
- Define the concepts of use, care, and storage of apparel products.
- Explain the difference between satisfaction and dissatisfaction.
- Identify the reasons why and how consumers dispose of apparel products.

Today is a great day! You have made your fashion product selection, purchased those jeans, and now you are admiring them in your home sweet home. You have definitely committed to your purchase selection, as you have removed all of the tags from the product. What is your next step? Are you going to put your jeans in the washing machine and dryer before you wear them? Are you so excited to wear them that you put them on as soon as you get home? Do you stuff the jeans in the closet with all of your many, many other fashion products? How do you feel about buying these jeans now that you own them? Are you scared to wear them because your friends and family members may not approve of them? Are you feeling guilty for buying one more item that you do not need and may never actually wear? While making an apparel purchase decision can be a complicated process, determining what to do with the product when you get home may be no less difficult for some buyers. In this chapter, we consider postpurchase behavior, including the last three steps in the fashion consumer decision process model. (Refer to the Consumer Decision Process Model in Figure 5.1 to refresh your memory about the steps in the model.) First, we discuss what you do with new apparel items when you get them to your home.

Your first moments together

What do you do when you finally get the apparel product that you purchased at the store or via the Internet home? You may think that whatever process you typically go through is the same process that other people go through with their new apparel purchases. However, as we discovered, this first postpurchase sequence of events is not exactly the same for every consumer.

While we were writing this book, we realized that we did not know very much about consumers' first moments together with their new purchases. To remedy this situation, we decided to find out what people do with apparel products after they bring them home. So we conducted an informal survey of consumers with the help of the undergraduate students enrolled in our classes. We asked our students to share with us what they did with their new apparel items once they got them home. We also asked our students to survey four additional people about what they did once they purchased a new apparel item. We discovered two main postpurchase behavior sequences.

One sequence of behavior is practiced by people who are committed to keeping the apparel item they purchased. These individuals cut the tags off of the apparel

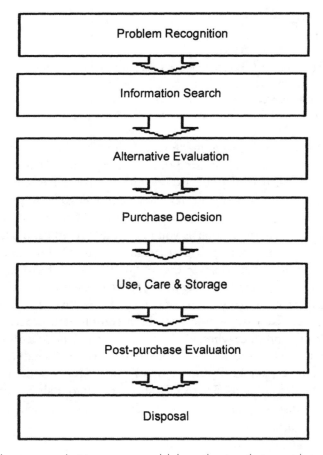

Figure 5.1 The consumer decision process model shows the steps that occur during the consumption process, including the postpurchase steps discussed in this chapter.

item and either wash it or dry clean it prior to wearing it. Because retailers typically do not allow consumers to return items once they have been cleaned, we felt that these consumers were the most committed to keeping the item they purchased and incorporating it into their wardrobes.

Another sequence of behavior was practiced by consumers who we felt were definitely not committed to keeping the item they purchased. These individuals stated that they did not cut the tags off of the apparel items as soon as they got them home. In fact, some of them retained the original shopping bag and receipt until they were certain they were going to keep the item they purchased. To make sure that they wanted to keep the new item, these individuals engaged in several additional postpurchase behaviors, such as trying on the apparel item again at home to make sure it fit and looking for other apparel items that they already owned that could coordinate with the newly purchased item. If these consumers eventually did commit to owning the new apparel item, they would cut the tags off and find a place for the item in their regular apparel use-care-store rotation.

Although none of the participants in our informal survey admitted to engaging in any nonnormative or unethical consumer behavior, we know from experience and research that some individuals wear apparel items without removing the tags because they intend to return the apparel items to the retail store after wearing them. This practice is referred to as merchandise borrowing and is discussed in the next chapter. Suffice it to say for now that there seem to be two levels of postpurchase commitment. To us, this process sounds a lot like dating—some people want to get married after one date, and other people continue to fear commitment even after years of dating the same person! Perhaps some of the same personality traits that influence interpersonal commitment also influence person-product commitment.

Step 5: Use, care, and storage of apparel products

Use

After you decide to commit to the apparel product that you have brought home, it is time to start using and caring for that product. **Usage** of apparel products is "considered to occur when the product is contributing to household well-being, whether functional or aesthetic" (Boyd & McConocha, 1996, p. 232). Obviously, wearing the apparel items you own contributes to your well-being. Your apparel items keep your body covered (and out of jail—as most countries around the world require individuals to wear apparel products of some sort when out in public). Your apparel items can also contribute to your sense of self. Individuals frequently wear apparel that reflects aspects of their identities (Roach-Higgins & Eicher, 1992) that are commented on and reacted to by others (Stone, 1962). Reactions of others can include praise that consequently enhances your self-worth.

The number of times you wear an apparel item is influenced by characteristics of your wardrobe as well as characteristics of the product (Fenner & Bruns, 2004).

Think for a minute about your favorite apparel item. Maybe this is easy for you because you are the type of person who likes to wear your favorite apparel item often. Maybe you do not have very many apparel items in your wardrobe, so an image of your favorite apparel item just pops right into your head. Or maybe you are the type of person who has a large, expansive wardrobe. In this case, thinking of your favorite apparel item may be very difficult because you have many favorite apparel items. It is hard to get a clear picture of a single favorite item in your mind because you have so many favorite apparel items to filter through. As you can see from this example, the size of your wardrobe affects how often and in what ways you use specific apparel items.

Similarly, the characteristics of the apparel products that you own have an impact on how often and in what ways you might use them. Some apparel products are meant to be worn very infrequently. If you own a tuxedo, chances are that you only wear this ensemble once or twice a year (unless you are a maître d' in a restaurant, in which case you may wear that tuxedo several times a week). Although brides often tell their bridesmaids that they will wear those purple taffeta dresses over and over again, this is very unlikely. For the most part, tuxedos and bridesmaids gowns are only worn once or twice, because, in Western cultures, social conventions direct our behavior to reserve these types of apparel items for special occasions like weddings and formal parties. Because we typically do not attend weddings and formal parties on a weekly basis, we do not wear these apparel items very often.

On the other hand, some apparel items are meant to be worn frequently. Do you have a job right now? If you do, do you have to wear a uniform? In many workplace environments, employers require employees to wear a specific type or color of shirt and a specific type or color of pants. If you work in this type of environment, you probably wear these shirts and pants many times each week. Even if you work in an environment that does not have such a dress code, you may find yourself wearing your work clothes, such as a business suit, on a more regular basis than your casual clothes or any special occasion clothing you may own. If you are currently not employed, it may be hard for you to imagine a time when you will wear "an interview suit" more often than your jeans and T-shirts. But if your life and career progress along the path that most college students' lives and careers progress, the major components of your wardrobe will soon be changing.

Care

Did you know that wearing a fashion product "can be hazardous to a garment's health" (Marshall, Jackson, Stanley, Kefgen, & Touchie-Specht, 2004, p. 354)? While in use, your apparel items are exposed to many dangers. How many times have you spilled something on a white shirt or khaki pants? Thank goodness for laundry detergents and stain removers.

Caring for apparel items is an act of physical maintenance because it is an "activity that helps restore or retain possession quality and usefulness and facilitates future usage of an item" (Boyd & McConocha, 1996, p. 234). The recommended manner of care for an apparel item varies by the fiber content. For instance, garments made of wool should not be washed in a washing machine (unless you want a new sweater for your Chihuahua). When garments made of wool fibers are laundered, the fibers become twisted and locked together as the washer agitates the apparel items (Kadolph & Langford, 2002). As a result, the garment overall will shrink and you will not be able to wear it again (but your Chihuahua will look fabulous). On the other hand, feel free to wash your cotton garments, like those jeans you purchased, in the washing machine. Cotton fibers do not lock together when agitated. But if you wear an acetate shirt with the new jeans, you should take it off before you get near the water of the washing machine. Acetate garments must be dry cleaned because water damages the fabric.

You may be wondering how in the world consumers remember all of the care methods for all of the fibers that their garments are made of. Well, in the United States at least, consumers do not need to think that hard about remembering because the Federal Trade Commission requires that apparel items sold in the United States contain care labels under its Care Labeling of Textile Wearing Apparel and Certain Piece Goods rule (16 CFR 423). The government cannot control whether consumers actually follow the suggested care methods, but it can make sure that consumers have access to this information in the form of a care label.

Because so many of the apparel items sold in the United States are manufactured outside of the United States, the Federal Trade Commission permits the care labels to contain either written care instructions in English or an approved set of care symbols. The set of symbols were developed in 1997 by the American Society of Testing and Materials, and they are intended to act as universal icons for the major care methods (e.g., machine washing, machine drying, hand washing, dry cleaning) that could be understood by anyone, regardless of native tongue (Magill, 1998). While it seemed like a good idea at the time—especially for the manufacturers producing apparel for individuals living in many different countries—the truth is that most consumers in the United States have absolutely no idea what these symbols mean (Swinker, Hines, & Schmitt, 1999). Hence, most apparel items still have the care instructions written out in English or appearing in both words and symbols. Take a look at the symbols in Boxed Case 5.1. See if you can match the icon with its meaning.

People residing in the United States clean their apparel items far more often than consumers from other countries (Fenner & Bruns, 2004). Excessive cleaning can be harmful to apparel items because the harsh chemicals in the detergents can degrade the fabrics (Marshall, Jackson, Stanley, Kefgen, & Touchie-Specht, 2004). Additionally, excessive cleaning wastes resources like water and electricity and produces waste when the water filled with detergent is disposed (Vezzoli, 1998). We have more to say about the environmental impacts of apparel in chapter 7. Suffice it to say that if we want our grandchildren to have a planet to live on, we all may want to reconsider our apparel care practices.

BOXED CASE 5.1. DO YOU KNOW YOUR APPAREL CARE SYMBOLS?

In 1997, the Federal Trade Commission approved the use of symbols instead of words on the care labels of apparel items sold in the United States. Do you know what these symbols stand for? Take the quiz below to find out how many of these symbols you are familiar with. Match the written care direction to the symbol that represents that direction.

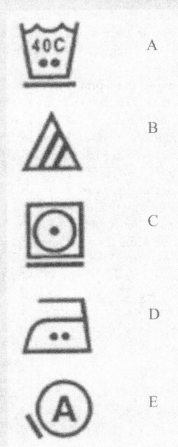

A

B

C

D

E

Clothing care symbols.

Written care directions

1. Dry clean short, any solvent
2. Only non-chlorine bleach when needed
3. Machine wash, 40 degrees C, permanent press
4. Tumble dry low, permanent press
5. Steam iron, medium

Answers—1E, 2B, 3A, 4C, 5D

When you are not wearing or caring for those jeans that you bought, you will need to find a place to store them. **Storage** is defined as "the placement of a household item during periods when it is not being used for its primary function" (Boyd & McConocha, 1996, p. 233). Most of us try to store our apparel items somewhere where they will be safe from dust, dirt, and moisture (Marshall, Jackson, Stanley, Kefgen, & Touchie-Specht, 2004). Of course, we all know someone who does not abide by this rule and stores his or her apparel items on the floor of his or her (but usually his—it is our experience that men tend to do this more often than women) bedroom. Figure 5.2 shows a very messy apparel storage technique.

While our undergraduates were asking people what they did with their new apparel products when they got them home, they also asked people where they stored their apparel products. We wanted to find out whether certain personality

Figure 5.2 Some consumers, especially boys and young men, store their apparel on the floor. Photo by Brian Balster.

characteristics were related to clothing storage behavior. From our undergraduates' informal survey, we found out that people who were more involved with apparel products tended to store their apparel products in more places than people who were less involved with apparel products. **Apparel product involvement** is "an unobservable state reflecting the amount of interest, arousal, or emotional attachment a consumer has" with apparel products (Bloch, 1986, p. 52). (To see how involved you are with apparel products, complete the questionnaire in Boxed Case 5.2.) The need for highly involved individuals to store their apparel products in multiple locations, such as closets, dresser drawers, and laundry hampers, may have something to do with the sheer number of apparel products these individuals own. It seems logical to assume that individuals who are more involved with apparel products would probably own more apparel products than individuals who are less involved with apparel products. The less involved individuals may choose to spend their money on other consumer products. If you need an example that more involved people own more apparel products, think about Carrie from the *Sex and the City* movie. Did Carrie want a big diamond ring from Mr. Big when they decided to get married? Oh no. Carrie, a consummate fashionista, just wanted Mr. Big to get her "a really big closet" for her apparel items (Brenner, Busby, & King, 2008). When highly involved individuals outgrow their current storage options, they can rent off-site storage for their apparel.

BOXED CASE 5.2. APPAREL PRODUCT INVOLVEMENT SCALE

Laurent and Kapferer (1985) conceptualized product involvement as being composed of five dimensions that are combined to create an involvement profile: the perceived importance and risk of the product class, the subjective probability of making a mispurchase, the symbolic or sign value attributed to the product class, the hedonic value of the product class, and interest. The perceived importance and risk of the product class relates to the significance a consumer attaches to a product class and the weight a consumer attaches to the consequences that might occur if he or she purchased an incorrect product from the class. The subjective probability of making a mispurchase relates to the likelihood that the consumer would select a poor product from the class. The symbolic or sign value attributed to the product class is associated with the level of meaning the consumer connects to the products from the class. The hedonic value of the product class is associated with the level of pleasure the consumer feels toward products in the class. And interest relates to the bond the consumer has with the product class.

Laurent and Kapferer (1985) developed a scale that could be used to assess consumers' level of involvement with any product category. You can complete the questionnaire to find out how involved you are with apparel products. Read the statements that follow and decide how much you agree or disagree with each statement. Remember, there are no right or wrong answers.

		Strongly Disagree				Strongly Agree
1.	When you choose apparel, it is not a big deal if you make a mistake.	1	2	3	4	5
2.	It is really annoying to purchase apparel that is not suitable.	1	2	3	4	5
3.	If, after I bought apparel, my choice(s) proved to be poor, I would be really upset.	1	2	3	4	5
4.	Whenever one buys apparel items, one never really knows whether they are the ones that should have been purchased.	1	2	3	4	5
5.	When I face a display of apparel, I always feel a bit at a loss to make my choice.	1	2	3	4	5
6.	Choosing apparel is rather complicated.	1	2	3	4	5
7.	When one purchases apparel, one is never certain of one's choices.	1	2	3	4	5
8.	You can tell a lot about a person by the apparel he or she chooses.	1	2	3	4	5
9.	The apparel I buy gives a glimpse of the type of man/woman I am.	1	2	3	4	5
10.	The apparel you buy tells a little about you.	1	2	3	4	5
11.	It gives me pleasure to purchase apparel.	1	2	3	4	5
12.	Buying apparel is like buying a gift for myself.	1	2	3	4	5
13.	Apparel is somewhat of a pleasure to me.	1	2	3	4	5
14.	I attach great importance to apparel.	1	2	3	4	5
15.	One can say apparel interests me a lot.	1	2	3	4	5
16.	Apparel is a topic that leaves me totally indifferent.	1	2	3	4	5

To score your questionnaire, first reverse your score for items 1 and 16. So if you circled 1, change your score to a 5. If you circled 2, change your score to a 4. If you circled 4, change your score to a 2. If you circled 5, change your score to a 1. Next, add the numbers you circled for 1, 2, and 3. This is your perceived product importance/risk dimension. Then add the numbers you circled for 4, 5, 6, and 7. This is your probability of a mispurchase dimension. The sum of items 8, 9, and 10 is your perceived symbolic/sign dimension. The hedonic dimension is represented by the sum of the numbers you circled for items 11, 12, and 13. Lastly, add the numbers you circled for items 14, 15, and 16 to obtain your interest dimension. Higher scores on each of the dimensions represent a greater degree of apparel product involvement.

———————————————————— Reference ————————————————————

Laurent, G., & Kapferer, J.-N. (1985). Measuring consumer involvement profiles. *Journal of Marketing Research, 22* (February), 41–53.

Our undergraduates' survey also revealed that more involved individuals tended to keep their clothing storage areas much more organized than less involved individuals. Highly involved individuals categorized their storage areas in a variety of ways, including organizing their collections by type of apparel (e.g., jeans in one section, pants in another section) or by color (see Figure 5.3). More than one survey participant mentioned storing apparel according to the order of the colors in the color spectrum. These people probably would not have any trouble finding a red shirt to wear with their new jeans, but they might have trouble deciding *which* red shirt to wear.

Step 6: Postpurchase evaluation of apparel products

Clearly, consumer behavior researchers know a lot about what influences individuals to make purchases of apparel products and about the general process that consumers engage in prior to making a purchase (remember problem recognition, information search, alternative evaluation, and purchase decision from chapter 3). But we do not know quite as much about what happens after consumers get the apparel products home (Hibbert, Horne, & Tagg, 2005). This emphasis on the prepurchase behavior of consumers may be a result of the fact that influencing consumers' decision-making process is, of course, important to apparel retailers who want to make money (as all apparel retailers want to do). If, say, the marketers at Top Shop find out what makes consumers buy their products as opposed to the products from Mango, then the marketers at Top Shop can use this information to encourage consumers to purchase their products and, consequently, make a profit.

So, obviously, understanding the prepurchase behavior of consumers is quite important. But understanding what consumers think about the apparel items that they buy as they wear them and care for them is equally, if not more, important. Think about this scenario. Let's say that, after you wear and wash your new jeans just one time, the zipper breaks and the stitching on the pocket unravels. Are you going to

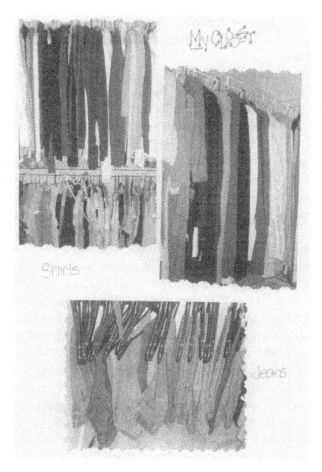

Figure 5.3 Some consumers, who are also highly involved with apparel products, have very organized closets, like the one seen here. Photo by Ashley Thompson.

be happy about this? Probably not. And do you think that the next time you are in the market for a pair of jeans you will rush back to the same store to buy the same brand again? Again, most likely, no. You will not be pleased with the quality of the jeans. **Apparel quality** refers to the degree to which an apparel item satisfies a consumer's needs (Yoon & Kijewski, 1997). These negative judgments about the quality of the apparel item you purchased will result in postpurchase dissatisfaction, and postpurchase (dis)satisfaction has obvious implications concerning repeat purchases.

Postpurchase satisfaction or dissatisfaction is "determined by the overall feelings, or attitude, a person has about a product after it has been purchased" (Solomon & Rabolt, 2004, p. 450). When the feelings are positive, we say that we are satisfied with the purchase. Conversely, when the feelings are negative, we say that we are dissatisfied with the purchase. Pretty simple, right? Of course it is. But, how do you decide whether you should feel positively or negatively about an apparel product? That is not so simple.

Before we make apparel purchases, we already have in mind what we think is going to happen after we purchase and use the product. In other words, we have expectations concerning the apparel product's likely performance, and we compare the product's actual performance against these expectations to assess the product's quality (O'Neal, 1992–1993). These expectations may be formed from our own personal prior experience with a particular apparel product or apparel brand. If we have purchased and worn T-shirts from Nike, then we are familiar with this brand's products. We have some expectation that the next time we buy a Nike T-shirt, it will perform the same way as the Nike T-shirts we own have performed for us in the past.

Our expectations may not always be based on our own past experience. We may have friends or family members who have purchased and used Nike T-shirts. They may have recommended this brand of T-shirt to us. Because we trust the opinion of our significant others, we form an expectation in our minds that we, too, will like the Nike T-shirt as much as our friends and family members do.

A third option concerning expectation formation is not based on anyone's past experience with a product. Sometimes we form our expectations concerning an apparel product's likely performance on the basis of the promises we see in marketing materials (Churchill & Surprenant, 1983). Maybe we saw an advertisement for Nike T-shirts while we were watching our favorite program on television. This advertisement promised that Nike T-shirts fit well, would wick the sweat away from our bodies while we were working out, and were easy to care for. Because of this advertisement, we would have an expectation that Nike T-shirts would perform as advertised.

If the Nike T-shirt that we bought fits poorly, keeps the sweat trapped next to our bodies while we are working out, and turns out to not be machine washable, then our expectations would not be met. In this case, we say that our expectations were disconfirmed. On the other hand, if the Nike T-shirt does exactly what the television advertisement or our friends and family members suggested, then we say that our expectations were confirmed. Does this mean that we will be satisfied? Well, not exactly. When our expectations are merely met or confirmed, we do not really feel positively or negatively about our purchases. We just feel neutral toward our purchase. In order for us to feel satisfied with an apparel purchase, our expectations must be exceeded. If our expectations have been exceeded, we say that our expectations have been positively disconfirmed. Referring to the Nike T-shirt example, we would only be satisfied with our purchase if the T-shirt went above and beyond our expectations. The T-shirt would have to not only do exactly what we expected it to do, but also wow us with some unexpected characteristic like being the softest T-shirt we have ever owned, being wrinkle resistant or stain resistant, or making us look ten pounds lighter when we wear it.

Although it may be difficult for retailers to satisfy consumers, it is well worth the effort. Satisfied consumers are likely to be loyal consumers (Anderson, Fornell, & Lehmann, 1994). Additionally, satisfied customers are likely to recommend the product or retailer to other consumers. (You can read about the success that one apparel manufacturing company is having as a result of satisfied consumers' comments in Boxed Case 5.3.) It is probably easier on a consumer, too, when he or she is satisfied as opposed to dissatisfied with a purchase. Returning products can sometimes be a hassle. And trying to find a new favorite brand of jeans can also be frustrating and time-consuming. So life is better for both buyers and sellers when buyers are satisfied.

BOXED CASE 5.3. SATISFIED CONSUMERS' COMMENTS CREATE A BUYING FRENZY

Michael Krinsky and Jeff Grosner are the owners of Mountain, an apparel manufacturing company in New Hampshire that makes the Three Wolf Moon T-shirt. Never heard of Mountain or the Three Wolf Moon T-shirt? Then you may be surprised to find out that the Three Wolf Moon T-shirt was Amazon.com's best-selling apparel item for May 2009 (Daum, 2009).

Of course, the Three Wolf Moon T-shirt was not always such a hot commodity. Mountain used to sell only about two or three of the shirts each day (Daum, 2009). The excitement about the shirt began after a satisfied consumer in New Jersey posted the following comment about the shirt on Amazon.com:

> "Pros: Fits my girthy frame, has wolves on it, attracts women. Cons: Only 3 wolves, cannot see wolves when sitting with arms crossed, wolves would have been better if they glowed in the dark" (Daum, 2009, p. A9).

This customer's comment was followed by additional comments by similarly satisfied consumers, such as:

> "I have been wearing this shirt for about 15 weeks and I have not needed to wash it! You don't put this shirt on your torso you put it on your soul."
> "Most shirts like this only contain one wolf. This shirt has three wolves, plus a moon. You are basically getting three wolves and a moon for the price of one wolf."
> "This is the T-shirt God would wear. If He wanted to look AWESOME" (Daum, 2009, p. A9).

Glowing reviews like these have created an Internet selling phenomenon. Although not all of the positive reviews are from actual customers, the posted comments are truly having an impact on sales of the T-shirt. Hopefully, the comments will not set the expectations of future purchasers too high. Otherwise, the future purchasers may risk being dissatisfied

──────────────────────── Reference ────────────────────────

Daum, M. (2009, June 2). One wolf T, and an Internet sensation. *Star Tribune* (Minneapolis), p. A9.

Step 7: Disposal of apparel products

How do people know when the time has come to part with an apparel item? **Disposal** of apparel "occurs when the garment leaves the possession of an individual" (Winakor, 1969, p. 631). In some cases, you may decide to dispose of an item when it becomes damaged from years of wear. In other cases, you may decide to rid yourself of a particular apparel item much sooner. Apparel retailers such as Zara, H&M, and Top Shop sell garments that are expected to be used fewer than ten times (McAfee, Dessain, & Sjoeman, 2004 cited in Birtwistle & Moore, 2007). Most people dispose of perfectly functional, wearable apparel at times. Perhaps you purchased—on impulse, of course—an apparel fad. After wearing it for one season, you probably do not have any real desire to keep wearing it, especially when everyone you know has stopped wearing it. Or suppose you bought something on a deep discount that never quite fit you correctly or that never really matched anything else in your closet. In these cases, you probably disposed of the item long before its useful life had passed.

As these examples demonstrate, there are many reasons why people decide to part with apparel items, just like there are many reasons why people decide to purchase apparel items. Some researchers (Hanson, 1980) have suggested that the product disposition process mirrors the product acquisition process. If this were the case, the product disposition process would begin with a problem recognition stage in which you would perceive that a discrepancy existed between your present state and your ideal state (Solomon & Rabolt, 2004). In your present state, you are an individual who owns an apparel product that you no longer desire. In your desired state, you are an individual who no longer owns that particular apparel item.

Sometimes the movement from your present state to your ideal state is motivated by a functional reason. For example, you may be driven to purchase new socks after you take your shoes off at the airport security gate and notice you have holes in the heel or toe area. On the other hand, sometimes disposal decisions are driven by emotional needs. We do not want to be embarrassed sporting a fanny pack if all of our friends are carrying hobo bags. So, even though our fanny packs are still perfectly functional, we decide to part with them.

Just as there are many reasons why we may decide to rid ourselves of certain apparel items, there are several different ways in which we can go about disposing of them. We can throw unwanted apparel in the garbage. To some people, this is the only appropriate method of disposal. These consumers feel that it is not hygienic and perhaps even unlucky to purchase and wear secondhand apparel products, especially those that belonged to people who are now deceased (Clark, 2005; Gregson & Crewe, 2003). Hence, disposing of unwanted apparel is an acceptable method of dealing with the taboo associated with wearing used apparel. To other people, there is not such a great stigma associated with wearing used apparel items. As a result, these people probably feel guilty about throwing apparel in the garbage, especially if they are disposing of apparel items whose useful life has not completely passed. So we may decide to donate unwanted apparel items to another person. Sometimes this person is a family member or a friend. One of the authors has four older sisters; you can imagine the chain of hand-me-downs. In fact, some family photos feature various sisters wearing the exact same outfit in different years!

If you do not know anyone to whom you can give your unwanted apparel item, you may wish to donate that item to a charitable organization. Organizations like the Salvation Army, Goodwill, and Oxfam receive apparel donations from individuals and resell them at a drastically reduced price. Donating unwanted apparel to charity shops makes consumers feel good (Birtwistle & Moore, 2007) because the proceeds from the sale of apparel items at these types of organizations help disadvantaged individuals in many ways. First, the inexpensive apparel available for purchase can be worn by individuals who cannot afford to purchase expensive apparel from department stores or specialty stores. Second, the stores associated with the charitable organizations reinvest the profits from the sales into community programs, which also help disadvantaged individuals. For example, proceeds from sales at a local Salvation Army Family Store may be reinvested into the programs offered by the Boys and Girls Club, an organization that helps disadvantaged young people become successful adults (Salvation Army, 2009). A third way in which donations to charitable organizations may help disadvantaged individuals also occurs. When donated items do not sell in a reasonable amount of time, the charitable organizations may resell them to apparel brokers, who then resell them to organizations overseas. This process provides jobs to people overseas as well as inexpensive apparel to consumers overseas. (You can read more about the process in Boxed Case 5.4.)

BOXED CASE 5.4. DONATED APPAREL PRODUCTS' EXCITING GLOBAL ADVENTURE

They call it *salaula* in Zambia (Durham, 2004) and *mivumba* in Uganda (Dougherty, 2004). Regardless of what it is called, the secondhand clothing market in Africa is big

POSTPURCHASE STEPS

business. In 2002, for instance, the value of secondhand clothing from the United States being exported to Africa for sale was $59.3 million (Dougherty, 2004).

Many apparel items that are donated to charitable organizations like the Salvation Army and Goodwill end up being worn by consumers in African countries. In fact, the majority of the apparel items that are donated to charitable organizations will end up being sold to consumers in other countries; only 10 percent to 20 percent of the donated apparel is purchased and worn by consumers in the country in which the apparel was originally donated (Durham, 2004). The remaining 80 percent to 90 percent of the donated apparel is sold in bulk to brokers who ship the secondhand apparel to countries overseas. When the shipments arrive overseas, the apparel is sold in large, open-air bazaars by local entrepreneurs.

Although the secondhand apparel business in Africa provides individuals with employment, not everyone is happy about the practice. Some people argue that the practice hurts the domestic apparel industry in the African countries. The African apparel manufacturers who are producing new items find it difficult to compete with the inexpensive secondhand apparel that is being imported from foreign countries (Dougherty, 2004). These manufacturers would like the practice to be banned. Until that day arrives, your donated apparel items will continue to acquire many frequent flyer miles after you discard them.

References

Dougherty, C. (2004, June 3). Trade theory vs. used clothes in Africa. New York Times. Retrieved June 16, 2009 from http://www.nytimes.com/2004/06/03/business/trade-theory-vs-used-clothes-in-africa.html?pagewanted=2

Durham, M. (2004, February 25). Clothes line. The Guardian. Retrieved June 16, 2009, from http://www.guardian.co.uk/society/2004/feb/25/voluntarysector.charitymanagement

If you have an apparel item that is really nice (or expensive) and that is in good condition, you may decide to resell the item when you no longer want to keep it. With the recent economic downturn, more consumers are purchasing secondhand clothing (Walker, 2008). Thus, the likelihood of your discarded apparel items being purchased by another individual is very high. You may decide to go it alone and sell the item yourself through a classified advertisement in the newspaper or on an Internet auction site such as e-Bay. On the other hand, you may decide to get together with some friends and sell your unwanted apparel items in a garage sale or a yard sale (see Figure 5.4). If you are ever in Covington, Kentucky, or Gadsden, Alabama (or anywhere in between the two), and you are interested in selling your items, you may want to take part in the largest garage sale in the United States. Every August, 450 miles along the highway 127 corridor are transformed into an outdoor shopping mall of used goods (Klaffke, 2003).

Figure 5.4 Unwanted apparel items can be sold at a garage sale or a yard sale. Photo by Brian Balster.

If it is not August and you would like to have help from others selling your used apparel items, you may want to consider utilizing the services provided by a consignment shop. A consignment shop is a store where the retailer does not own the merchandise. Individuals bring their slightly used and gently worn apparel and the shop owner provides a selling space for the items to be offered for sale to consumers (Berman & Evans, 2001). Consignment shop owners price the apparel items, merchandise the apparel items, promote the items, and ring up the sales. In exchange for the services provided by the consignment shop owner, you will be required to pay a percentage of the selling price to the consignment shop owner. In most cases, the consignment shop owner keeps 60 percent of the selling price, and you get 40 percent of the selling price.

As long as you do not throw out your apparel items in the trash, your apparel items will have another life without you. What is the end of the line with you becomes the beginning of the line with another consumer who purchases your unwanted apparel items. The new consumer will go on to use, care for, store, and eventually discard your unwanted apparel items. Depending upon the condition of the apparel items at the end of the second cycle of ownership, your unwanted apparel items may have a third, fourth, or even fifth life. In this way, your apparel items may travel further and remain on the planet longer than you, especially if those apparel items are made of synthetic materials, like polyester. We discuss the environmental impact of apparel consumption in chapter 7.

Summary

The fact that a consumer has purchased an apparel item does not necessarily indicate that he or she is committed to keeping and using the item. Several factors may motivate the consumer to return the item prior to use. Just like there are differences in commitment to an apparel item, consumers also differ in how they use, care for, and store apparel items. Some of these differences are tied to personal traits of consumers such as degree of product involvement. Consumers also have different options for the disposal of unwanted apparel items. Some of these options are growing in popularity as consumers are becoming more willing to purchase slightly used or gently worn apparel items.

Key Terms

- apparel product involvement
- apparel quality
- caring
- disposal

- postpurchase satisfaction/dissatisfaction
- storage
- usage

Questions for review and discussion

1. Describe the steps you generally undertake once you have made an apparel purchase. Explain the reasoning for your behavior.
2. What is your favorite apparel item? Why do you like this item so much? How often do you wear this item? Is the amount of time you wear this item related to the characteristics of the item itself, the characteristics of your entire wardrobe, your demographic and psychographic characteristics, or a combination of these characteristics? Why do you think this?
3. Consumers care for their apparel items in a variety of ways. Reflect on your own care practices. Do you see your wardrobe as an important investment of time and resources or as disposable?
4. What is the benefit associated with using apparel care symbols on a label instead of using written apparel care directions on the label? What can be done to increase consumers' understanding of these symbols?
5. Think about a time when you were satisfied with an apparel item. In what ways did the item exceed your expectations? Think about a time when you were dissatisfied with an apparel item. In what ways did the item not meet your expectations?
6. Consumers' expectations play an important role in their postpurchase experience with apparel products. In addition to quality, what apparel characteristics influence your expectations and why?
7. Which method of disposal do you use most often for your unwanted apparel items? Why do you use this method? Next, think about how your grandparents or parents dispose of unwanted items. How are your practices alike and how are they different?

Suggested Readings

If you are interested in the topics in chapter 5, you may also like reading these other articles and books:

Bloch, P. H. (1986). The product enthusiast: Implications for marketing strategy. *Journal of Consumer Marketing, 3*(3), 51–62.

Boyd, T. C., & McConocha, D. M. (1996). Consumer household materials and logistics management: Inventory ownership cycle. *Journal of Consumer Affairs, 30*(1), 218–249.

Hansen, K. T. (2000). *Salaula: The world of secondhand clothing and Zambia.* Chicago: University of Chicago Press.

Marshall, S. G., Jackson, H. O., Stanley, M. S., Kefgen, M., & Touchie-Specht, P. (2004). *Individuality in clothing selection and personal appearance* (6th ed.). Upper Saddle River, NJ: Pearson Prentice Hall.

Winakor, G. (1969). The process of clothing consumption. *Journal of Home Economics, 61*(8), 629–634.

References

Anderson, E. W., Fornell, C., & Lehmann, D. R. (1994). Customer satisfaction, market share, and profitability: Findings from Sweden. *Journal of Marketing, 58*(3), 53–66.

Berman, B., & Evans, J. (2001). *Retail management* (8th ed.). Upper Saddle River, NJ: Prentice Hall.

Birtwistle, G., & Moore, C. (2007). Fashion clothing—Where does it all end up? *International Journal of Retail and Distribution Management, 35*(3), 210–216.

Bloch, P. H. (1986). The product enthusiast: Implications for marketing strategy. *Journal of Consumer Marketing, 3*(3), 51–62.

Boyd, T. C., & McConocha, D. M. (1996). Consumer household materials and logistics management: Inventory ownership cycle. *Journal of Consumer Affairs, 30*(1), 218–249.

Brener, R., Busby, K. A. (Producers), & King, M. P. (Director). (2008). *Sex and the city* [Motion picture]. United States: New Line Cinema.

Churchill, G. A., Jr., & Surprenant, C. F. (1983). An investigation into the determinants of customer satisfaction. *Journal of Marketing Research, 19,* 491–504.

Clark, H. (2005). Second hand fashion, culture, and identity in Hong Kong. In A. Palmer & H. Clark (Eds.), *Old clothes, new looks: Second hand fashion* (pp. 155–172). Oxford, England: Berg.

Fenner, A., & Bruns, S. (2004). *Dress smart: A guide to effective personal packaging* (2nd ed.). New York: Fairchild Books.

Gregson, N., & Crewe, L. (2003). *Second-hand cultures.* Oxford, England: Berg.

Hanson, J. W. (1980). A proposed paradigm for consumer product disposition processes. *Journal of Consumer Affairs, 14*(1), 49–67.

Hibbert, S. A., Horne, S., & Tagg, S. (2005). Charity retailers in competition for merchandise: Examining how consumers dispose of used goods. *Journal of Business Research, 58,* 819–828.

Kadolph, S. J., & Langford, A. L. (2002). *Textiles* (9th ed.). Upper Saddle River, NJ: Prentice Hall.

Klaffke, P. (2003). *Spree: A cultural history of shopping.* Vancouver, BC, Canada: Arsenal Pulp Press.

Magill, R. (1998). Keeping pace with permanent care labeling processes. *Bobbin, 39*(9), 36–41.

Marshall, S. G., Jackson, H. O., Stanley, M. S., Kefgen, M., & Touchie-Specht, P. (2004). *Individuality in clothing selection and personal appearance* (6th ed.). Upper Saddle River, NJ: Pearson Prentice Hall.

POSTPURCHASE STEPS

O'Neal, G. S. (1992–1993). A conceptual model of consumer perception of apparel quality. *Themis: Journal of Theory in Home Economics, 2*(1), 1–25.

Roach-Higgins, M., & Eicher, J. (1992). Dress and identity. *Clothing and Textiles Research Journal, 10*(4), 1–8.

Salvation Army. (2009). *Family store*. Retrieved June 16, 2009, from http://www.uss.salvationarmy. org/uss/www_uss_greensboro_nc.nsf/vw-text-index/f31fd1f10ab1e4a08525747100501370?opendocument

Solomon, M. R., & Rabolt, N. J. (2004). *Consumer behavior in fashion*. Upper Saddle River, NJ: Prentice Hall.

Stone, G. (1962). Appearance and the self. In A. Rose (Ed.), *Human behavior and the social process: An interactionist approach* (pp. 86–116). New York: Houghton Mifflin.

Swinker, M. E., Hines, J. D., & Schmitt, J. C. (1999, November). *Consumers' use of care labels and their understanding of the international symbols*. Paper presented at the annual meeting of the International Textile and Apparel Association, Santa Fe, NM.

Vezzoli, C. (1998, November). *Clothing care in the sustainable household*. Paper presented at the Greening of Industry Network Conference, Rome, Italy.

Walker, R. (2008, October 31). Goodwill hunting. *New York Times Magazine* [Online]. Retrieved March 13, 2009, from http://www.nytimes.com/2008/11/02/magazine/02wwln-consumed-t.html

Winakor, G. (1969). The process of clothing consumption. *Journal of Home Economics, 61*(8), 629–634.

Yoon, E., & Kijewski, V. (1997). Dynamics of the relationship between product features, quality evaluation, and pricing. *Pricing Strategy and Practice, 5*(2), 45–60.

6

NONNORMATIVE APPAREL CONSUMPTION: MISBEHAVIOR

After you have read this chapter, you should be able to

- Summarize the scope of consumer misbehavior.
- Characterize types of consumer misbehavior.
- Describe motivations that underlie specific categories of misbehavior.
- Identify harms linked with each category of misbehavior.

Consumer misbehavior

The focus of the preceding chapters has been on understanding consumers and how they behave in the marketplace under most circumstances. In other words, attention has been paid to how consumers act routinely. This chapter focuses on nonnormative apparel consumption, which is also called consumer misbehavior. **Consumer misbehavior** refers to "behavioral acts by consumers which violate the generally accepted norms of conduct in consumption situations and thus, disrupt the consumption order" (Fullerton & Punj, 2004, p. 1239). Consumer misbehavior is a significant part of the consumption experience (Fullerton & Punj, 2004). We spend time and effort understanding consumer misbehavior because of the financial losses and psychological damage it can cause to both retailers and consumers.

Many consumers misbehave at least some of the time. For example, Wilkes (1978) investigated the extent to which consumers engaged in different fraudulent behaviors. Participants reported that they knew people who frequently engaged in several fraudulent consumer acts such as allowing a retailer to undercharge them for an item, not being charged at all for an item, allowing a retailer to give them too much change for a purchase, and returning an apparel item after having worn it. Not only do some consumers misbehave, but their misbehavior affects other consumers who do not misbehave.

Some researchers have studied consumer misbehavior under the term *consumer unfairness* (Berry & Seiders, 2008). Berry and Seiders use the term **consumer unfairness** to refer to instances "when a customer behaves in a manner that is devoid of common decency, reasonableness, and respect for the rights of others, creating inequity and causing harm for a company and in some cases, its employees and other customers" (p. 1). The difference between the terms *consumer misbehavior* and *consumer unfairness* appears to be whether attention is focused on the potential motivation of the consumer (i.e., being unfair) or the actions of the consumer (i.e., what the consumer does). Another distinction between the two terms is that consumer misbehavior can include consumption acts that are legal as well as illegal, whereas behaving unfairly is typically not an illegal act. Berry and Seiders (2008) developed a **typology** of unfair customers reflecting the most common and problematic types. Each category features a different side of consumer unfairness. (Read the descriptions of the types of unfair consumers in Table 6.1.) Perhaps you have seen someone acting like this while you have been shopping for apparel products.

Whether the approach is to understand motivations or to examine behavior, understanding unacceptable behavior can be as important as understanding acceptable or normative consumption. O'Guinn and Faber (1989) argued that by understanding and analyzing what is undesirable behavior, we clearly know what desirable behavior is. Outlining what is acceptable consumer behavior on an international scale is particularly important as individual consumers are dealing with retailers around the world that may not share similar expectations for behavior and vice versa.

What is it that causes one type of consumer behavior to be labeled as acceptable or proper and another type to be labeled as unacceptable and improper? This **labeling process** is a reflection of norms and expectations for behavior within a selling or exchange environment (Fullerton & Punj, 2004). Customers, when they enter a marketplace, have expectations for how they should act, how other consumers should act, and how retailers should act. Those expectations have been shaped by the culture in which the business was developed and the culture in which the customer has been socialized (Pitta, Fung, & Isberg, 1999). Think about this idea for a minute. When you go to purchase apparel at a department store in London or New York, the salesperson expects you to pay the price indicated on the price tag. It is not expected that you will bring the item to the cash register and negotiate the price for a shirt when you are shopping at Marks and Spencer or Saks Fifth Avenue. Imagine the strange looks you would get from the salespeople and other customers! However, if you were shopping for apparel with a merchant located in Camden Lock or with a street vendor on Canal Street, asking for a better price would be perfectly acceptable consumer behavior. Thus, the cultural environment influences what behaviors are expected and consequently labeled appropriate and which are

Table 6.1 Categories of Unfair Customers

Category	Description
Verbal abusers	Verbal abusers are customers who deride, bully, and verbally abuse sales associates; they commonly make threats to report employees to higher authorities within the organization. They often have negative effects on other customers by their bad behavior. These threats can extend the negative experience after the incident has ended. An example is a customer who brings a garment back to a retailer after wearing it, and the retailer refuses to take it back for an exchange. The customer then makes a scene, berating the sales associate for not giving her what she wants.
Blamers	Blamers accuse a retailer's products, policies, and people at all levels for any perceived negative outcome they experience. Blamers do not see themselves in any way responsible for the outcome. An example is a customer who fails to follow care label instructions for cleaning and holds the retailer responsible when the garment changes color after cleaning.
Rule breakers	Rule breakers pay no attention to store procedures when the procedures are at odds with their own goals. They seek to optimize their rewards at the expense of the company. A specific type of rule breaker is a rule maker. These are customers who believe the policies of the store do not apply to them because they hold some type of superior status or are extra special customers. Examples are a customer who demands that his purchases be shipped to his home free of charge or one who believes she should receive a discount after a promotional event has ended because she did not have time to get to the store.
Opportunists	An opportunist is an individual who capitalizes on chances to take financial advantage of a retailer. They often demand some form of compensation by exaggerating problems they encounter or a state they encounter. An example is an individual who returns a pair of jeans for a refund to a store that offers a satisfaction guarantee after wearing the jeans for several years with the complaint that the jeans should have lasted longer.
Returnaholics (also called merchandise borrowers, deshoppers)	Labeled as a hybrid, these customers share characteristics with rule breakers and opportunists but engage in a specific type of activity: they purchase, use, and then return items to the store. An example is a customer who purchases products with a credit card to earn rewards and then returns the products at a point in time when the rewards cannot be removed.

From "Serving Unfair Customers," by L. Berry and K. Seiders, 2008, *Retailing Issues Letter, 19*(1), pp. 1–8.

inappropriate. As a result, both consumers and retailers, as they conduct business outside of their traditional home markets, are likely to experience deviations from their expectations that can cause either to label any departure from expected behavior as misbehavior.

CONSUMER MISBEHAVIOR

Types of consumer misbehavior

Similar to Berry and Seiders's (2008) typology of unfair consumers, Fullerton and Punj (2004) created a typology of consumer misbehaviors. They developed five categories focused on the target of the misbehavior. They suggested that consumers' misbehaviors could be aimed at the retailer's premises, employees, financial assets, merchandise and services, and other consumers (see Table 6.2). There is some overlap between the typology of consumer unfairness and the typology of consumer misbehaviors. We continue with a discussion of what may motivate consumers to misbehave in general, a discussion of different types of consumer misbehaviors, and what harm is associated with these types of misbehaviors.

What general factors motivate consumer misbehavior?

Two broad sets of factors are related to consumers' misbehavior: consumer traits/ dispositions and characteristics of the exchange setting and marketing institutions (Fullerton & Punj, 1993). Next, we look closely at each of these factors.

Consumer traits

Characteristics proposed to explain consumers' propensities to misbehave include demographic characteristics, psychological characteristics, social group influences, and a consumer's state of mind at the time of the event (Fullerton & Punj, 1993). Demographic characteristics include age, sex, economic status, and education. It is reasonable to assume that demographic characteristics may make a difference, because different types of misbehaviors are more likely to occur during different life

Table 6.2 Typology of Consumer Misbehavior

Category of Misbehavior	Examples
Directed at retailer's employees	Verbal abusers, physical abusers; incidents of consumer rage; disobedience of rules; bizarre behavior
Directed at other consumers	Grabbing items from other consumers; intimidating others; butting and budging in line
Directed toward financial assets	Failing to notify retailer of billing errors; retail fraud; warranty frauds; rumor generation; bad check passing
Directed at merchandise and services	Theft of merchandise; altering price tags; use of forged or stolen tickets; buying counterfeits; copyright violations; merchandise borrowing
Directed at premises	Vandalism, arson, computer viruses

From "Repercussions of Promoting an Ideology of Consumption: Consumer Misbehavior, by R. A. Fullerton and G. Punj, 2004, *Journal of Business Research, 57*(11), pp. 1239–1249.

stages. For example, shoplifting occurs more frequently with adolescents than with adults. On the other hand, adults are more likely to commit credit card fraud than adolescents (Cox, Cox, & Moschis, 1990). Forms of consumer misbehavior may also vary on the basis of sex. For example, because women do more shopping in general than men, women may engage in more merchandise borrowing than men. Forms of consumer misbehavior also may be tied to education level. Some fraud—including check and credit card fraud—is more likely to be committed by well-educated individuals because increased education may enhance consumers' ability to think of and carry out some misbehavior. For example, in 2006, a $60 million shoplifting ring was uncovered (Marco, 2008). The ring consisted of a team of shoplifters and a team of individuals with no criminal records. The shoplifters would steal expensive beauty and health items and pass them to individuals who had no criminal records, who would then offer the stolen items for sale on auction sites (e.g., eBay) and at outdoor markets. The team sold items on eBay through a site called Lola's Discount Health and Beauty. The individual overseeing the site explained the business in her seller's profile as follows. "We buy overstock, discontinued and shelf pull items by the case or pallet. Some things we almost always stock on a regular basis and other items we only get on a one-time basis . . . check back regularly as there is always something new up for auction here!" (Marco, 2008).

Personality characteristics also may be tied to consumer misbehavior. Materialism (Belk, 1985) might be one such characteristic. Materialism can be characterized by three main traits: possessiveness, nongenerosity, and envy. Materialistic individuals prefer to own and keep things. They are possessive and generally unwilling to share what they have with others. And they tend to envy others who have possessions that they themselves do not have. It is the envy aspect of materialism that may be tied to consumer misbehaviors such as theft or vandalism (Belk, 1985). Other personal characteristics that could be tied to consumer misbehaviors include level of moral development and propensity for thrill seeking. Evidence exists that some consumers engage in misbehaviors to enliven their otherwise boring lives (Moore, 1984).

The social groups that one belongs to can influence consumer misbehavior. Consumers can be socialized into acts of misbehavior (Cox, Cox, & Moschis, 1990). Misbehavior can serve as an initiation ritual into some social groups, particularly during adolescence; some forms of misbehavior may be learned in a group setting but performed on an individual basis. Additionally, a consumer's frame of mind at the time of the event can increase tendency to misbehave as a result of weakened self-control. Fulleron and Punj (1993) suggest that, when this happens, consumers may attribute their actions to influences beyond their control. In this case, these consumers may say something like, "The devil made me do it."

Characteristics of the exchange setting

Certain conditions of the marketplace can influence consumers' willingness to engage in misbehaviors. Included in this set of factors is the type of products and services offered. How merchandise is presented to the customer and how much the customers are allowed to serve themselves plays a role in access to merchandise and offers more or less opportunity for misbehavior. When you go shopping, you may notice that small, expensive items (items that are easy to steal) are often kept behind locked glass cabinets to deter theft. At Tiffany & Co., for instance, the diamond rings are not sitting on top of the counter but inside a case.

The type of security or deterrence efforts presented plays a role as well. Visible and active security measures deter some consumers from misbehavior. A relatively new technology that helps to deter theft is RFID (radio frequency identification). If you have ever purchased a pair of pants that has a tag in it that says, "Please remove this tag before washing," chances are you have purchased an apparel item that contains an RFID tag. RFID tags are small computer chips that can be used to track the movement of apparel goods similarly to the way your movements can be tracked using your cell phone. If consumers attempt to leave the store without paying for an item that contains an RFID tag, the computer chip will set off alarms at the front door of the store until the RFID tag is deactivated by the salesperson. Retailers' willingness to prosecute shoplifters as one example can aid in deterring this type of misbehavior.

The attitude of employees is also a characteristic of the setting that has an effect on customer behaviors. The degree to which sales associates are alert, attentive, and polite can enhance or hinder customers' willingness to misbehave. The public's image of the retailer can also influence customer behavior. Is the retailer a good citizen of the community? Is the retailer perceived as a friendly or caring store? Stores that represent large chains and report huge profits may be more likely to be victimized than locally owned small retailers.

Characteristics of consumers and characteristics of the exchange setting can combine to influence consumer misbehavior. For example, the larger and more impersonal a retailer is and the more a retailer allows the customer to roam the store unaided and unassisted, the greater is the situational opportunity to misbehave. This opportunity would more likely be acted upon if the customer had certain characteristics, including being materialistic and holding positive attitudes toward misbehavior.

Consumer misbehavior: buying counterfeits or pirated products

A type of misbehavior that is directed toward the merchandise is the buying of counterfeits (Fullerton & Punj, 2004). Counterfeits continue to exist in the marketplace because consumers continue to purchase them. A **counterfeit** product is defined as an identical copy of an authentic product, including packaging, trademarks, and labeling (Kay, 1990). A related term frequently used to describe fake copies of software or compact discs is **pirated goods**. A counterfeit differs from a **knock-off** or an imitation product. A knock-off is a line-for-line copy that sells under a different brand name (Kim & Nelson, 2000). The copy is often done in different fabrications.

In the United States, it is illegal to sell counterfeit or pirated products, but it is not illegal to purchase them. Several European Union countries have different rules. Buying and using counterfeit products is legal in the United Kingdom, the Czech Republic, and Germany. However, in Italy, France, and Portugal, you risk large fines if you buy a counterfeit product. This applies regardless of whether you know that it is illegal ("Is Buying and Using," n.d.). Some counterfeit products are so well made that it is difficult to tell the difference between the original and the counterfeit product. (See if you can tell which of the two purses is the original and which is the counterfeit in Figure 6.1.)

In the 1980s, most firms affected by the production of fake products were in the luxury sector (Guttierez, Verheugen, Mandelson, & Schwab, 2006). Demand for luxury counterfeits has been fueled by the linking of personal and social characteristics to the public display of high fashion brands. This process, as well as the lack of access of some consumers to these expensive brands, fueled demand for counterfeits in the luxury sector (Juggessur & Cohen, 2009). Since the 1980s, the fake product market has expanded to include the medical and agricultural industries along with computers, hardware, electrical appliances, car parts, airplane parts, and toys (Guttierez et al., 2006).

Estimates of the cost of counterfeiting to manufacturers are in the billions, as it has been suggested that the sale of fakes makes up approximately 7 percent of

Figure 6.1 Consumers indicate that they can tell the genuine article from the counterfeit. Which of these handbags is the genuine one and which one is the fake? If you thought the handbag on the right was the fake, you are correct! Photo by Riane Johnson.

global trade (Thomas, 2008). In 2008, the U.S. Customs and Border Protection (2009) and Immigration and Customs Enforcement made seizures of counterfeit and pirated goods representing $272.7 million. This amount represents a 38 percent increase over fiscal year 2007. Footwear was the number-one apparel-related product seized. Fake products seized that might pose risks to health and safety included sunglasses, medications, and perfume. The largest part of the counterfeit industry is made up of products such as automobile parts, airplane parts, toys and software; fakes of luxury goods such as Louis Vuitton represent about 4 percent.

Seizures of counterfeits have also increased at the borders of the European Union. In 2007, customs registered over 43,000 seizures of fake goods. Counterfeit cigarettes represented the largest category of goods followed by apparel. Although several countries are home to counterfeit operations, China leads the way ("Rise in Counterfeit," 2008).

Consumer demand for counterfeits

Several researchers have examined factors fueling consumer demand for counterfeit products (Albers-Miller, 1999; Ang, Cheng, Lim, & Tambyah, 2001; Cordell, Wongtada, & Kieschnick, 1996; Tom, Garibaldi, Zeng, & Pilcher, 1998; Wee, Tan, & Cheok, 1995). Not too surprising is the ample evidence that price is one of the most important motivators to a consumer decision to purchase known apparel counterfeits (Albers-Miller, 1999; Tom et al., 1998). Consumers who knowingly purchase fakes are drawn to apparel counterfeits because they are often priced at 60 percent to 70 percent less than originals. Do not assume, however, that all counterfeits are sold at reduced prices. Sometimes consumers are unaware that they are purchasing a counterfeit of a luxury item. For example, luxury products purchased on auction sites such as eBay have been found to be fakes (Hafner, 2006).

Variables other than price have been investigated for their relationship to a consumer's intention to purchase counterfeits. These variables include qualities of consumers, including personality, attitudes, and demographic characteristics. For example, Wee, Tan, and Cheok (1995) found that individuals who held a favorable attitude toward counterfeiting and who had low household incomes reported that they intended to purchase counterfeit products as compared to individuals who held negative attitudes and had high household incomes.

Consumer characteristics such as moral viewpoints influence attitudes toward counterfeits and willingness to purchase counterfeits (Tan, 2002; Moores & Chang, 2006). Remember the Forsyth (1980) taxonomy of ethical ideologies from chapter 1? It seems logical to assume that consumers with different ethical viewpoints might have different attitudes toward counterfeit products and toward purchasing such products, right? Well, the relationship is not quite that simple. In general, no differences in consumers' attitudes concerning counterfeits have been tied to ethical viewpoint. Consumers representing different viewpoints are somewhat neutral on anticounterfeiting opinions, suggesting they are uncertain of their attitude or perhaps ambivalent about them (Cho, Yoo, & Johnson, 2005). Interestingly, in Cho, Yoo, and Johnson's (2005) study, all participants displayed positive attitudes concerning product reliability, suggesting they believed that the quality of counterfeits was high. Additionally, all participants indicated that they liked to shop for and intended to purchase counterfeits in the future. These findings seem to indicate that consumers do not feel badly about purchasing counterfeit goods.

One possible explanation for the lack of significant connection between ethical viewpoints and attitudes toward counterfeits is the **normalization** of purchasing counterfeits. Normalization occurs over time and results in behavior that is initially labeled as aberrant or inappropriate becoming viewed as normal or acceptable. This initially deemed inappropriate behavior becomes appropriate or normal because of the large number of people who engage in it. Counterfeits are increasingly common, and people are presented with opportunities to purchase counterfeits through street vendors as well as through private parties held in the home. (See Boxed Case 6.1.) Evidence that purchasing counterfeits may have become normalized comes from the Cho, Yoo, and Johnson (2005) research. One of the participants, in response to the question of why she purchased counterfeits, commented "It [counterfeiting] really doesn't matter to me. The designers are getting enough money already. Do they really need all the money that is lost in counterfeits?"

BOXED CASE 6.1. HOUSE PARTIES AND COUNTERFEITS

When you think of where fake apparel items and leather goods are offered for sale to consumers in the United States, you might think of locations such as the garment district in Los Angeles or in Chinatown in New York. You may be surprised to learn that counterfeits are also sold in the suburbs of major cities. For several months, a team of investigators from 12 News in Milwaukee, Wisconsin, went undercover to examine the purse party phenomenon. Producer Susan MacDonald attended three purse parties held in locations including a strip mall and an individual's private home during the investigation. "Dozens of purses, everywhere, living room, dining room, kitchen, family room," MacDonald said. "There was Kate Spade. There was Prada, Gucci, Louis Vuitton." At prices reflecting discounts of 80 percent, these fake designer handbags were flying out the door. The problem is huge. The trademark attorney for handbag designer Kate Spade indicated that the company's number-one problem relative to fakes is the purse party. The attorney estimated that, on the street, the ratio of fake Kate Spade handbags to real ones is one to one.

The purse party phenomenon is not confined to the United States. During November 2008, the London Detachment of the Royal Canadian Mounted Police arrested a London resident for the sale and distribution of counterfeit purses and jewelry. The resident was selling the purses in her home under the business name of Katie's Unique Boutique.

----- References -----

Counterfeit bags may have links to organized crime, terrorism. (2003, May). *Milwaukee News*. Retrieved June 4, 2009, from http://www.wisn.com/news/2191330/detail.html

RCMP crash counterfeit purse party. (2008). Retrieved June 4, 2009, from www.rcmp-grc.gc.ca

What is the harm in purchasing fashion counterfeits?

As noted, many people believe that buying and using fashion counterfeits is a relatively harmless activity. Luxury goods are expensive and represent large profits. Even though profits for the owners of luxury brands are lost through the sale of counterfeits, there exists the attitude that these brand owners make so much money that they can afford to have others benefit through the manufacture of fakes. So what is the harm?

First, counterfeits negatively impact the image of the original brand, especially in instances when the consumer is unaware that he or she is purchasing a fake. (See Boxed Case 6.2 for luxury consumers' view of fakes.) Consider the consumer who has saved to purchase a luxury handbag or wallet that he or she believes will provide good design, longevity, and durability. How does his or her attitude toward that brand change when he or she finds the handbag or wallet falls apart after a few uses? Further, what does he or she think about the brand when he or she attempts to have the item replaced or repaired, only to find out that the item he or she spent several hundred dollars for is a fake?

BOXED CASE 6.2. WEALTHY CONSUMERS SAY FAKE PRODUCTS DAMAGE THE FASHION INDUSTRY

In 2006, the Luxury Institute surveyed a sample of U.S. households with a minimum of $200,000 in gross annual income and a minimum net worth of $1 million. Four out of five of the participants indicated that fakes have a negative impact on brands. Most participants are not fooled by the quality of fakes. Most participants (75%) said that they could tell the difference between real and fake products. Forty percent of the participants said that they knew individuals who purchased fakes, and 56 percent indicated that the purchase of fakes was going to get worse in the coming years. Participants had little respect for those who purchase fake goods or the countries that allow the production of fakes. Over 66 percent indicated that governments should impose sanctions on countries that allow the production, distribution, and sale of fake luxury goods. The majority of participants (85%) indicated that China was doing the least to combat this problem.

FASHION AND THE CONSUMER

	Reference	

Luxury institute wealth survey: Wealthy consumers say counterfeits hurt the luxury goods industry. (2006, January). *Business Wire*, p. 1.

Second, the dollars lost to manufacturers as a result of the sale of fashion counterfeits is in the billions. Thomas (2008) reported that the World Customs Organization believes the fashion industry loses up to $9.2 billion per year to counterfeiting. Since these businesses are illegal, they do not pay business taxes, which is a loss to local governments. Counterfeiting also costs jobs. For example, it has been estimated that job loss within the European Union is 100,000 annually (Union des Fabricants, 2003).

Third, there is mounting evidence that the profits generated from the sale of apparel counterfeits support terrorist activities (INTERPOL, 2003; Johnston, 2003; Thomas, 2008; Ungoed-Thomas, 2005; Union des Fabricants, 2003). In a 2003 report to the U.S. House of Representatives Committee on International Relations, then Secretary General Ronald Noble shared growing evidence that the sales of counterfeits was funding terrorist activities (INTERPOL, 2003). The Federal Bureau of Investigation in the United States believes that the first bombing of the World Trade Center in 1993 was funded with the sale of fake T-shirts. In addition to funding terrorist activities, because the production of counterfeits is illegal, it is reasonable to assume that fakes are not produced under safe and proper working conditions. So the next time you have the option of buying a counterfeit good, ask yourself whether you want to be a part of the illegal activities that accompany the counterfeit fashion goods industry. Is that low price for a pair of counterfeit True Religion jeans really a good price when you consider the high price that you or others may have to pay for other items in the future?

Consumer misbehavior: merchandise borrowing

Another area of consumer misbehavior that is directed toward the merchandise is merchandise borrowing (Fullerton & Punj, 2004). **Merchandise borrowing** occurs when consumers purchase items, use them, and then return them to retailers (Piron & Young, 2000). Another form of borrowing involves the exchanging of a purchased item after use for a new item. The purchases in these instances involve deceit, because there is no intention of keeping the merchandise. Merchandise borrowing can be perceived as a type of shoplifting (Piron & Young, 2000), because some of the value of the item is lost because it has been used by the borrowers. In some instances, when an apparel item is borrowed, it can be resold to another consumer as new, but in many instances (depending on the condition of the returned item), the item will be offered for sale at a reduced price or it will be destroyed by the retailer. Both actions reduce or eliminate the profitability of the item.

Merchandise borrowing is facilitated by retailers who offer their customers generous return policies (King & Dennis, 2003). Under a policy of guaranteed satisfaction, a consumer can easily purchase an item online, from a catalog, or directly from a retailer's store; wear the item for an event; and then return the item. Consumers who engage in this type of behavior have been called **returnaholics** (Berry & Seiders, 2008), **deshoppers** (King & Dennis, 2003), and serial wardrobers (Speights & Hilinski, 2005), and they have been labeled as engaging in **retail return fraud** (Chandler, 2005). When customers engage in merchandise borrowing, they are using retailers like they use a public library. Public libraries do not charge members to borrow books and other materials. Thus, merchandise borrowing as discussed here should not be confused with the rental of items. Some businesses rent luxury items to consumers for a fee. For example, Bag, Borrow, or Steal rents designer handbags for a monthly fee (Windfield, 2005). Users of this service can have an expensive luxury bag for their use and trade it in for another one any time they wish, as long as they continue to pay the rental fee.

Retailers are aware of the practice of merchandise borrowing (Chandler, 2005; Kang, 2004; King, Dennis, & McHendry, 2007; Merrick & Brat, 2005). It is estimated that 12 percent of all returns involve merchandise borrowing (Zabriskie, 1972–1973), and the cost of merchandise borrowing is about $16 billion a year (Kang, 2004; Merrick & Brat, 2005). Applying this number to an individual rather than presenting an aggregate number, merchandise borrowing costs the average household of four $225 annually (Speights & Hilinski, 2005). Merchandise borrowing is important to those who are interested in apparel consumption, because clothing is a frequently borrowed item (Johnson & Rhee, 2008; Piron &Young, 2000). Other items are borrowed as well, including furniture, televisions, power tools, and luggage. Any items that do not easily show wear can be borrowed. Retailers today have enacted strict return policies in an attempt to inhibit this behavior, as can be seen in Figure 6.2.

Why do people borrow?

Individuals provide several explanations for their borrowing behavior. Piron and Young (2000) asked participants in their research to supply the reasons that they borrowed apparel. Participants shared that they borrowed for social, economic, professional, and altruistic reasons along with personal satisfaction. Social reasons include borrowing clothing items to attend and participate in social events such as holiday parties, weddings, and other special occasions. These individuals shared that they needed something nice to wear to these social events. Not surprisingly, participants indicated they also borrowed for economic reasons. These participants said that they had a low income but they wanted to experience expensive items, so they bought them, used them, and then returned them. They were also interested in saving money.

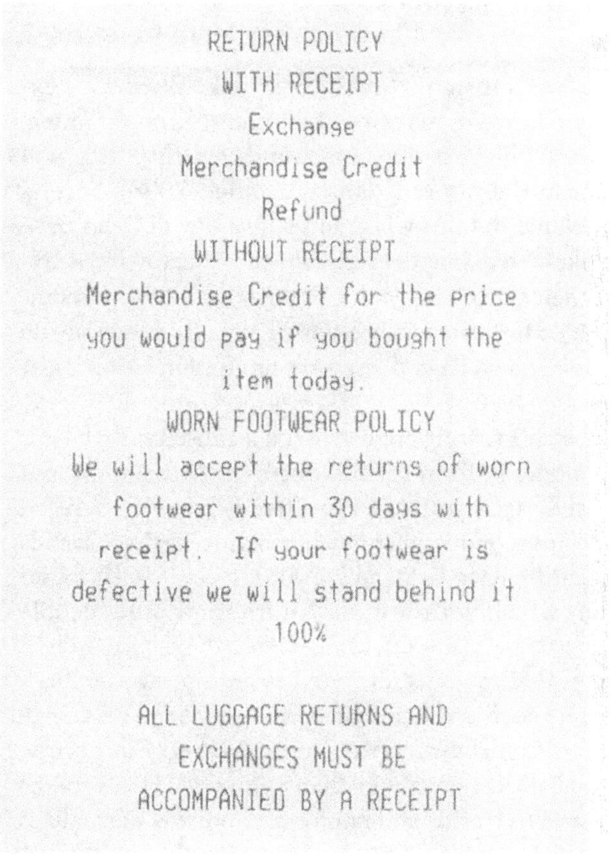

```
          RETURN POLICY
          WITH RECEIPT
           Exchange
       Merchandise Credit
            Refund
         WITHOUT RECEIPT
   Merchandise Credit for the price
   you would pay if you bought the
              item today.
       WORN FOOTWEAR POLICY
   We will accept the returns of worn
     footwear within 30 days with
     receipt.  If your footwear is
   defective we will stand behind it
               100%


       ALL LUGGAGE RETURNS AND
         EXCHANGES MUST BE
      ACCOMPANIED BY A RECEIPT
```

Figure 6.2 One of the methods retailers have employed to deter merchandise borrowing is to tighten their policies concerning returns. Customers may find these policies printed on the back of receipts that they receive when they make purchases. See the amount of detail in this example of one retailer's return and exchange policies. Photo by Kim Johnson.

Participants who borrowed for professional reasons did so because they needed a nice outfit for a job interview or to wear something that would impress their supervisor. Participants who borrowed for what the researchers labeled as altruistic reasons indicated that they borrowed not for themselves but because they wanted to look good for others. For example, a mother might borrow an expensive outfit to wear to her daughter's graduation because she wants her daughter to feel good about her and be proud to be associated with her. Or a man might want to look good for a girlfriend or wife, so he borrows some apparel and accessories for an evening out. Others reported borrowing for personal satisfaction. These individuals borrowed because they wanted to meet needs for self-fulfillment. They wanted "to feel good," "to feel better," or "to get noticed." In other words, they desired to feel good, if only for a short while, as a result of having temporary possession of an expensive item. Overall, borrowing enabled the consumers to either "maintain or acquire social acceptability, and was seen as a tool toward that goal, thus justifying the behavior" (Piron & Young, 2000, p. 123).

CONSUMER MISBEHAVIOR

Merchandise borrowers tend to be women (Schmidt, Sturrock, Ward, & Lea-Greenwood, 1999), borrowing four times more often than men (Piron & Young, (2000). Borrowers do not work in retailing and generally indicate that they will continue their borrowing behavior in the future (Johnson & Rhee, 2008). Several psychological variables might be related to borrowing, and only a few of them have been investigated. Borrowers are likely to blame the seller for their borrowing activity and are likely to indicate that their borrowing is due to "uncontrollable circumstances" (Rosenbaum & Kuntze, 2003). Borrowers are not necessarily materialistic individuals, so they do not feel the need to keep possession of an item (Johnson & Rhee, 2008).

In terms of sociological influences, borrowing appears to be a consumer behavior that is learned from others in the home or from friends. Borrowers often indicated that they learned borrowing from their family members or friends, were encouraged to borrow by others who held positive opinions about borrowing, or had friends who borrowed (Johnson & Rhee, 2008; King & Dennis, 2003). Cole (1989) found that individuals who indicated they would borrow in the future knew other people who had engaged in borrowing activities.

There are also cultural influences that can be interpreted as promoting merchandise borrowing. Television characters such as Donna on *The West Wing* and Carrie on the *King of Queens* popular television shows in the United States both borrow expensive apparel to wear on special occasions and then return it. This type of media treatment along with exposure to friends and family who borrow normalizes merchandise borrowing.

There is clearly the potential for merchandise borrowing as a form of consumer misbehavior to increase and spread around the world. For example, with the sale of apparel items via the Internet increasing, borrowing is likely to increase because Internet apparel retailers generally have to accept returns or exchanges because consumers are unlikely to purchase using the Internet unless they can return items. One of the ways that U.S. retailers are trying to halt this practice is through developing restrictive return policies and charging restocking fees for returned items (King, Dennis, & McHendry, 2007). Restrictive policies alone may not curtail borrowing and may be a detriment to customers' perceptions of service.

There is a need to understand consumer motivations behind borrowing behavior, and we may gain greater knowledge if we study these variables across cultures. Several variables that might prove to be important psychological influences on merchandise borrowing and thus that might be worthy of investigation include need for affiliation and compliance. In addition, other social group variables, including need for social approval and social validation, might exert an influence on borrowing behaviors. An examination of these variables cross-culturally would allow investigation of additional demographic variables such as income, age, ethnicity, and education on both attitudes toward and actual borrowing behavior.

What is the harm in merchandise borrowing?

There are costs associated with borrowing apparel merchandise. As noted, some merchandise cannot be returned to the selling floor so it cannot be offered for sale and consequently reduces a retailer's profits. To counter this, a retailer may increase its markup percentage to compensate. This simply means that retailers will charge a little more for items than they would otherwise to counter the impact of the borrowing activities of their customers. The result is that all customers pay for the borrowing.

Merchandise borrowing is a form of theft, because borrowers are stealing a part of the value of the item. When customers purchase a new item, they expect that it has not been used by someone else. So when they actually get a used item, it can alter their perceptions of both the product and the retailer. Of course, they can return the item, but often they may be scrutinized by the retailer because it is their word that the item had been used before they got it and they may need to provide some proof that they themselves did not use it!

Consumer misbehavior: shoplifting

Referred to by several different terms, including lifting, five-finger discount, jacking, racking, nicking, and boosting, shoplifting occurs by both customers and employees and is another example of misbehavior directed at merchandise. In this discussion, we limit our treatment of shoplifting to customers' behavior. **Shoplifting** is defined as "the theft of merchandise during store hours by someone who is shopping or pretending to shop" (Cameron, 1964). According to the National Association for Shoplifting Prevention, one in every eleven people in the United States is a shoplifter (Granato, 2007; "Shoplifting Statistics," 2006). Another source suggests that 60 percent of consumers have shoplifted at some time in their life (Klemke, 1992). Estimates vary, but goods worth more than $13 billion are stolen from retailers each year. That figure translates to about $35 million per day. The typical shoplifter steals from $2 to $200 per incident, often buying and stealing in the same visit ("Shoplifting Statistics," 2006). Referred to by retailers as **shrinkage**, theft from the store is calculated into a retailer's markup policy and thus is paid for by honest customers.

Similar statistics have been reported for retailers in the United Kingdom ("Shoplifting Up," 2006) with reported stealing per incident as slightly higher (£149 per incident). The British Retail Consortium reported that shoplifting was to blame for nearly 66 percent of violent incidents in stores and had caused some stores to close ("Shoplifting Up," 2006). Some strategies used by shoplifters are presented in

Boxed Case 6.3. We present these strategies to demonstrate that shoplifting can be a complicated crime, not to give you ideas about how to shoplift.

BOXED CASE 6.3. STRATEGIES USED FOR SHOPLIFTING

Shoplifters use a variety of strategies to assist them in their shoplifting efforts. Listed below are some common tactics.

Umbrellas: Having a closed umbrella hanging on your elbow while browsing through the aisles or leaning up against a counter allows the shoplifter to easily drop items inside.

Folded or rolled newspapers: Shopping with a folded or rolled newspaper allows the shoplifter to place small items inside.

Baby strollers: Since strollers typically have baby blankets and other baby items inside, shoplifters can use these materials to hide items. Some shoplifters build false bottoms into strollers.

Diaper bags: Shoplifters may hide items under diapers, baby clothing, and other items typically carried in these bags.

Large coats: Shoplifters cut slits into the lining of their coat pockets so that they can reach out and grab items and place them in their coats. They inspect items with one hand and use the other to reach out and grab.

Shopping bags: Shoplifters will bring bags from other retailers into the store and try to put stolen items from the second store underneath the items they already purchased from the first store. This is one of the reasons underlying retail policy that requires customers to check bags from other stores or to have them stapled shut.

Fitting rooms: Shoplifters will wear old baggy clothing to put new clothing underneath or to leave their old clothing and put on new clothing.

One-employee stores: A shoplifter enters a store and indicates that something he or she wants is not on the shelf. This sends the one employee into the back to look for the item, during which time the shoplifter takes items and leaves the store.

Crotch walking: Women shoplifters wear full skirts and place items between their thighs and walk out of the store with them.

Reference

Granato, S. (2007). Shoplifting statistics and tactics: 75% of adults are guilty of the five finger discount. Retrieved June 8, 2009, from www.associatedcontent.com

Why do people shoplift?

Reasons that individuals shoplift vary by age. When adolescents were caught shoplifting, they mentioned that they stole because they were "bored and had nothing better to do" (Granato, 2007). They also shared that peer pressure was a factor.

They shared that they felt the need to keep up with peers who wore the latest clothing styles. Some teens also shoplift on a dare or because they desire attention from friends or from family members ("Teen Shoplifting Statistics," n.d.) or to gain friends' approval (Cox, Cox, & Moschis, 1990). These adolescents explained their behavior by suggesting their friends wanted them to shoplift, their friends needed the item, or because they wanted to please their friends.

Adolescents mentioned that they shoplifted because of the excitement and risk involved (Cox, Cox, & Moschis, 1990). Participants indicated they stole for the fun, the excitement, or to see whether they could get away with it. Another reason provided by adolescents for shoplifting was economic and had two sides (Cox, Cox, & Moschis, 1990). One side reflected the idea that items were stolen because the shoplifters did not want to pay for them. The other side reflected the idea that items were stolen for the purpose of reselling them.

Adults provide somewhat different explanations for their shoplifting behavior. In simple terms, some adults steal because they want something for nothing (Berlin, 2006). Getting something for nothing provides a reward, which provides some consumers with a psychological lift. Everyone feels better when they get something new, and it is the same for shoplifters.

It is more than the value of the merchandise that adult shoplifters get from their stealing (Berlin, 2006). For some individuals, shoplifting provides them a "substitute for a loss." These consumers feel that they have been unjustly disadvantaged in some way, and the item they shoplift is compensation. Others feel they are justified in their shoplifting because they are owed for all that they give to others. And, similar to adolescents, for some adults, shoplifting is a relief from boredom, stress, and depression. The link between shoplifting and depression helps to explain why so many shoplifters steal from stores around their birthdays and holidays (Berlin, 2006).

Shoplifters also steal because they believe that they will not get caught (Tonglet, 2001). This is not an irrational belief, because shoplifters report they are caught only once every forty-eight times that they steal ("Shoplifting Statistics," 2006). If caught, they are turned over to the police only half of the time ("Shoplifting Statistics," 2006).

Shoplifting can also become addictive (Berlin, 2006; Lawson, 2006) because the excitement generated from getting away with shoplifting produces an increase in adrenaline and dopamine, resulting in what shoplifters describe as a rush or high feeling. Shoplifters note that this high eliminates or reduces their unwanted feelings (e.g., of depression or anger) and, wanting to experience those good feelings again, are motivated to repeat their behavior.

Characteristics of shoplifters and factors that characterize their shoplifting

In the United States, the National Association for Shoplifting Prevention ("Shoplifting Statistics," 2006) reports that that 75 percent of all shoplifters are adults, 55 percent of adult shoplifters began shoplifting in their teen years, and the majority of shoplifters are not professionals. Additionally, an equal percentage of men and women are shoplifters, with men showing slightly higher odds of being shoplifters than women (Blanco et al., 2008). Being never married and relatively young (aged 18 to 29) also increases the probably of being a shoplifter (Blanco et al., 2008). Shoplifting is common with individuals who have at least some college education and have annual incomes of over $35,000 (Blanco et al., 2008). Habitual shoplifters steal approximately 1.6 times per week ("Shoplifting Statistics," 2006). They generally do not plan their shoplifting and are the type of people who do not commit other types of crimes (Berlin, 2006).

In a study of shoplifting in the United Kingdom, Tonglet (2001) found that men were more likely to shoplift than women, and over 52 percent of the recent shoplifters thought it was likely they would shoplift again in the future. (To read more about the different types of shoplifters that exist, see Boxed Case 6.4.)

BOXED CASE 6.4. TYPOLOGY OF SHOPLIFTERS

Moore (1984) created a typology of shoplifting types by interviewing 300 convicted shoplifters. He categorized individuals on the basis of five dimensions: frequency; precipitating factors; attitude toward shoplifting; use of stolen goods; and reaction to detection, prosecution, and conviction. What follows is a brief description of each type. It is important to recognize that this typology is based on a small percentage of all shoplifters. But it does serve as a starting point to analysis of distinctions between shoplifters and suggests that not all can be treated the same in terms of prevention efforts.

Impulse shoplifters—Shoplifting for this group was infrequent and unplanned, and they typically took one inexpensive item. When caught, they experienced guilt and shame. Getting caught was such a traumatic experience that they were unlikely to shoplift again.

Occasional shoplifters—This group was motivated to shoplift by peer and economic pressures. When caught, they admitted to shoplifting and viewed their behavior with mild embarrassment. They tend to minimize the seriousness of their behavior, but consideration of prosecution and the embarrassment associated with it to family members was a sufficient enough shock to prevent these consumers from shoplifting again.

Episodic shoplifters—This group was the smallest in total numbers. Shoplifting for these consumers reflected ritual behavior that was tied to self-punishment. Shoplifting occurred infrequently and was typically caused by psychosocial stressors. When caught, they recognized that shoplifting was wrong. Participation in psychotherapy was found to be a successful means to prevent further shoplifting for these shoplifters.

Amateur shoplifters—This group was the largest. These shoplifters stole weekly and found lifting to be profitable. They developed shoplifting techniques and tended to steal small items that were easy to conceal. When caught, they claimed minimal experience in shoplifting and employed various strategies to avoid punishment. Individuals in this group would continue to steal until they got caught.

Semiprofessional shoplifters—For these consumers, stealing was a lifestyle. They stole weekly and resold items. They tended to perceive themselves as being unfairly treated by society; thus, shoplifting was a means to compensate for how the world treated them. Individuals in this group believed that shoplifting was not wrong and did not exhibit guilt about their behavior. When caught, they tried to talk their way out of legal consequences and, if this did not work, became angry about being treated unfairly. Many individuals in this group continued to shoplift after being caught and fined.

--- Reference ---

Moore, R. (1984). Shoplifting in middle America: Patterns and motivational correlates. *International Journal of Offender Therapy and Comparative Criminology, 28*, 53–64.

What's the harm in shoplifting?

Honest consumers generally pay for the costs of shoplifting. When retailers are deciding how much to charge for their merchandise, they must estimate their losses from shoplifting. Because they estimate that customers will steal merchandise, they try to recoup that loss by charging more for all items that they sell than they would have to if customers (and employees) did not steal. Thus, everyone pays a little more for things because of shoplifting. Shoplifting also adds to costs because retailers use additional security devices such as security cameras to deter shoplifting, which are also paid for by customers, because retailers again add the cost security to the items they sell.

Shoplifting is also an added cost to government, as people are charged with the crime and police and court resources are used to prosecute shoplifters. When caught, shoplifters expend additional resources as they are jailed and may suffer loss of income as a result of not being able to return to work or as a result of having to miss work to participate in court-ordered community service activities as payment for their crime.

Consumer misbehavior: extreme consumption

The last category of consumer misbehavior is directed toward the retailer's employees or toward other consumers. This area of research is referred to it as **extreme consumption**. The example of extreme consumption we'll examine occurs on the Friday after Thanksgiving, otherwise known as **Black Friday**.

In the United States, Thanksgiving is a holiday that is celebrated on the fourth Thursday of the month of November. Traditionally, the Friday after Thanksgiving marked the beginning of the holiday selling season. Retailers opened their stores early and offered consumers special sales and other promotional events to lure shoppers into their stores. The Friday after Thanksgiving came to be known as Black Friday because the promotions targeting consumers generated significant sales. The end result was that this day was the first day that many retailers began to run their businesses in the black (i.e., began to show a profit for the year). Another term used to describe this day is **Green Friday**, because retailers generally make significant amounts of money on this day, and paper money is green in the United States.

Black Friday is the beginning of an incredible shopping weekend in the United States. The National Retail Federation (2007) reported that, in 2007, 147 million shoppers went shopping on this weekend. Each consumer spent an average of $347, and all types of consumers went shopping. All types of retailers offer consumers deals. As a result, consumers in 2007 shopped at discount stores (55.1%), traditional department stores (38.7%), specialty retailers (43.2%), and online (31.6%) (National Retail Federation, 2007). Consumers were out shopping for clothing (46.8%), consumer electronics (35.7%), and toys (28.2%), among other items. Consumers begin their shopping early. The trend in the last few years has been for stores to open at midnight on Friday. Some stores opened even earlier. This strategy appeared to pay off, as 14.3 percent of consumers were out shopping before 4:00 A.M. on Black Friday, compared to 12.4 percent the previous year (National Retail Federation, 2007).

Consumers are highly motivated to shop early, because retailers offer what they refer to as door busters. **Door busters** are promoted items with prices so low they motivate consumers to arrive early and line up outside the store waiting for it to open. Some consumers will begin lining up as much as seventeen hours before a store opens. (Figure 6.3 shows consumers lined up in the snow waiting for stores to open.)

Consumer misbehavior may be an unintended consequence of marketing activities that promote consumption (Fullerton & Punj, 2004). If retailers, for example, advertise items at greatly reduced prices but do not stock sufficient items, consumers may feel deceived and believe that a norm of reciprocity has been violated. If consumers feel retailers have taken advantage of them, emotional reactions may occur, leading to riots, boycotts, or other types of misbehavior.

In 2007, Lennon and Johnson conducted a study of Black Friday shopping. They found that shoppers went to great lengths to participate in Black Friday shopping. Consumers came to the United States from several countries—including France, Japan, Latin America, Mexico, Brazil, and the Caribbean—to shop (Lennon & Johnson, 2007). Deals attracted shoppers, who became angry and frustrated to learn that few products (such as $600 flat-screen televisions) were in stock at the advertised prices.

The lack of reciprocity experienced by customers could have generated their negative emotions (Lennon & Johnson, 2007) and misbehavior. **Reciprocity** in this

Figure 6.3 Customers frequently line up for hours prior to the opening of a store on Black Friday. Photo by Jaeha Lee.

instance refers to a norm for behavior that suggests if someone does something for you (e.g., a favor) at some point in the future, you need to return the favor and do something for that individual. Applied to this situation, retailers offered customers incredible deals if they came to the store when the store opened (i.e., door busters). Customers came to the store early, sometimes standing in line for hours waiting to get in. However, the retailers failed to honor their offer by not having sufficient items available for the large number of customers. The customer did something for the retailer (came early, waited for the store to open) as requested, but the retailer did not do something for the customer (did not have merchandise as advertised). Not having sufficient quantities of merchandise led to several forms of reported consumer misbehavior, including pushing and shoving other customers, pinning employees against stacks of merchandise, aggressively grabbing merchandise, over-turning piles of clothing, and ransacking stores. Much of the consumer misbehavior occurred at stores offering the most (or most remarkable) promotions (e.g., Wal-Mart, Best Buy, Kohl's).[1]

For the past several years, there have been accounts of consumer misbehavior on Black Friday (e.g., people pushing to get into the store, grabbing merchandise from each other, fighting over merchandise). What happened in 2008 is perhaps the most egregious example of the extent of the aggression that some consumers will demonstrate to locate and purchase deals. Two thousand customers lined up outside of

CONSUMER MISBEHAVIOR

a Wal-Mart store in Long Island, New York, waiting for the store to open. Chanting "push the doors in," the crowds pressed up against the doors. To get the door buster deals, eyewitnesses reported that shoppers took the doors down and rushed in. In the process, shoppers trampled to death a 28-year-old employee and injured four other shoppers. After customers trampled the employee, they initially refused to stop shopping, even after being asked to leave because an employee had been seriously injured. Deals offered to shoppers at the store included a $798 Samsung fifty-inch plasma HDTV, a Bissell compact upright vacuum for $28, and men's Wrangler jeans for $8. The store was eventually closed but it reopened at 1:00 P.M. and was packed within minutes (Gould, Trapasso, & Schapiro, 2008).

Research on Black Friday consumers and their behaviors is limited. We have not been able to locate evidence of the type of individuals who are willing to misbehave on Black Friday or reasons underlying their misbehaviors, other than to get an otherwise expensive item for an incredibly discounted price. It is quite possible that all types of people are willing to misbehave in pursuit of an incredible deal. Because of the high profits that are generated on this day, it is unlikely that retailers will discontinue the practice of offering heavily discounted items to entice customers into their stores during the early morning hours. Of several potential areas for future research, perhaps attention can be paid to how retailers can better manage customers' expectations on this day to avoid incidents of misbehavior. For example, advertisements that share information on merchandise quantities might alter consumers' behaviors.

Summary

Although we may not all agree on what is good consumer behavior and what is misbehavior, understanding consumer misbehavior can assist us in understanding what an appropriate business exchange is between a retailer and a consumer and is important to facilitating good consumer behavior within and across borders. Many consumers engage in fraudulent acts for a variety of reasons. Some of these reasons are tied to characteristics of the individual and others are tied to social influences and circumstances. All forms of consumer misbehavior result in harm to other consumers, to retailers, and to society overall.

Key Terms

- Black Friday
- consumer misbehavior
- consumer unfairness
- counterfeit
- deshoppers

- door buster
- extreme consumption
- Green Friday
- knock-off
- labeling process

- merchandise borrowing
- normalization
- pirated goods
- reciprocity
- retail return fraud
- returnaholics
- RFID
- shoplifting
- shrinkage

Questions for review and discussion

1. What commonalities exist across the types of consumer misbehavior presented?
2. How is branding related to consumer demand for counterfeits?
3. If you were offered the opportunity to purchase a counterfeit handbag or wallet, would you make the purchase? Why or why not?
4. Develop a return policy for an apparel retailer that would deter merchandise borrowing but not deter legitimate apparel returns.
5. Explain how merchandise borrowing is a form of shoplifting.
6. What are some policies that retailers can implement to halt consumer misbehavior on Black Friday?

Note

1. Best Buy is a consumer electronics store, and Kohl's is a department store featuring apparel for women, men, and children and home furnishings.

Suggested Readings

If you liked the topics in chapter 6, you may also like reading the following books:

Naim, M. (2005). *Illicit: How smugglers, traffickers and copycats are hijacking the global economy.* New York: Doubleday.
Phillips, T. (2005). *Knockoff: The deadly trade in counterfeit goods.* London: Kogan Page.

References

Albers-Miller, N. D. (1999). Consumer misbehavior: Why people buy illicit goods. *Journal of Consumer Marketing, 16*(3), 273–287.
Ang, S. H., Cheng, P. S., Lim, E.A.C., & Tambyah, S. K. (2001). Spot the difference: Consumer responses towards counterfeits. *Journal of Consumer Marketing, 18*(3), 219–235.
Belk, R. (1985). Materialism: Trait aspects of living in the material world. *Journal of Consumer Research, 12,* 265–280.
Berlin, P. (2006). Why do shoplifters steal? Retrieved June 8, 2009, from www.shopliftingprevention.org
Berry, L., & Seiders, K. (2008). Serving unfair customers. *Retailing Issues Letter, 19*(1), 1–8.

CONSUMER MISBEHAVIOR

Blanco, C., Grant, J., Petry, N., Simpson, H., Alegria, A., Liu, S., & Hasin, D. (2008). Prevalence and correlates of shoplifting in the United States: Results from the National Epidemiologic Survey on Alcohol and Related Conditions (NESARC). *American Journal of Psychiatry, 165*(7), 905–913.

Cameron, M.O. (1964). *The booster and the snitch: Department store shoplifting.* New York: Free Press.

Chandler, M. (2005, December 26). Retailers reconsider their return policies. *Contra Costa Times,* D1.

Cho, H., Yoo, J., & Johnson, K. P. (2005). Ethical ideologies: Do they affect shopping behaviors and perceptions of morality? *Journal of Family and Consumer Sciences, 97*(3), 48–55.

Cole, C. A (1989). Deterrence and consumer fraud. *Journal of Retailing, 65*(1), 107–120.

Cordell, V.V., Wongtada, N., & Kieschnick, R.L., Jr. (1996). Counterfeit purchase intentions: Role of lawfulness attitudes and product traits as determinants. *Journal of Business Research, 35*(1), 41–53.

Cox, D., Cox, A.D., & Moschis, G. (1990). When consumer behavior goes bad: An investigation of adolescent shoplifting. *Journal of Consumer Research, 17,* 149–159.

Fullerton, R.A., & Punj, G. (1993). Choosing to misbehave: A structural model of aberrant consumer behavior. *Advances in Consumer Research, 20, 570–574.*

Fullerton, R.A., & Punj, G. (2004). Repercussions of promoting an ideology of consumption: Consumer misbehavior. *Journal of Business Research, 57*(11), 1239–1249.

Forsyth, D.R. (1980). A taxonomy of ethical ideologies. *Journal of Personality and Social Psychology, 39*(1), 175–184.

Gould, J., Trapasso, C., & Schapiro, R. (2008). Worker dies at Long Island WalMart after being trampled in Black Friday stampede. *New York Daily News.* Retrieved June 9, 2009, from http://www.nydailynews.com/ny_local/2008/11/28/2008-11-28_worker_dies_at_long_island_walmart_after.html

Granato, S. (2007). Shoplifting statistics and tactics: 75% of adults are guilty of the five finger discount. Retrieved June 8, 2009, from http://www.associatedcontent.com

Gutierrez, C., Verheugen, G., Mandelson, P., & Schwab, S. (2006, June 20). Countering counterfeiters. *Wall Street Journal,* A20.

Hafner, K. (2006, January 29). Seeing fakes, angry traders confront EBay. *New York Times.* Retrieved May 31, 2009, from http://www.nytimes.com/2006/01/29/technology/29ebay.html

INTERPOL. (2003). INTERPOL warns of link between counterfeiting and terrorism. Cites evidence that terrorists fund operations from proceeds. Retrieved June 4, 2009, from http://www.interpol.int/public/icpo/pressreleases/pr2003/pr200319.asp

Is buying and using a counterfeit illegal? (n.d.). Retrieved May 31, 2009, from http://www.forbru gereuropa.dk/english/facts/counterfeitproducts/buycounterfeit

Johnson, K.K.P., & Rhee, J. (2008). An investigation of consumer traits and their relationship to merchandise borrowing with undergraduates. *Journal of Family and Consumer Sciences Education, 26*(1). [Online journal] www.natefacs.org/JFCSE/v26no1/v26n1k_johnson.pdf

Johnston, D. (2003, July 16). Fake goods support terrorism, Interpol official is to testify. *New York Times,* A11.

Juggessur, J., & Cohen, G. (2009). Is fashion promoting counterfeit brands? *Brand Management, 16*(5/6), 383–394.

Kang, S. (2004, December 5). Retailers say "no" to serial exchangers. *Desert News,* 3A.

Kay, H. (1990). Fakes progress. *Management Today,* 54–58.

Kim, L., & Nelson, R. (2000). *Technology, learning, and innovation.* Cambridge, England: Cambridge University Press.

King, T., & Dennis, C. (2003). Interviews of deshopping behavior: An analysis of theory of planned behavior. *International Journal of Retail and Distribution Management, 31*(3), 153–163.

King, T., Dennis, C., & McHendry, J. (2007). The management of deshopping and its effect on service. *International Journal of Retail and Distribution Management, 35*(9), 720–733.

Klemke, L. (1992). *The sociology of shoplifting: Boosters and snitches today.* Westport, CT: Praeger.

Lawson, W. (2006). Doped up on shopping. *Psychology Today.* Retrieved June 8, 2009, from www. psychologytoday.com

Lennon, S., & Johnson, K.K.P. (2007, November). *Black Friday: Shopping on the dark side.* Paper presented at the International Textile and Apparel Association annual meeting, Los Angeles, CA.

Marco, M. (2008, January). $60 million shoplifting ring busted in Florida. *The Consumerist.* Retrieved June 15, 2009, from http://consumerist.com/349005/60-million-shoplifting-ring-busted-in-florida#c

Merrick, A., & Brat, I. (2005, December 15). Taking back that blender gets harder; Sears is the latest retailer to tighten returns policy; how to avoid being refused. *Wall Street Journal* (Eastern ed.), D1.

Moore, R. (1984). Shoplifting in middle America: Patterns and motivational correlates. *International Journal of Offender Therapy and Comparative Criminology, 28,* 53–64.

Moores, T., & Chang, J. (2006). Ethical decision making in software piracy: Initial development and test of a four-component model. *MIS Quarterly, 30*(1), 167–180.

National Retail Federation. (2007, November 25). Black Friday weekend traffic up 4.8 percent as consumers shop for smaller ticket items. Retrieved July 19, 2010, from http://www.nrf.com/modules.php?name=News&op=viewlive&sp_id=420

O'Guinn, T.C., & Faber, O.J. (1989). Compulsive buying: A phenomenological exploration. *Journal of Consumer Research, 16,* 147–157.

Pitta, D., Fung, H., & Isberg, S. (1999). Ethical issues across cultures: Managing the differing perspectives of China versus USA. *Journal of Consumer Marketing, 16*(3), 240–256.

Piron, F., & Young, M. (2000). Retail borrowing: Insights and implications on returning used merchandise. *International Journal of Retail and Distribution Management, 28*(1), 27–36.

Rise in counterfeit seizures "threat" to Europeans. (2008, May). Retrieved May 7, 2009, from www. euractiv.com/en/trade/rise-counterfeit-seizures-threat-europeans/article

Rosenbaum, M., & Kuntze, R. (2003). The relationship between anomie and unethical retail disposition. *Psychology and Marketing, 20*(12), 1067–1093.

Schmidt, R., Sturrock, F., Ward, P., & Lea-Greenwood, G. (1999). Deshopping—The art of illicit consumption. *International Journal of Retail and Distribution Management, 27*(8), 290–301.

Shoplifting statistics. (2006). Retrieved June 8, 2009, from www.shopliftingprevention.org

Shoplifting up 70% since 2000. (2006). Retrieved June 8, 2009, from www.newsvote.bbc.co.uk

Speights, D., & Hilinski, M. (2005). Return fraud and abuse: How to protect profits. *Retailing Issues Letter, 17*(1), 1–6.

Tan, B. (2002). Understanding consumer ethical decision making with respect to purchase of pirated software. *Journal of Consumer Marketing, 19*(2), 96–111.

Teen shoplifting statistics. (n.d.). Retrieved June 8, 2009, from http://www.familyfirstaid.org/shoplifting-statitics.html

Thomas, D. (2008). The cost of counterfeiting. *Lost Magazine.* Retrieved June 4, 2009, from http://www.lostmag.com/issue29/counterfeiting.php

Tom, G., Garibaldi, B., Zeng, Y., & Pilcher, J. (1998). Consumer demand for counterfeit goods. *Psychology and Marketing, 15*(5), 405–421.

Tonglet, M. (2001). Consumer misbehavior: An exploratory study of shoplifting. *Journal of Consumer Behavior, 1*(4), 336–354.

Ungoed-Thomas, J. (2005). Designer fakes are funding Al-Qaeda. *Timesonline*. Retrieved June 4, 2009, from http://www.timesonline.co.uk/tol/news/uk/article432410.ece

Union des Fabricants. (2003). *Counterfeiting and organized crime*. (2003). Paris: Author.

U.S. Customs and Border Protection. (2009, January 8). CBP, ICE release annual report on counterfeit goods seized. Retrieved May 7, 2009, from http://www.cbp.gov/xp/cgov/newsroom/news_releases/archives/2009_news_releases/january_2009/01082009.xml

Wee, C., Tan, S., & Cheok, K. (1995). Non-price determinants of intention to purchase counterfeit goods. *International Marketing Review, 12*(6), 19–46.

Wilkes, R. (1978). Fraudulent behavior by consumers. *Journal of Marketing, 42,* 67–75.

Windfield, N. (2005, October 17). In a dizzying world, one way to keep up: Renting possessions. *Wall Street Journal*, A1.

Zabriskie, N. (1972–1973). Fraud by consumers. *Journal of Retailing, 48*(4), 22–27.

7

SOCIAL RESPONSIBILITY RELATED
TO FASHION CONSUMPTION

After you have read this chapter, you should be able to

- Explain the concept of social responsibility in the apparel industry
- Define the triple bottom line system of accounting.
- Discuss the environmental impact of the apparel industry.
- Identify ways the apparel industry can reduce environmental damage.
- Explain the benefits of the practice of fair trade in the apparel industry.
- Define the concept of cause-related marketing.
- Explain the dangers associated with overconsumption of apparel products.
- Discuss the benefits associated with the voluntary simplicity movement.

Although previous chapters have suggested the existence of a socially responsible consumer movement, this chapter discusses social responsibility related to fashion consumption in depth. **Social responsibility**[1] "embraces all of the social issues surrounding the relationships between workers and small and large businesses, the health and safety of workers, environmental sustainability, and communities and economic growth" (Dickson, Loker, & Eckman, 2009, p. 29). Our decisions for what apparel to consume and how to dispose of apparel once we have decided that we no longer want to wear it or store it can be motivated by our personal needs. These decisions can also be motivated by our social and environmental concerns. When we make decisions that include concerns beyond the personal to include social and environmental issues, we are attempting to consume in a socially responsible manner.

Early definitions of the concept of social responsibility were developed in the business literature (Carroll, 1999). To determine what being socially responsible means within the fashion industry, Dickson and Eckman (2006) conducted a survey of academics asking them to define the term *socially responsible apparel and textile business.* From participants' responses, the researchers developed the following conceptual definition. "Socially responsible apparel and textile business involves . . .

- An orientation encompassing the environment, its people, the apparel/textile products made and consumed, and the systematic impact that production, marketing, and consumption of these products and their component parts has on multiple stakeholders and the environment.
- A philosophy that balances ethics/morality with profitability, which is achieved through accountability-based business decisions and strategies.
- A desire for outcomes that positively affect or do very little harm to the world and its people" (p. 188).

Social responsibility is a concept that will affect consumers and future fashion businesspersons. An ever-increasing number of consumers are demanding that businesses account for more than just their financial situation using the triple bottom line system of accounting. The **triple bottom line** system of accounting suggests "that a corporation's ultimate success or health can and should be measured not just by the traditional financial bottom line, but also by its social/ethical and environmental performance" (Norman & McDonald, 2004, p. 243).

Recent magazine and newspaper articles, books, feature-length documentaries such as *An Inconvenient Truth* and *The Corporation*, and popular movies such as *Blood Diamond* have heightened consumers' awareness of social and environmental issues related to the production and consumption cycle. In turn, consumers' interest in the activities of the businesses from which they purchase apparel products has also increased (Strong, 1996). The number of consumers who want to purchase apparel from businesses that attempt to limit harm to the environment or to the people who make that apparel has increased. A survey of 1,554 U.S. college students revealed that 41 percent of undergraduates and graduate students wanted to purchase apparel products from socially and environmentally responsible brands. The students believed that socially responsible brands were those that donated money to charity or a cause, used eco-friendly or green business practices, and employed fair labor practices (Bush, 2008). Yet how easy is it to locate such businesses? Joergens (2006), in her research with young adults in England and in Germany, found that focus group participants were unable to name a fashion company that they thought was or was not socially responsible. Furthermore, these participants had never studied the corporate responsibility of an apparel brand they liked. In contrast to young consumers in the United States, Joergens found her participants were not concerned about the ethical issues facing the fashion industry, did not take these issues into account when shopping, and would rather forego ethical issues in order to buy more items than one or two ethically produced items. All participants admitted they would purchase clothing made by an unethical company because they wanted the style and would not be interested in paying more for an ethically produced item, even if they could afford it.

In contrast to Joergens's (2006) findings, Shaw and Tomolillo (2004) found that consumers in Scotland were similar to the students in the United States. The Scottish consumers shared they were anxious about a number of issues, including the use of chemicals in the production of textiles, the use of animal fur, and the general ethos and conduct of the fashion industry. Participants also held negative views of the fashion industry, because they perceived the industry as being domineering and superficial. The following participant quote illustrates this view: "it's hard to pinpoint whether that's actually how you want to look or whether you think you want to look a certain way because the fashion industry is telling you to look that way" (p. 146). The participants also noted that trying to purchase ethical clothing products was difficult due to the lack of information about companies and how they make products, the lack of a formal regulatory system that oversees the industry, and the higher prices charged for ethical clothing.

As you can see, socially responsible consumption is a complex and important topic. Of course, not every consumer, retailer, manufacturer, and designer is equally committed to engagement in socially responsible business practices within the apparel industry. Doing the socially responsible thing is more important to some people than to others. Regardless of your personal opinions on the subject, social responsibility is an issue that you will need to know about as a consumer and as a potential future apparel industry professional. For the rest of the chapter, we will look at some of the most relevant topics related to socially responsible production and consumption in the apparel industry.

Environmental impact of fashion consumption

Although this book is about apparel consumer behavior, the fact of the matter is that consumption does not occur without production. The textile and apparel production cycle is plagued with environmental concerns at every stage of the development process: from decisions concerning the production of fibers through the cutting and sewing of fabrics into garments. At the fiber stage, the processing of both natural and manmade fibers has the potential to wreak havoc on the planet and all its inhabitants. It is quite easy to find fault with petroleum-based fibers, such as polyester, due to their dependence on fossil fuels, a nonrenewable resource, for production. As Claudio (2007) explains, "The manufacture of polyester and other synthetic fabrics is an energy-intensive process requiring large amounts of crude oil and releasing emissions including volatile organic compounds, particulate matter, and acid gases such as hydrogen chloride, all of which can cause or aggravate respiratory disease" (p. 450). Manmade fiber production can cause environmental and health problems for people and animals living near or using the same water supply as the textile factories.

Natural fibers can be just as, if not more, destructive to the planet than manmade fibers. Commercial cotton farming uses more pesticides than any other agricultural crop during growth and cultivation (Claudio, 2007; Sanfilippo, 2007). All of the pesticides that are sprayed on the crops eventually end up in the water supply, causing pollution of the water itself as well as harming the creatures living in the water. In fact, cotton pesticides used by farmers in Australia are being blamed, in part, for destruction of the Great Barrier Reef (Sanfilippo, 2007). In addition to plant fibers, animal fibers often rely on environmentally harmful products in their production.

Commercial wool farmers often use parasiticides on their sheep to promote healthy coat growth, and these parasiticides can also end up in the water supply (Mole, 2007). After shearing, the wool goes through several stages of cleaning and processing. Although wool is a natural fiber, the cleaning and processing stages often involve the use of petroleum-based products (Mole, 2007). So, in this way, even natural fibers can cause environmental damage as a result of their dependence on fossil fuels for production.

In response to concerns about the environmental issues associated with fiber production, many apparel designers and producers have begun using organic fibers. The T-shirt pictured in Figure 7.1 is made of organic cotton. Organic fiber production must "follow standards that nurture the soil or animal from which it comes" and must "not use toxic insecticides, herbicides or fungicides" (Chamberlin, 2009). Certified organic cotton cannot be grown from genetically engineered seeds or with the use of synthetic fertilizers (Organic Trade Association, 2008). To be certified as organic wool, the sheep cannot be dipped in parasiticides and no petroleum-based products can be used to clean and process the wool (Mole, 2007). Consumers are interested in purchasing apparel made with organic fibers; sales of apparel made with organic cotton has been steadily increasing since 2001, and almost 20 million pounds of apparel made with organic cotton were purchased by consumers worldwide in 2005 (Mowbray, 2007).

In addition to the use of organic fibers, environmentally minded consumers and producers can reduce textile and apparel waste by recycling fibers, yarns, fabrics,

Figure 7.1 The public's interest in protecting the environment extends to apparel products, like this eco-friendly, organic cotton T-shirt. Photo by Jennifer Yurchisin.

and even entire garments. For instance, Patagonia makes polyester fibers for many of its apparel products by collecting and reusing the polyester in plastic beverage bottles, second-quality fabrics, and apparel items disposed of by consumers (Patagonia, Inc., 2009). You can recycle denim jeans if you participate in Cotton Incorporated's Cotton's Dirty Laundry Tour. The cotton fibers contained in any donated denim jeans are recycled and used as insulation material for housing or made into other consumer products (Cotton Incorporated, 2009).

It is not just fibers that are problematic. The coloring processes are some of the most environmentally harmful stages of the apparel production process (Maycumber, 2008; Orzada & Moore, 2008). To get the most vibrant colors on a fiber or a fabric, it is necessary to use clean, unpolluted water in the dyeing process. Unfortunately, many of the countries in which apparel is manufactured barely have enough clean water for drinking, let alone manufacturing purposes. One of the largest producers of textile products is China. Mainland China is, quite literally, running out of water (Mowbray, 2007). The Yellow River is being sucked dry because the water is being diverted to support the country's recent manufacturing boom (Larmer, 2008). If it was not bad enough that a great deal of clean water is used to color apparel products, the chemicals used in the dyeing processes often end up back in the water supply. Many of these chemicals are toxic to humans and animals. An estimated 81 percent of all of the water pollution associated with the textile sector occurs in developing countries, which becomes extremely problematic for people living in these countries (Braungardt, 2007). The people in developing countries barely have enough water to drink, and what little water they do have becomes poisoned with chemicals from the apparel manufacturing process.

Fortunately for individuals all over the globe, alternatives for applying color to apparel products do exist. Many types of sheep exist, so wool can be grown in a variety of natural hues, including black, gray, silver, brown, beige, red, and blonde (Natural Colored Wool Growers Association, 2009). Naturally colored cottons are also being developed. One such producer is Sally Fox, who markets her fibers under the trade name of Fox Fibre. Today, Fox Fibre cotton is available in several colors, such as brown, mocha, rust, red, green, gray, and even pink (Vreseis, Inc., n.d.). Advances are being made in terms of chemical dyeing also. Instead of using water to apply dyes, methods have been developed to use air and foam in the color application process (Maycumber, 2008). These new application techniques not only save water during the processing stage but also reduce the amount of chemicals that could potentially end up in the water supply (Maycumber, 2008).

Fair trade apparel consumption

As mentioned in chapter 2, new areas of the world are becoming increasingly industrialized, thanks, in large part, to the production of apparel items being manufactured for sale in Western countries, such as the United States and European

Union countries. Some consumers in the United States are concerned about the lives of apparel-sector workers in the United States as well as in foreign countries (Dickson, 1999). As these developing countries expand their production facilities to meet the demands of foreign consumers, there is little thought given to the long-term effects of such large-scale and, in many cases, unregulated industrialization (Claudio, 2007). Western consumers have expressed a desire to avoid duplicating in developing countries many of the social injustices that occurred in developed countries as a result of the Industrial Revolution. (To read more about the dangers of working in a textile factory during the Industrial Revolution, read the excerpt in Boxed Case 7.1.)

BOXED CASE 7.1. EXCERPT FROM "THE PHYSICAL DETERIORATION OF THE TEXTILE WORKERS," IN P. GASKELL'S (1833) *THE MANUFACTURING POPULATION OF ENGLAND*

"Any man who has stood at twelve o'clock at the single narrow door-way, which serves as the place of exit for the hands employed in the great cotton-mills, must acknowledge, that an uglier set of men and women, of boys and girls, taking them in the mass, it would be impossible to congregate in a smaller compass. Their complexion is sallow and pallid—with a peculiar flatness of feature, caused by the want of a proper quantity of adipose substance to cushion out the cheeks. Their stature low—the average height of four hundred men, measured at different times, and different places, being five feet six inches. Their limbs slender, and playing badly and ungracefully. A very general bowing of the legs. Great numbers of girls and women walking lamely or awkwardly, with raised chests and spinal flexures. Nearly all have flat feet, accompanied with a down-tread, differing very widely from the elasticity of action in the foot and ankle, attendant upon perfect formation. Hair thin and straight—many of the men having but little beard, and that in patches of a few hairs, much resembling its growth among the red men of America. A spiritless and dejected air, a sprawling and wide action of the legs, and an appearance, taken as a whole, giving the world but 'little assurance of a man,' or if so, 'most sadly cheated of his fair proportions" (Gaskell, 1833, pp. 161–162).

"Factory labor is a species of work, in some respects singularly unfitted for children. Cooped up in a heated atmosphere, debarred the necessary exercise, remaining in one position for a series of hours, one set or system of muscles alone called into activity, it cannot be wondered at—that its effects are injurious to the physical growth of a child. Where the bony system is still imperfect, the vertical position it is compelled to retain, influences its direction; the spinal column bends beneath the weight of the head, bulges out laterally, or is dragged forward by the weight of the parts composing the chest, the pelvis yields beneath the opposing pressure downwards, and the resistance given by the thigh-bones; its capacity is lessened, sometimes more and sometimes less; the legs curve, and the

whole body loses height, in consequence of this general yielding and bending of its parts"
(Gaskell, 1833, pp. 202–203).

Credit: http://www.victorianweb.org/history/workers2.html

———————————————————————— Reference ————————————————————————

Gaskell, P. (1833). *The manufacturing population of England.* London: Baldwin and Crad-
dock.

Of course, no one purchasing apparel from a department store in New York or London or Tokyo wants anyone to suffer mentally or physically as a result of making that apparel. (How would you feel if you knew that the shirt you are wearing right now was made by a young child who was forced to work for eighteen hours a day with only a fifteen-minute rest break?) It would be inhumane for you not to feel guilty about this. If you want to avoid purchasing apparel that was manufactured in situations like this, you can look for the No-Sweat label. Only apparel from certified factories will contain this label (Kunz & Garner, 2007).

Despite wishing otherwise, negative working conditions exist in apparel factories all over the world. One way that apparel designers and retailers can attempt to avoid using factories in which unhealthy employment practices are in place is to develop a code of conduct that the factories must abide by. A **code of conduct** is "a statement of principles and standards by which business decisions are made" (Kunz & Garner, 2007, p. 125). Designers and retailers who contract work with factories can refuse to pay for apparel that is produced by the factory if the factory that has agreed to honor the designer's or retailer's code of conduct violates aspects of that code of conduct. Say, for example, that Top Shop has a code of conduct that states that employees in the factories that produce their apparel must only work eight hours a day and must be given two short breaks during those eight-hour shifts. One day, executives from Top Shop visit the factory and discover that the employers in the factory are forcing employees to work for fifteen hours a day without any breaks. In addition to being upset, the executives from Top Shop can demand that the working conditions be brought up to code before they pay for the products that are being produced by this factory. By imposing codes of conduct on factories that produce their apparel, designers and retailers can assure consumers that the apparel they are buying has been made by employees who are treated fairly.

However, for a segment of consumers, codes of conduct in industrialized factories are not enough. This segment of apparel consumers believes that individuals who are living in developing countries should not be required to change their traditional ways of producing apparel products in order to participate in the global market-place. These consumers feel that viable alternative forms of economic development

SOCIAL RESPONSIBILITY

to the factory system exist and should be encouraged in developing countries. One of these alternative forms of economic development involves the production and sale of fair trade products.

Fair trade consumption promotes "social responsibility through a compatible, non-exploitive, and humanizing system of international exchange" (Littrell & Dickson, 1999, p. 4). Fair trade products are those that "seek to improve the prospects of suppliers" to improve their working conditions, health, safety, and to help them get out of poverty (Crane & Matten, 2004, p. 331). In other words, rather than being produced in large quantities in gigantic factories, apparel products can be produced using traditional methods and sold to consumers in developed countries. In this way, people in developing countries can participate in the global apparel market and the economies of the developing countries can grow without destroying traditional ways of life. Certified fair trade products will contain the fair trade label. Such products can be purchased at stores that specialize in fair trade products, like Ten Thousand Villages and Worldly Goods (see Figure 7.2).

Figure 7.2 These earrings were purchased from Ten Thousand Villages, a store that specializes in fair trade products. Photo by Jennifer Yurchisin.

FASHION AND THE CONSUMER

Fair trade consumers tend to place a high value on fairness and responsibility (Caruana, 2007; Crane & Desmond, 2002). They tend to have an outward focus as opposed to being self-centered (Dickson & Littrell, 1997). Fair trade consumers also like fair trade products because they are unique and not mass produced (Dickson & Littrell, 1998; Kim, Littrell, & Ogle, 1999; Randall, 2005). These consumers enjoy the fact that, because very few other consumers have the same apparel items, the fair trade products they purchase allow them to express their individuality (Kim, Littrell, & Ogle, 1999; Shaw & Shiu, 2003).

Cause-related fashion consumption

Even if you do not purchase fair trade products, you can still help individuals with your consumption. **Cause-related products** are created through "a general alliance between businesses and non-profit causes" (Cui, Trent, Sullivan, & Matiru, 2003, p. 310). When you purchase a cause-related product, a for-profit business will make a monetary donation to a specific nonprofit organization (Trimble & Rifon, 2006). Typically, when consumers purchase a cause-related product, they do so because they have some sort of personal involvement with the cause being supported (Hajjat, 2003).

Figure 7.3 Rubber bracelets like the ones in this photograph have been a very popular cause-related apparel item. Photo by Jennifer Yurchisin. With thanks to Kittichai Watchravesringkan.

SOCIAL RESPONSIBILITY

There are many examples of cause-related fashion products in the marketplace. If you want to help people living with HIV in Africa, you can purchase any number of fashion products from (RED), including a suit and sunglasses from Giorgio Armani's Emporio Armani line, a T-shirt from Gap, and a pair of Converse All-Star high-top tennis shoes. A popular and inexpensive cause-related fashion product a few years ago was the silicone rubber charity bracelet (Dodes, 2005; Webster, 2005). The proceeds of the sales of these colorful bracelets (see Figure 7.3) were donated to a wide range of charities such as the Livestrong Lance Armstrong Foundation for cancer research and the Hot Topic Foundation to support programs and organizations that encourage youth in art and music.

Overconsumption

As you learned in chapter 2, U.S. consumers spend the most on apparel each year. Americans spend 11 percent of their income on apparel and apparel services in contrast to people in the European Union, who spend 7 percent of their income on apparel and apparel services. Europeans have fewer apparel items because they tend to pay more per item for their apparel and tend to wear the items longer than Americans (Brosdahl, 2007). Some might suggest that Americans suffer from a condition known as **affluenza**. Affluenza is "a painful, contagious, socially transmitted condition of overload, debt, anxiety, and waste resulting from the dogged pursuit of more" (de Graaf, Wann, & Naylor, 2001, p. 2). As evidence of Americans' interest in purchasing over every other activity, de Graaf, Wann, and Naylor (2001) cite interesting bits of information, including the fact that there are twice as many shopping centers as high schools in the United States and that Americans spent more on shoes, clothing, and jewelry ($80 billion) than on higher education ($65 billion) in 1999. It is doubtful that the situation has changed much since 1999. While shopping and buying things definitely helps improve the nation's economic situation, researchers (Kasser, 2002; Schor, 1998) have found that the endless pursuit of material possessions, in the absence of a pursuit of any other human need (e.g., companionship, education, spiritual enlightenment), leads to unhappiness. Hence, affluenza can be a serious problem. (To see if you suffer from affluenza, complete the questionnaire in Boxed Case 7.2.)

BOXED CASE 7.2. DIAGNOSING AFFLUENZA

Are you interested in learning whether you suffer from affluenza? You can complete a simple true-false test to find out. The test is located on the Web site of the Public Broadcasting Service, along with other resources related to the Affluenza movie. Indicate whether the following statements are true or false concerning your behavior.

1. I'm willing to pay more for a T-shirt if it has a cool corporate logo on it.
2. I believe that if I buy the cocktail dress, the cocktail party will come.
3. I have a shoe collection Imelda Marcos would envy.
4. When I'm cold, I take my clothes off and turn up the heat.
5. I'm willing to work 40 years at a job I hate so I can buy lots of stuff.
6. When I'm feeling blue, I like to go shopping and treat myself.
7. I want a sports utility vehicle, although I rarely drive in conditions that warrant one.
8. I usually make just the minimum payment on my credit cards.
9. I believe that whoever dies with the most toys wins.
10. Most of the things my friends/family and I enjoy doing together are free.
11. I don't measure my self-worth (or that of others) by what I own.
12. I know how to pinch a dollar until it screams.
13. I worry about the effects of advertising on children.
14. To get to work, I carpool, ride my bike, or use public transportation.
15. I'd rather be shopping right now.

To score your test, give yourself two points for every true response and one point for every false response for items 1 through 9 and 15. For items 10 through 14, give yourself zero points for every true response, and give yourself two points for every false response. If the sum of your score for items 1 through 9 and 15 is 10 to 15, you are experiencing no dangerous signs of affluenza at this time. If the sum of your score for items 1 through 9 and 15 is 16 to 22, you are suffering from mild affluenza. If the sum of your score for items 1 through 9 and 15 is 23 to 30, you are experiencing severe affluenza.

Reference

Do you have it? (n.d.). Retrieved June 17, 2009, from http://www.pbs.org/kcts/afflu-
enza/diag/have.html

Voluntary simplicity

In response to affluenza are individuals participating in the **voluntary simplicity movement**. Voluntary simplicity refers to the choice to "limit expenditures on consumer goods and services and to cultivate non-materialistic sources of satisfaction and meaning" (Etzioni, 1998, p. 620). Voluntary simplifiers consist of a group of consumers who, for many reasons, decide to live with less. Referred to by some as socially conscious consumers, these anticonsumers express a variety of concerns about the environment, overconsumption, abuse of developing nations, and extensive advertising (Craig-Lees & Hill, 2002). These individuals engage in a variety of anticonsumption activities, including selecting products based on ethical or ecological considerations, reducing consumption, and boycotting specific product categories (Craig-Lees & Hill, 2002).

Voluntary simplicity as

> a way of life is not a static condition to be achieved, but an ever-changing balance that must be continuously and consciously made real. Simplicity in this sense is not simple. To maintain a skillful balance between the inner and outer aspects of our lives is an enormously challenging and continuously changing process. The objective is not dogmatically to live with less, but is a more demanding intention of living with balance in order to find a life of greater purpose, fulfillment, and satisfaction. (Elgin, 2000, p. 398)

Etzioni (1998) wrote that voluntary simplicity is practiced at three levels of intensity. He labeled these as downshifters, strong simplifiers, and those practicing simple living. **Downshifters** are characterized as consumers who give up some luxuries that they can afford but in other areas live a rich and consumption-oriented lifestyle. For example, they may wear jeans with an Armani blazer or drive to their vacation home in a beat-up pick-up truck. Consumers who are members of this group of simplifiers adhere to the tenets of voluntary simplicity in some areas but not in others.

Strong simplifiers include consumers who have given up high-income occupations to live on less income. A large number of these consumers retire early in order to increase their leisure time. Consumers who practice **simple living** adjust all of their living patterns. They frequently move from living in affluent neighborhoods to small towns and less affluent areas of cities. Their behavior is motivated by a philosophy rather than just a change in income.

Craig-Lees and Hill (2002) compared Australian voluntary simplifiers to nonsimplifiers to further understand the differences between these two groups in terms of what each believes is important in their lives, what they would change in their lives, what possessions are important, and what they consider when choosing products. (See Table 7.1 for a comparison of simplifiers and nonsimplifiers). In general, both value goods for the functions they perform and the experience they deliver. Compared to simplifiers, more nonsimplifiers linked the idea of status to goods, used brand names and fashion as status, and, if women, talked positively about clothes and cosmetics. Products and services that were sacrificed as a result of the lowered income of simplifiers included going to movies and theaters, dining in restaurants, travel, and purchasing image brands.

What are the long-term effects of living a simple life?

Etzioni (1998) noted that a simple lifestyle would enhance society's ability to protect the environment. Voluntary simplifiers use fewer resources than average consumers. They are also more likely to recycle, build compost heaps, and engage in other civic activities. Etzioni also suggests that voluntary simplicity "might be the best source to create the societal conditions under which limited reallocation of wealth—needed to ensure the basic needs of all—could become politically possible" (p. 640). He argues that, to the extent that the wealthy will find value and meaning in pursuits

Table 7.1 Voluntary Simplifiers Compared to Nonsimplifiers

Characteristic	Simplifier	Nonsimplifier
What is important in life?	Family Self Relationships, community	Family Work Health
What would change in their lives?	Quality of life Change house, car	Investments Travel
What possessions are important?	Mementos, heirlooms, Bible Hobbies Letters, diaries	Photos Documents Mementos, heirlooms, Bible
What do they consider when selecting products?	How products are produced Quality Price	Quality Price Brand name (value)

From "Understanding Voluntary Simplifiers," by M. Craig-Lees and C. Hill, 2002, *Psychology and Marketing*, *19*(2), pp. 187–210.

other than wealth, they can be expected to give up some of their wealth and income. These freed resources can be shifted to those in need without resistance.

We now leave it up to you to decide how you want to behave in the marketplace. We have given you information with which to make those decisions. The choice and the consequences associated with that choice lie with you.

Summary

Being a socially responsible apparel consumer is a complex process reflecting decision making at several stages of production as well as consumption and disposal. Consumers, through their apparel choices, have opportunities to make consumption decisions that can reduce the impact apparel production has on the environment as well as on the people involved in apparel production. Being a socially responsible consumer may also mean reducing total expenditures on apparel, wearing items longer, and thoughtful consideration of how apparel items are to be discarded.

Key Terms

- affluenza
- cause-related products
- code of conduct
- downshifters
- fair trade consumption
- simple living
- social responsibility
- strong simplifiers
- triple bottom line
- voluntary simplicity movement

Questions for review and discussion

1. Reflecting on the definition of social responsibility for a textile and apparel business, complete the following statement: A socially responsible apparel consumer is an individual who . . .
2. Why is the textile and apparel industry so often associated with environmental damage?
3. Suppose you are working as the sourcing manager for an apparel retailer. You are required to write a code of conduct for the facilities that produce your apparel. Write at least two rules that the manufacturing facilities will need to abide by if they want to continue to conduct business with your company. Why did you write those two rules? Why are those two rules important to you? Why are they important to your consumers?
4. What is fair trade consumption? What arguments could retailers present to consumers to increase the demand for fairly traded apparel products and to encourage more consumers to purchase fairly traded apparel products?
5. What is a cause-related product? Do you think there are certain causes that are better suited for apparel products than others? Why or why not? What do you think it was about the rubber charity bracelets that made those cause-related products so popular? What advice would you give to apparel designers who wanted to create a new cause-related apparel product to ensure success of that product?
6. Why do you think Americans suffer from affluenza more than consumers in other countries? Do you think, as consumers in developing countries gain access to more products, they will also become inflicted with affluenza? Why or why not?
7. Imagine that you want to live a simple life. Describe your current lifestyle and apparel consumption patterns. Indicate what changes you would need to make, if any, to live a simple life with respect to your apparel consumption.

Note

1. Other terms used to describe social and environmental issues tied to apparel design, production, consumption, and disposal include eco-fashion, green clothing, ethical fashion, ethical consumption, future fashion, and sustainability (Bostic, 2008; Joergens, 2006; Shaw & Tomolillo, 2004).

Suggested Readings

If you are interested in the topics in chapter 7, you may also like reading these other books:

Blanchard, T. (2007). Green is the new black: How to change the world with style. London: Hodder & Stoughton.

de Graaf, J., Wann, D., & Naylor, T. H. (2001). Affluenza: The all-consuming epidemic. San Francisco: Berrett-Koehler.

Fletcher, K. (2008). Sustainable fashion and textiles. London: Earthscan.

Hethorn, J., & Ulasewicz, C. (Eds.). (2008). Sustainable fashion: Why now? A conversation about issues, practices, and possibilities. New York: Fairchild Books.

Hoffman, L. (Ed.). (2007). Future fashion: White papers. New York: Earth Pledge.

Kasser, T. (2002). The high price of materialism. Cambridge, MA: MIT Press.

Schor, J. B. (1998). The overspent American. New York: HarperPerennial.

References

Bostic, N. (2008). *Knowledge, attitudes, and behaviors of college students in family and consumer sciences toward environmentally friendly apparel*. Unpublished doctoral dissertation, North Carolina State University, Raleigh.

Braungart, M. (2007). Eco-effective fashion. In L. Hoffman (Ed.), *Future fashion: White papers* (pp. 189–196). New York: Earth Pledge.

Brosdahl, D.J.C. (2007). The consumption crisis. In L. Hoffman (Ed.), *Future fashion: White papers* (pp. 7–16). New York: Earth Pledge.

Bush, M. (2008). Students rank social responsibility. *Advertising Age, 79*(30), 11.

Carroll, A. (1999). Corporate social responsibility. *Business and Society, 38*(3), 268–295.

Caruana, R. (2007). Morality and consumption: Towards a multidisciplinary perspective. *Journal of Marketing Management, 23*(3/4), 207–225.

Chamberlin, C. (2009). Introduction to organic fibers. Organic.org. Retrieved June 17, 2009, from http://www.organic.org/articles/showarticle/article-224

Claudio, L. (2007). Waste couture: Environmental impact of the clothing industry. *Environmental Health Perspectives, 115*(9), 450–454.

Cotton Incorporated. (2009). Cotton today—About cotton sustainability: Recycling. Retrieved May 16, 2009, from http://cottontoday.cottoninc.com/sustainability-about/recycling/

Crane, A., & Desmond, J. (2002). Societal marketing and morality. *European Journal of Marketing, 36*(5/6), 548–569.

Crane, A., & Matten, D. (2004). *Business ethics*. Oxford, England: Oxford University Press.

Craig-Lees, M., & Hill, C. (2002). Understanding voluntary simplifiers. *Psychology and Marketing, 19*(2), 187–210.

Cui, Y., Trent, E.S., Sullivan, P.M., & Matiru, G.N. (2003). Cause-related marketing: How generation Y responds. *International Journal of Retail and Distribution Management, 31*(6/7), 310–320.

de Graaf, J., Wann, D., & Naylor, T.H. (2001). *Affluenza: The all-consuming epidemic*. San Francisco: Berrett-Koehler.

Dickson, M.A. (1999). US consumers' knowledge of and concern with apparel sweatshops. *Journal of Fashion Marketing and Management, 3*(1), 44–55.

Dickson, M.A., & Eckman, M. (2006). Social responsibility: The concept as defined by apparel and textile scholars. *Clothing and Textiles Research Journal, 24*(3), 178–191.

Dickson, M.A., & Littrell, M.A. (1997). Consumers of clothing from alternative trading organizations: Societal attitudes and purchase evaluative criteria. *Clothing and Textiles Research Journal, 15*(1), 21–33.

Dickson, M.A., & Littrell, M.A. (1998). Consumers of ethnic apparel from alternative trading organizations: A multifaceted market. *Clothing and Textiles Research Journal, 16*(1), 1–10.

Dickson, M.A., Loker, S., & Eckman, M. (2009). *Social responsibility in the global apparel industry*. New York: Fairchild Books.

Dodes, R. (2005, September 17). Style—accessories: Charity begins at the mall. *Wall Street Journal*, P11.

Elgin, D. (2000). Voluntary simplicity and the new global challenge. In J.B. Schor & D.B. Holt (Eds.), *The consumer society reader* (pp. 397–413). New York: New Press.

Etzioni, A. (1998). Voluntary simplicity: Characterization, select psychological implications, and societal consequences. *Journal of Economic Psychology, 19*, 619–643.

Hajjat, Mahmood M. (2003). Effect of cause-related marketing on attitudes and purchase intentions: The moderating role of cause involvement and donation size. *Journal of Nonprofit and Public Sector Marketing, 11*(1), 93–109.

Joergens, C. (2006). Ethical fashion: Myth or future trend? *Journal of Fashion Marketing and Management, 10*(3), 360–371.

Kasser, T. (2002). *The high price of materialism.* Cambridge, MA: MIT Press.

Kim, S., Littrell, M.A., & Ogle, J.L.P. (1999). The relative importance of social responsibility as a predictor of purchase intentions. *Journal of Fashion Marketing and Management, 3*(3), 207–218.

Kunz, G.I., & Garner, M.B. (2007). *Going global: The textile and apparel industry.* New York: Fairchild Books.

Larmer, B. (2008, May). Bitter waters. *National Geographic, 213*(5), 146–169.

Littrell, M.A., & Dickson, M.A. (1999). *Social responsibility in the global market: Fair trade of cultural products.* Thousand Oaks, CA: Sage.

Maycumber, S.G. (2008, July/August). Textile sustainability: More than just fiber—It's also how you deal with it. *Textile Insight, 6.*

Mole, M. (2007). Dreaming of organic sheep. In L. Hoffman (Ed.), *Future fashion: White papers* (pp. 150–159). New York: Earth Pledge.

Mowbray, J. (2007). Can sustainability stay the distance? In L. Hoffman (Ed.), *Future fashion: White papers* (pp. 263–274). New York: Earth Pledge.

Natural Colored Wool Growers Association. (2009). *The history of natural colored sheep.* Retrieved June 17, 2009, from http://www.ncwga.org/index.html

Norman, W., & MacDonald, C. (2004). Getting to the bottom of "triple bottom line." *Business Ethics Quarterly, 14*(2), 243–262.

Organic Trade Association. (2008). *Organic cotton facts.* Retrieved June 17, 2009, from http://www.ota.com/organic/mt/organic_cotton.html

Orzada, B.T., & Moore, M.A. (2008). Environmental impact of textile production. In J. Hethorn & C. Ulasewicz (Eds.), *Sustainable fashion: Why now? A conversation about issues, practices, and possibilities* (pp. 299–325). New York: Fairchild Books.

Patagonia, Inc. (2009). *Fabric: Recycled polyester.* Retrieved May 16, 2009, from http://www.patagonia.com/web/us/patagonia.go?slc=en_US&sct=US&assetid=2791

Randall, D.C. (2005). An exploration of opportunities for the growth of the fair trade market: Three case studies of craft organizations. *Journal of Business Ethics, 56,* 55–67.

Sanfilippo, D. (2007). A fair deal for farmers. In L. Hoffman (Ed.), *Future fashion: White papers* (pp. 137–149). New York: Earth Pledge.

Schor, J.B. (1998). The overspent American. New York: HarperPerennial.

Shaw, D.S., & Shiu, E. (2003). Ethics in consumer choice: A multivariate modelling approach. *European Journal of Marketing, 37*(10), 1485–1498.

Shaw, D., & Tomolillo, D. (2004). Undressing the ethical issues in fashion: A consumer perspective. In M. Bruce, C. Moore, & G. Birtwistle (Eds.), *International retail marketing* (pp. 141–154). New York: Elsevier.

Strong, C. (1996). Features contributing to the growth of ethical consumerism: A preliminary investigation. *Marketing Intelligence and Planning, 14*(5), 5–13.

Trimble, C.S., & Rifon, N.J. (2006). Consumer perceptions of compatibility in cause-related marketing messages. *International Journal of Nonprofit and Voluntary Sector Marketing, 11*(1), 29–47.

Vreseis, Inc. (n.d.). *A message from Sally.* Retrieved June 17, 2009, from http://www.foxfibre.com/

Webster, N.C. (2005). Livestrong color coded causes. *Advertising Age, 76*(24), 31, 35.

INDEX

natural fibers, 28
need, 60
   physiological, 60
   psychogenic, 60–1
nonnormative apparel consumption
   defining misbehavior, 129–30
   deshoppers, 140
   extreme consumption, 147–50
   merchandise borrowing, 111, 139–43
   motivating factors, 132–4
   retail return fraud, 140
   returnaholics, 140
   shoplifting, 143–7
   shrinkage, 143
   types, 132
normalization, 137
norms, 14

pirated goods, 134
planned obsolescence, 62–3
postpurchase dissatisfaction, 119
postpurchase satisfaction, 119

qualitative research, 21
   advantages of, 21
   disadvantages of, 21–2
   see also research methods

radio frequency identification (RFID), 134
ready-to-wear, 31, 33
reciprocity, 148–9
recreational shoppers, 78
research methods
   experiments, 20
   field observations, 22
   interview, 21
   qualitative, 21
   quantitative, 16
   questionnaire, 16
   response rate, 20
   surveys, 16

secondhand apparel, 123–4
shopping
   across cultures, 47
   age differences, 88–9

arenas, 27
   department store, 32
   during ancient times, 27
   during end of twentieth century, 35
   during Industrial Revolution, 30
   during twentieth century, 34
   during twenty-first century, 39
   gender differences, 87–8
   hedonic, 40
   home television shopping, 37
   Internet shopping, 38
   mall, 35
socially conscious consumers, 165
   see also fashion consumption,
      social responsibility; voluntary
      simplicity
sources of information
   marketer-controlled, 66
   objective, 66
   personal, 66
   public, 66
subcultures, 100
surveys, 16
   advantages of, 17
   disadvantages of, 17
   see also research methods

taste, 8
time poverty, 36
total income, 101
   see also fashion consumption, economic
      influences on
trend, 8
triple bottom line accounting, 156
tunic, 28
typology, 130, 146

value retailer, 46–7
voluntary simplicity, 165–7
   downshifters, 166
   simple living, 166
   strong simplifiers, 166

wants, 61

CPSIA information can be obtained
at www.ICGtesting.com
Printed in the USA
LVHW101735190819
628158LV00008B/32/P